Sounds in Motion and Monorail Minds

BY THE SAME AUTHOR:

Music and the Art of Peace Maintenance
As in Music, So in Life

Sounds in Motion and Monorail Minds

Musicians' Adventures and Scientific Trips

Johnny Woods

*To Vivian all —
one of my favorite
classmates and "co-play
actors" who remembered me
50 years later.
All my very best regards!
Johnny Woods*

*22 aug. 1998
Helsingborg
Sweden*

The Pentland Press Limited
Edinburgh • Cambridge • Durham • USA

First published in 1997 by
The Pentland Press Ltd.
1 Hutton Close
South Church
Bishop Auckland
Durham

British Library Cataloguing in Publication Data.
A Catalogue record for this book is available
from the British Library.

ISBN 1 85821 501 3

Typeset by CBS, Felixstowe, Suffolk
Printed and bound by Antony Rowe Ltd., Chippenham

DEDICATION

In memory of Loren Eiseley who revealed that great scientific achievements are merely projections of shadows dancing on the brain, and Louis Armstrong who proved that it is actually the joy of jazz that moves our spirit into joining the dance of life itself.

MUSES DANCE

Oh friends, no more these sounds
Let us sing more cheerful songs
More full of joy!

Opening lines of Friedrich von Schiller's poem 'Ode To Joy' which inspired Beethoven to write a fitting melody to be sung in the final movement of his Ninth Symphony.

'Come,' said the Muse
Sing me a song no poet has yet chanted,
Sing me the Universal

from Walt Whitman's epic
poem 'Leaves of Grass'.

KILLJOY'S MARCH

This new type of man turns his interest away from life, persons, nature and ideas. He transforms all life into things including himself. He aspires to make robots as one of the greatest achievements of his technical mind. The world of life has become a world of 'no life'. Living persons have become 'non-persons', a world of death.

Psychiatrist Erich Fromm: *Anatomy of Human Destructiveness* (1974)

CONTENTS

A PRELUDE

With penetrating insight the brilliant English intellectual, Isaiah Berlin, once said, 'Solitude doesn't mean that you live far away from other people. It means that people don't understand what you're saying.' This prompts me to recall Ludwig Wittgenstein - the twentieth century genius of philosophy - who regarded his own thinking as being alien to the scientific and mathematical spirit of the age in which he lived. He felt as if he were writing for people who belonged to a different culture. Playing clarinet and listening to classical music was the greatest pleasure in his life. Curiously enough the father of modern science, Francis Bacon, (1561-1626) had positive humane visions for the progress of science far beyond our present day technological 'Supermen'. Unfortunately Bacon experts inform us that there is a tendency to vulgarize and misinterpret his ideas today. Incidentally Bacon empathized with Orpheus (not the myth but the actual living person) the pioneer Greek musician and dynamic peacemaker.

In this period of disruption with its irrationality and glorification of scientism, the spin-off effects have produced technology for the industrialization of music - the brave new world of the electronic sound industry - making it possible for a handful of conglomerates to control 85 per cent of the world's recordings (less than 10 per cent are acoustic jazz or classical music). This assembly line production 'manufactures' dozens of amateur players into 'Super-Stars' overnight. No wonder that thousands of young gifted college educated musicians feel alienated while hundreds of highly skilled professionals are under-employed. If time speaks another language then it appears that natural acoustic music is being excommunicated from society for the sake of technological 'progress' and big business sound powers.

Solitude leads to contemplation and in the leisure of my retirement (merely another kind of 'gig' with more free time for writing and performing) I was inspired to write this story of my alter-ego, Monk Freeman, a professional musician who finished his graduate work before joining a Navy Band (Korean War) for a two year stint of the Pacific, toured all of the US and most of Europe, and lived, taught and performed in New York, the West Indies, New Mexico and Sweden (where I now live as a permanent resident). A white jazz clarinetist, Monk was blessed with good fortune early in life, sharing a similar family background to Bix Beiderbecke, Fletcher Henderson, Duke Ellington, Coleman Hawkins, Miles Davis and countless others who contradicted the old 'poor black' myths.

As I wrote I could not help but philosophize about the past and wonder in what direction music is headed. What more new scientific sound miracles lie just around the very 'square' corners as we approach the third millennium? Historical research revealed to me that for thousands of years, long before 'info-tech' computers replaced the wisdom of ancient tribes (American Indians, Chinese, Egyptians, Greeks, etc.) music was revered as the only unified field of all knowledge: superior even to science, religion, economics and politics. Naturally only sensibly inspired music making deserved this kind of respect. These primitive people believed that music not only reflected the values of a culture but possessed the secret power to direct its destiny. Later on philosophers professed a close relationship between ethics and aesthetics. In one chapter Monk discusses this area in which he did research for his Master's degree.

In the story of Monk Freeman's life he moves on to Santa Fé where the reader is introduced to a prominent but disillusioned nuclear physicist who was once a promising jazz pianist. The scientist, one Barry Stein, reaches a crucial turning point in his life where he reveals his deepest thoughts and feelings about the scientific mind and the heart of music. His conscience haunts him and he is deeply disturbed by the unharnessed energies of scientific progress since the beginning of the atomic age: its

2200 bomb tests, the production of over 30,000 missiles, 500 nuclear reactors worldwide, the multi-billion dollar space race, the 'Star Wars' project, nefarious genetic food technology and – the 'Final Solution' – nanotechnology, a molecular witch's brew which can make everything out of anything. Barry was convinced that we must question the arrogant authority of this kind of science. Above all he felt it was time to challenge the lockstep engineering behind the technocratic troika of big power interests consisting of computerized robot men, global business tycoons (like the secretive Bilderberg Group) and the conniving 'New Right' social democrats. Barry warns that this Orwellian project is a systematic scheme to manipulate people as mere laboratory objects in a grandiose One World experiment. In order to control this process the technicians are required to maintain a scientific attitude of 'pure objectivity'. One example of this infectious form of Techno-Urban Fascism is obvious in the rising power of the present day European Union, with its momentum of a monorail locomotive. Be this as it may, as an author-musician I had little time or patience for the triteness of over-zealous technocracies. Instead I preferred to concentrate my writing on the organic unity of real life values in music rather than the dead inorganic matter of technology.

Music was Monk's mistress and as long as his guardian angel Cecilia guided him along the way he had every reason to be content with his life. Extremely fortunate he was too, especially when he considered how unlucky some of his more gifted colleagues were in being forced to seek other work. Monk's adventures gave him the reputation of being some sort of a maverick among his fellow musicians until they realized that he had a dream to fulfill not long after settling down in enchanting Santa Fé, New Mexico. Here he organizes several dynamic music projects which the reader will discover as the story develops into a joyful climax.

In this mean-time Monk Freeman is keenly aware of the acoustic musicians' fight for survival and refuses to be distracted by the degenerate forces of goose-stepping killjoys. Instead he is conscious of the fact that the rigid logic of science is inadequate and cripples us emotionally. He asks what has happened to our lack of feeling, sensitivity, compassion, dullness of spirit and the vitality of joy? Is it possible that our 'realistic' macho-utilitarian society has suppressed our ability to be compassionate? Other ways of thinking are necessary but at least equally important are newer ways of expressing positive feelings, using our creative energies and imaginative forces which may lead us on to a more holistic world view.

Who knows but what a small touch of mysticism might be sufficient to enhance our intellectual vision to the point where we could learn to transcend beyond ourselves? Perhaps the dancing muses have a part to play after all!

The dance of life swings onward and upward.

Have a good read.

J.W.

Chapter I

JAZZ CAME UP THIS RIVER

What else is the whole jazz trip? You take your seat in the cat's head, like you're stepping into one of those little cars in a funhouse. Then pulled by some strong dark chain that you can't shut off, you plunge into the darkness, down the inclines, up the slopes, around the sharp bends and into the dead ends; past bizarre, grotesque window displays and gooney, lurid frights with spectacles and whistles and sirens and scares and even along a dark moody tunnel of love. It's all a trip, and the best of it that you haven't the faintest idea where you're going!!

Ladies and Gentlemen - Lenny Bruce

1

In looking back over the adventurous life of a maverick jazz musician, one might describe Monk Freeman as a free spirited existentialist, an agnostic humanist who nevertheless believed he was guided by the musicians' guardian angel, St Cecilia. Often after playing a gig he would ask her, 'How am I doing, CC, will I ever make it big?' Once Monk claimed she answered this question by saying, 'Monk, you are a highly gifted musician but in the time of your life you will see fewer jazz artists of your calibre get the fame they deserve. Unfortunately the trend is toward industrialization of music with technology producing instant amateur super-stars. But I promise you that you'll always make a living playing. Keep right on swinging, Monk!' A bittersweet prediction from the 1940s but he learned to live with it and did manage to make a relatively

1

successful career both as a performer and as a college music teacher. He had faith in Cecilia and felt certain that she steered him in the right direction in spite of some low periods in his life. Considering the whole scene, Monk had every reason to be grateful for her guidance and most of all the early support that came from his parents. Indeed, his fortunate family background made it possible for him to make the right choice from the beginning.

Born several years before the Great Depression, while the Golden Age of Jazz was in full swing, this musical mistress had already seduced Monk Freeman by the age of eleven. Running on track during those lean years of the thirties was an investment in the advanced research of nuclear physicists to prepare the world for the birth of the Atomic Age. Fortunately the hard times of this decade barely affected the family economy as his father was a successful banker who had sold short his blue chip investments in early 1929. This made it possible for them to live quite well in a large family home with a full time black maid and a late model Ford sedan, extremely lucky circumstances for those days. His home town of Sewickley, Pennsylvania happened to be an upper class suburb of Pittsburgh where steel tycoons built their mansions in the hills surrounding the town. Monk's mother was a professional dancer and his father a soloist in their church choir. He attended a private Pre-school (Kindergarten) where the new Carl Orff music methods were taught to all two and a half to six year old children, a unique privilege which gave him an early start. Twice a week his mother taught at Miss Molly's Ballroom Dancing School with lessons at the exclusive Edgeworth Club: required attendance in spite of his kicking and screaming resistance when he started at the age of seven.

Although unemployment was high, few people deprived themselves of the special need for live entertainment. Jazz musicians never had it better but circuses for the masses were in even higher demand. The famous Ringling Brothers and Barnum and Bailey circuses filled Big Top tents nightly in tours all over the country. Every year in May, clowns, elephants and a one-hundred piece band marched through Sewickley 'bally-hooing' to invite everyone to the big show in the main tent that evening. Monk was ecstatic when he heard the triumphant tones of the band booming through his neighborhood. On cue he hopped on to his bicycle to fall in line with the parade, usually closing in on the clarinet section. The clowns and elephants took over the show while the monkeys flirted with the little boys and girls lined up along the street. It thrilled him just to be a part of the spectacle.

When he reached the fairgrounds down by the Ohio riverside he went through the usual routine of asking the foreman what he could do to work for a free ticket. After two hours of sweeping platforms and cutting high weeds he earned his ticket for the main show that evening. Feeling like a real circus roustabout he bragged to his mother about the experience. That night the whole family including his two sisters and a brother followed him to the Big Top.

This exciting live production became a lifetime inspiration, as it was for the famous mobile artist Alexander Calder.*

Radios and record players were somewhat of a luxury in those days but the father of his childhood playmate Bill Mullan owned an electric appliance store and the family possessed the first electric gramophone in town: a miracle for Monk as his family still had an old grind up 'His Masters Voice' Victrola. The 78 'pancake' records were expensive and the best jazz records – especially of black artists – not easy to find. However, Bill's older brother worked in his father's store and ordered anything available at a discount.

Instead of playing baseball or football after school, Bill and Monk spent many hours digging the latest sounds of jazz. Lester Young, Coleman Hawkins, Louis Armstrong and Duke Ellington were among their favorites. Up and coming Buddy Rich inspired Bill to take up the drums while master jazz clarinetist Edmund Hall impressed Monk more than the debonair and stylized playing of Benny Goodman. With the exception of the Goodman Sextet along with some Fletcher Henderson and Eddie Sauter big band arrangements, Monk felt that Hall had a lot to teach

---

Contemporary carnival culture is reduced to the size of a squared off screen, a little toy 'picture box' which hypnotizes billions of viewers.

Benny about jazz clarinet playing. He knew what he liked and liked what he knew. In fact at eleven years old his taste was so sophisticated that when the family's black maid played him her favorite 'Race' records (a very early version of rhythm and blues popular in black bar-room juke boxes) he thought it repulsive and wondered how she could listen to such junk.*

For Monk a yearly musical event happened in August just before school started. As the Ohio river rolled on down from Pittsburgh on its way to the Mississippi many river boats of all sizes were continually sailing back and forth loaded from bow to stern. Now the principal of his school was married to a steam boat captain who often cruised on down to the end of the line to the port of New Orleans. In some way he persuaded the owner and the captain of a grand old showboat – the *Dan D. Burk* – to pull in to Sewickley on its yearly cruise to Pittsburgh.

About the middle of August Monk began counting the days and listening each morning when he awoke anxiously waiting to hear the explosive jet stream tones of that ancient steam pressure organ, the calliope, which erupted into the river valley like a volcano when the *Dan D. Burk* belched out its arrival. Immediately after breakfast one morning a piercing blast suddenly shook the house and Monk could feel the vibrations quivering up his back and his eardrums ringing. Before symptoms of the St Vitus dance broke out his mother knew it was time for the annual family boat ride on the river.

'All right, Monk, I know how you feel. I'll ask your father if he will take us all on the Saturday afternoon cruise.'

High noon Saturday and the calliope tones were deafening with its explosive music firing away in all directions. Holding their ears, they all climbed aboard the seventy-year-old paddle-wheel steamboat just in time to be served real southern fried chicken with piles of french fries. For

---

*Little did he realize that twenty years later the roots of rhythm and blues would develop into the rock and roll craze belted out by lily white hillbillies such as Bill Haley and Elvis 'The Pelvis', and finally be whitewashed clean by those cute little Edwardian boys from Liverpool. These middle class racists hardly ever included any black talent which was what their rhythm sections needed most.

4

dessert they ordered a favorite from Georgia, pecan and peach ice cream. As the boat pulled out from the dock a seven-piece Dixieland band marched proudly around the main deck before ducking into the ship's dance floor. Monk had little time to enjoy the scenery but spent all afternoon digging the happy sounds of real authentic New Orleans jazz. They generated a vitality of joy that made him dizzy with delight. Although he almost felt like dancing he knew his ballroom dance steps were no help in this situation. He remembered a New Orleans classic named 'King Porter Stomp' and asked the band if they could play it. To his surprise they launched into it as if they had been waiting for someone to ask for it all along.

Time and the river rolled on until all too soon the *Dan D. Burk* gradually slowed down as it approached the Sewickley dock. As Monk and his parents got up to leave he waved to the band and they waved back, breaking into a chorus of 'High Society'. Monk was so overjoyed he stayed awake half the night humming that song and dreaming about one of the last of the old Mississippi river showboats.

Usually on a Sunday afternoon once a month an old friend of the family, Lydia Pinkerton, stopped by to take the Freeman children for a ride around the town in her old-time Fisher body style electric car. Custom made and driven by special high power batteries it floated down the street like a cloud. She drove for nearly an hour as Monk waved at his astonished friends along the way. Miss Pinkerton, a ninety-year-old spinster, actually owned the only electric automobile in Sewickley and she took special pride in showing it off. The only other vehicles driven by batteries were the Railway Express delivery trucks equipped with solid hard rubber tyres. Years later Monk wondered why electric cars were not more popular with the public until he realized that oil monopolies and automobile manufacturers conspired together to eliminate research or promotion for this more rational alternative. Madison Avenue brainwashed the rising middle class to believe in this myth and the government confirmed it by building thousands of miles of super-highways all over the US.

2

During the 1930s trains were a blessing for both commuters and long distance travelling. Monk took his first long trip by train when invited by his aunt to spend the summer with her and his cousins at their seashore home north of Boston. He looked forward to this adventure with wild anticipation as it involved taking a twenty-hour train ride from Pittsburgh to Boston. Reservations were made far in advance for his berth in a Pullman sleeping car. The day arrived and all the way to the station he sang Glenn Miller's 'Chattanooga Choo-Choo'. After kissing his mother farewell, he climbed aboard. The black porter, dressed in a neatly pressed white uniform, greeted him with a Louis Armstrong smile.

'Hello theyah, young man, you must be Mistah Monk. Youah mothuh say you gwine all de way to Boston. Wowie! You is such a lucky young man. Well suh, you is very welcome aboard and right hyah is youah seat beside this gentleman who is also gwine to Boston, so no problem. So now you just sit right down and have a real nice trip. You just let me know anytime at all what you need by pressing this button.'

Hard core 'realists' today would label this porter as a typical 'Uncle Tom' of the thirties but the facts say otherwise. Not only did these servicemen have security and good pay while millions of whites were unemployed but they had professional style training along with membership in one of the first highly organized unions in America. What's more, with dozens of Pullman train trips he experienced later in his life Monk found all these porters to be consistently proud and happy workers who truly enjoyed being hospitable. And of course it paid off as hardly anyone could resist leaving them a generous tip. (Regretfully for train romantics those days are gone forever but for Monk and classic writers like Thomas Wolfe the memories lingered on.)

This Pullman trip turned out to be half the fun of Monk's vacation. He discovered his companion to be the star pitcher for the famous Boston Braves baseball team. After such an adventurous train ride and a rather sleepless night looking out the window at all the scenery along the way he arrived in Boston where his aunt and cousins greeted him as he descended from his Pullman car.

During this most delightful summer at the seashore near Swampscott where the family lived he and his cousin Johnny 'trapped' several boatfuls of lobster. Johnny's mother thought that enough was more than enough and helped Johnny sell them at the local fish market. Lobster trapping and swimming at the beach in front of their house were the highlights of this six-week vacation. Several times a week, especially on rainy days, Johnny took Monk down to his 'chemistry lab' in the basement where they conducted experiments, with noxious gases and minor explosions threatening the entire household. Already at thirteen Johnny had plans to study chemistry and make it his career. Monk thought it looked like lots of fun, a pleasant plaything, a hobby at best, but to spend a lifetime mixing liquids in bottles staring at the same old apparatus following exact formulas seemed to place one on a narrow path with no time for feelings or imagination. Apparently this scientific bent came from Johnny's father, a teacher of astronomy at Boston University. Monk's Uncle Andy had a portable telescope which he placed in the backyard on clear evenings when many constellations were visible. Often he invited the boys out to participate in observing certain star patterns. With great enthusiasm he explained fascinating things about the universe and its galaxies. Monk looked forward to these evenings looking through space at faraway stars and Uncle Andy made it sound as if Monk was on board his personal rocket ship guiding him into the galaxies. One evening Monk recalled his uncle being more inspired than usual and waxing eloquently about his subject.

'Did you ever stop to think that here we are now placed between a microscopic earth and a telescopic universe but we understand so little about how we fit into it all? Some scientists say that we are all like atoms on a grain of sand simply lost somewhere in the stars. For example, if we could squeeze the entire galaxy including the Milky Way into the size of North America then our earth in proportion would shrink into an apple lying on the ground somewhere in the USA. To a person from another galaxy our sun would shine no more than a needle point. Actually, it's sometimes good for all of us to know just exactly how tiny we are. More than any other science, astronomy teaches humility.'

Then Johnny asked, 'Dad, about how far is it to the farthest star in our universe?'

'Well, it's about like this. If it were possible to take a rocket ship moving as fast as the speed of light – that's 185,000 miles per second – it would take a hundred thousand years to reach the furthest star in our universe!'

Monk followed with this question, 'Does anyone know how old the earth is or any of the stars?'

That's a good question, it shows you are thinking. Let me explain it like this. As far as we know the earth is about five billion years old. However, certain layers of the earth's soil are only five hundred million years old. If one were to stand on a piece of that land on a starry night and look at a visible faraway star you would have to realize that the light we see at that very moment took almost five hundred million years to reach us. To top it all off there are ten billion galaxies, each containing ten billion stars. You see now that the universe is so vast that man will never find the end of the trail!'

About one week before Monk had to leave, Uncle Andy invited them to visit the new planetarium in Boston. As they approached the city his uncle predicted that within our lifetime we would enter the space age by landing the first man on the moon. Uncle Andy was proud of this new planetarium and hoped that more would be spent on similar projects to educate the public in the near future. He felt strongly that every large city in America ought to be obligated to prepare the taxpayers for future space projects. In a democracy this kind of research was what every citizen was entitled to be informed about.*

Stepping into the main lobby, Monk noticed a long pendulum hanging from the ceiling swinging back and forth over a clock-like circle on the floor.

---

*More than a few astro-physicists claim that ninety per cent of all we need to know about space can be learned from earth-bound research. However, super power science believes in producing supermen. We must now look forward to more Olympic style space races in the future, astronomically expensive joy rides where the sky is literally the limit.

'This is a Foucault pendulum you are looking at,' said Uncle Andy. 'It moves with the rotation of the earth here in the northern hemisphere. If it were placed on the equator there would be no movement whatever.'

Then Monk asked, 'You mean that as we move around in space this pendulum swings on forever like a clock keeping time?'

'Yes, why, that's excellent insight, Monk. Without knowing it you have related space and time, the ABC of Einstein's theory of relativity.'

Before leaving Monk told Uncle Andy how astronomy enchanted him and asked what kind of prerequisites were needed to pursue further studies. He was told that as in all science a keen interest in mathematics was essential and that astronomy was the most accurate mathematically of all sciences.

'I wonder how it is possible to measure all that time and space in the cosmos. Why must everything in the universe be measured with numbers? And what about lots of valuable things that science can never measure. It looks as if math is much too rigid for my way of thinking, but astronomy will always be my favorite science. Thanks for introducing me to the subject, Uncle Andy!'

3

Monk's vacation days gradually came to a close and he expressed gratefulness to his aunt and uncle for the wonderful summer memories. They took him to the train and wished him a pleasant trip, reminding him to get off at Grand Central Station in New York where he would be met by his Great Uncle Ed. There he planned to spend a few days sightseeing with his family. After meeting his uncle he was driven to their home on Long Island. At dinner that night they announced that they had tickets for Benny Goodman's Carnegie Hall concert the following evening and were sure that he might like to join them. In 1941, Goodman's band swung more than ever with Dave Tough drumming and Peggy Lee singing along with Eddie Sauter's arrangements, and Monk was completely entranced. He kept on hearing the influence of Edmund Hall in

Goodman's playing but the overall production sounded magnificent to his ears.

The following day they guided him around Manhattan including the jazz 'Mecca', 52nd Street, which he had read so much about. It amazed him to discover that so many of those famous clubs resembled cozy cellar closets. At any rate this impressed him more than riding to the top of the Empire State building. Monk slept well that night dreaming about dropping into one of those little jazz clubs and staying all night until none other than Edmund Hall invited him to sit in on a blues number. He awoke in the morning hoping that some day he would make the rounds of some of these jazz spots.

The whole family had breakfast together and afterwards his aunt helped him pack and get ready to be driven to the Pennsylvania station where he boarded the 6.30 train for Pittsburgh. He thanked his uncle and aunt profusely as he hopped on the coach just as it started to pull out. Passing through a Pullman car on his way to the day coach, he was greeted by the same black porter who had served him on the way to Boston.

'Oh hello theah, Mistah Monk. So youse on the way home? Ah hope you done had a good time theah in Boston. You get off in Pittsburgh so you gonna sit up in the next coach! Have a nice trip back!'

Monk thanked him and found his seat by a window where he gazed at the rolling green landscape scenery as the train pounded down upon the Pennsylvania countryside all the way to Pittsburgh. With a certain amount of wistfulness he recalled his summer memories. At about 10.45 p.m. the train pulled into the station where his parents greeted him immediately as he stepped down from his coach. On the way to Sewickley Monk bubbled over describing his adventures in Boston and New York.

'And Dad, do you know something? I heard Benny Goodman at Carnegie Hall and I would just love to learn to play the clarinet!'

Several weeks later his father came home with a long leather case and presented it to Monk. When he opened it he discovered a clarinet made of metal. Surprised and a little startled, he exclaimed, 'But Dad, are you sure this is a real clarinet? Benny Goodman played on a black wooden clarinet!'

'The man who sold it to me at the music store said this is the kind of clarinet beginners start on. Whats more he plays the clarinet and has offered to give you lessons.'

Monk made such rapid progress that his teacher recommended him to a Pittsburgh Symphony clarinetist, an Italian named Domenic Caputo who taught part-time at the music department of Carnegie Tech. After two years of lessons he joined the college summer orchestra and enrolled in a theory class where one of his classmates happened to be young Henry Mancini. Henry was already a gifted arranger and an accomplished jazz pianist who loved to play transcribed Fats Waller solos for him after class.

Occasionally Cecilia's soft voice entered his mind to inspire him with the following words, 'This is it for you, Monk! You've found your happiness in playing the clarinet!' At last he felt that he had joined a full time partnership in the dance of life. However, his clarinet teacher expected him to spend his practice time learning the 'great masters'. As a budding young clarinetist he performed with other string orchestras too, learning the important solo passages, reading the notes as written and carefully following the conductor's interpretation, but what chance did he have to become creative as a mere spot of color within an orchestra performing a typical extended work? Why were drummers (percussion) so relatively unused? There was no driving pulse, no rhythm being generated, and it seemed that symphony orchestra percussionists never played within the orchestra as an active functioning section. I'll bet good jazz drummers could teach them something, thought Monk. Besides his orchestra work Monk was obligated to play in the high school football marching band, a spectacle which he looked upon with disdain. The band director knew that Monk really loved jazz and supported him in his effort to organize a sixteen-piece dance band which later played for all the school parties. But he got his biggest kicks 'sitting in' with older professional musicians at local jams. One of them, a highly gifted self-taught black tenor sax player named Hiawatha Edmundson taught him how to transcribe jazz solos from records.

One Sunday afternoon in August, following an especially ecstatic jam session, Monk heard the devastating news that America's miracle men of the military science complex had given birth to the atomic age by vaporizing two hundred thousand innocent members of the yellow race with two cute little atomic bombs affectionately called 'Little Boy' and 'Fat Man'. They were the ultimate weapon for arriving at America's own 'Final Solution' and a portentous specter of things to come – 2,200 atomic bomb tests later.

4

With only two years to go before graduation Monk planned to attend a good college music school. Besides participating in three school music activities he had to practice daily and maintain good grades in the standard college preparatory subjects, like anyone planning to become a science major, for example. In addition to all this it was necessary for him to take piano lessons and extra training in theory, both of which were required as part of his entrance exam. Occasionally he teased several classmates who planned medical and engineering careers, spoofing them with, 'What a snap it is for you guys! All you do in high school is take the same courses to meet the same grade requirements I have and then begin studying your major area from zero! And no auditions nor entrance exams.'

Monk was aware that he would not be auditioned on his jazz improvisation abilities but tested strictly on his 'serious' classical talents.

His girl friend played excellent piano and offered to accompany him when he played solos in church on Sundays. At the same time he began to select pieces appropriate for his future audition. During the summers Dr Louis Carroll heard him play and invited him to join his select one-hundred piece concert band at the Pennsylvania State Fair in Harrisburg. Several of the musicians in the band were students at the Ohio State University school of music and one clarinetist had nothing but praise for his new clarinet professor who also played principal clarinet in the Columbus Symphony Orchestra.

Monk had one more year of high school and later in the fall he decided to apply at Ohio State. His clarinet, piano and theory teachers encouraged him and promised to recommend him. He studied hard to keep up his grade average and worked intensely on two required solos and one of his own choice. Finally, at the beginning of February he received his appointment for an audition and music examination on his birthday in April.

The big day arrived and he appeared in the music school office fifteen minutes before his audition time. Ten minutes later Dr McPherson walked over to meet him and guide him to his studio. Appearing to be somewhat of a martinet on first impression, he gradually revealed his charm and humor to make Monk feel at ease. Professor McPherson listened intently to his solos, saying very little until Monk finished sight reading some new music. Then, praising him highly, he asked if Monk had applied for a scholarship.

'No', said Monk, 'I really felt the competition was too keen for me'.

'You are an exceptional clarinetist and I will recommend you. Just go ahead and apply.'

What a wonderful birthday present, thought Monk and he literally danced for joy down the hallway to his piano and theory exam presided over by the department head. It seemed like a breeze to him and he whizzed through it in two hours.

In May he heard that his scholarship was approved, allowing him more than enough to pay his tuition and dormitory expenses for the coming school year. If he maintained grades high enough to be placed in the top ten per cent of his class he could apply for the same scholarship for each following year. During the summer he practised every day and played week-end gigs with various local bands.

5

The sub-conscious works 30,000 times faster than the conscious mind.

Finally September rolled around. Monk bade farewell to his parents and friends and boarded the Greyhound bus for Columbus, Ohio. Arriving on a cold windy day, he spent the entire afternoon enrolling and getting settled in his dormitory. Fortunately his room-mate was a music major, a French horn player in his third year. Sharing the same interests with a fellow musician made Monk feel more secure right from the beginning. Also he had the advantage of obtaining inside information on the workings of the music department.

Monk's schedule consisted of four classes daily, two hours in his practice room and another hour playing piano. Twice weekly he rehearsed with the concert band and two hours per week with the big band jazz ensemble, doubling on alto saxophone. Ambitious musicians have a deep sense of self-discipline as well as self-criticism and Monk was no exception to this rule. After the first day of classes he fitted himself into the groove for the long goal ahead.

One Sunday afternoon his room-mate, Henry Markowitz, followed him to a jam session at the Student Union where he, other soloists and the rhythm section from the big band enjoyed playing together. In between sets he sat with Henry having a beer.

'Did you ever feel like playing jazz on your horn, Henry?'

'Well, I guess the French horn has its limits in jazz. It's just not built to be so flexible. Maybe that's why Gunther Schuller decided to be a composer rather than a player. And frankly I never got inspired to learn. However, I'm damn curious how in the world you can stand up there and blow out all those notes so freely from the top of your head. You all look like you're having so much fun. Tell me, how do you do it?'

'Creating jazz ideas is not so easy to explain but basically one starts by doing a lot of listening to the language, various styles and the overall idiom of jazz. Listening to the great soloists you begin to get a rhythmic feeling for what they are doing. Then in order to get a grip on the methods behind improvisation you must learn the rules of theory and harmony just like we do at school but applying it in a more practical way. Jazzmen not only learn to play all the scales and spell out chords but they listen carefully to bass lines and chord progressions of a melody as they swing along with a rhythm section. More than in classical performance jazz musicians find that balance between individual freedom and fulfilling

14

the demands of a group. Instead of being tied to the black and white notes and the "one-way" interpretation of a conductor the jazz player involves himself in free wheeling interplay with his colleagues expressing his musical ideas unself-consciously. A good jazz artist masters his basic harmonic material then lets the sub-conscious mind take over as he composes his ideas spontaneously in performing. By the way, did you know that the sub-conscious works 30,000 times faster than the conscious mind? This whole exciting process goes on as musicians communicate sounds and exchange feelings with each other with never any fear of being vulnerable. That's about all I can tell you in a nutshell, except we're all a bunch of nuts anyway and I guess that helps.'

Things were going so well for him at OSU that during the spring quarter he decided to continue studying straight through the summer term and try to graduate in three years. Fortunately Ohio State worked on the quarter system with abundant course offerings for the summer sessions which fitted well into the required subjects he needed to graduate. For the next two years he maintained a straight 'A' average, kept his scholarship and planned to graduate at the end of his last summer term. His undergraduate work wound him up with such momentum that it stimulated his appetite to dig further into graduate work. However he felt he had 'paid his dues' in classical clarinet training in order to graduate with a teacher's degree in music. Adding a spot of colour to a symphony orchestra never appealed to him nor did he have any ambitions to become a 'Funky Winkerbean' high school band director. In this age of over-specialized scientists Monk was more aware than ever that serious professional musicians (not the ephemeral electronic players) were expected to be accomplished general practitioners covering all areas of music – arranging, composing, conducting, teaching, maintaining fine solo abilities, with a working knowledge of all musical instruments, feeling at home on the piano to accompany if necessary and finally being familiar with the latest recording techniques. Furthermore he felt he had earned the privilege and deserved the freedom to play the kind of music he had always loved the most – JAZZ!

Considering the present world condition at this time of his life there were still three sensible options to pursue in order to survive and perhaps evolve further. Adapt to the reality of the situation as he perceives it while preserving his own integrity. Improvise – keeping an open mind to new ideas while using his intuition and creative imagination to make his life a work of art. And finally overcome the problem by choosing among several solutions.

In considering these options it was entirely too obvious to Monk that the canyon wide gap between assembly line amateurs and creative professional artists altogether made him realize that music is not a circus full of fun and frolics constantly demanding new acts, that great music is actually timeless while real creativity is a matter of refinement as well as innovation. This was simply an aesthetic fact of life. Musical circus lovers on the other hand are almost thankful for the technology of scientism which makes it possible to give birth to a 'super star' every minute (the old circus king Barnum said there's a sucker born that often). Early on Monk had learned to ignore such obvious and banal sounds as they are unworthy of the listening ear. What's more, he was convinced that there is more vitality of human joy in acoustic folk music and jazz improvisation than can ever be manufactured by the electronic sound industry. The gullible simply rationalize fads and trends as part of the 'modern' world we live in.

And, as he looked around he could not help but notice that live jazz playing opportunities were going into a rapid decline. The industrialization of popular music using assembly line production methods not only reduced contemporary music to its lowest common denominator but the establishment of an electronic sound industry threatened the jobs of many serious career professionals. During the 1960s nearly ninety per cent of AFM music union members were either unemployed or under-employed. Monk realised early on that as these manufactured sounds were gradually coming under control of a few global monopolies their ruthless promotional techniques deceived people into believing that this was the kind of progressive music the world had been waiting for. It seemed obvious to him that a gullible public had fooled themselves into thinking that there was no right or wrong in music and that it could only be judged good or bad by its function, mainly as a frill for fun and frolics. Apparently this sophisticated concept of relativism infected the masses to the extent that they smugly presumed themselves to be perfectly adequate judges of this new sound commodity.* In fact some of them cultivated a form of reverse snobbery when they condescended to comment upon old fashioned acoustic music making, especially if no electronics were included. From his studies, Monk knew very well that several ancient civilizations believed that intelligent - and natural - musicmaking was the highest of all the arts. They were convinced that music led the way to spiritual enlightenment and a harmonious society. They knew that the power of creating music must never fall into the hands of the evil or the ignorant, otherwise civilization was doomed. Only in the hands of the enlightened could music become an instrument of beauty which would then lead to peace and harmony.

Seeing the present scene in music and contemplating his future, Monk remembered one of his favorite courses outside of music, the philosophy of aesthetics as taught by the department head, a prominent Guggenheim fellow. From his lectures he learned that music has the power to reflect the values of a civilization and to direct its destiny. Professor Morris Weitz taught him that the most important lesson one can apply in aesthetics includes an ethical value - to make one's entire life some kind of a work of art. As a realistic-idealist Monk wanted to believe deeply in this idea and hoped some day to apply it. He talked to Dr Weitz who advised him to contact a former student of his who now headed the department of philosophy at the University of California at Berkley. As

---

* *Monk recalled reading about the experiment of a prominent ear specialist who took three of his totally deaf patients to a famous discotek. The doctor led them in while holding his ears but as he looked around to check his patients they were nowhere to be seen. Searching for them he walked out the main entrance and spotted them braced against the marquee pillars with their bodies quivering wildly. One of them lunged toward the doctor shaking his finger exclaiming, 'Don't you ever take us to that torture chamber again.' Later Monk discovered in his research that the most notorious Chinese torture method consisted of placing a huge metal bell over the victim's head and beating upon it until an incurable case of tinnitus developed (a lifetime ringing in the ears) and he reflected how perverse it is that today trendy masochists pay high prices for a somewhat similar treatment!*

far as he knew this school was one of the few which offered graduate level courses in aesthetics. Monk wrote to him immediately and two weeks later received a cordial letter encouraging him to apply for entrance. An application form was included along with a catalog listing the curriculum. Monk studied this carefully and noticed that it was possible to take elective courses in ethnomusicology while majoring in aesthetics. This convinced him that he had made the right decision so without hesitation he filled out the application and mailed it the next day.

Just before his summer graduation Monk received his letter of acceptance to the University of California to begin in the autumn term. Although overjoyed at being admitted it meant that he had to borrow money from his father to cover the cost of one more year to earn his master's degree. His scholarship at OSU plus part time work had covered his undergraduate expenses so his father felt it was time to help him with a loan.

During his vacation breaks Monk played occasional gigs with his friend Hiawatha Edmundson in local Pittsburgh jazz clubs. 'Hi', as he called him, planned to go to New York City about the middle of August shortly after Monk graduated and asked if he might like to follow along with him. Hi's aunt had a nice roomy apartment in Harlem where they could stay for a week while they toured the jazz clubs. One of his close colleagues was Tadd Dameron who had been making a big name for himself arranging for Dizzy Gillespie's band. If Hi had given him five minutes to pack he would have wondered what to do with the other three. It was a positively exciting invitation that was impossible to turn down even if he had to beg, borrow or steal the money to make it.

'I'll be delighted to dig the New York scene with you, Hi, but I've got to graduate first. You just let me know exactly what day and time your bus leaves and I'll be there.'

6

There are 479,001,600 combinations of the twelve tones of the chromatic scale. With rhythmic variety added to the internal universe of melodic patterns there is no likelihood that new music will die of internal starvation in the next 1000 years.
Nicolas Slonimsky (prominent music theorist). Stated in 1947.

Graduation day arrived and Monk received Cum Laude award along with his BS degree in Music. His parents were beaming with pride throughout the ceremonies and his grandparents who attended gave him a check to pay for his New York vacation. Two days later Monk found himself on the Greyhound bus with his friend Hiawatha. Both of them took their instruments in preparation for jam sessions to come. Hi told him all about his aunt and Tadd Dameron whom he had known for many years and all he knew about the leading jazz clubs. He predicted that they would do more listening than playing but hopefully join in on several jam sessions which were not as regular as they used to be.

'But Hi, do you really think I'm up to the level of any of these New York musicians?'

'Hell, man, you have as much or more technique than any clarinetist I've ever heard in that city. In fact there are a few so called big names I know who don't play half as well as you do. You know how it is, Monk, we all have something different to contribute. They have more routine and experience but they don't have a lot to say. Like you've got a personal style, man, and lots of real joy in your playing!'

'Well, thanks for all that praise and encouragement, Hi, something tells me I'll need it all.'

'Don't you worry bout a thing, man. You just blow like you do back home and you may burn out some of those cats.'

They arrived that evening and took a taxi to Hi's aunt's place where they arrived in time for dinner. His aunt was an exuberant host and treated them like two royal princes. She had a well paid job as a social welfare secretary for a large part of Harlem and she and her husband lived in a nice spacious apartment. Their two children had grown up, found jobs and lived in their own homes. Aunt Rebecca and Uncle Louis both liked jazz and thought they might join them on nights when they were free.

Hiawatha called Tadd right after dinner and they planned to meet at Birdland the following night. Friday night all four of them took a taxi to the club and found a table up front near the stage where Tadd and his quintet were about to play. Tadd sat at the piano and glanced down to see them, greeting, 'Howdy there, Hi. Glad you brought your friends. See you all after this set.'

Monk had heard numerous records of Dameron's original bop-swing style but this was a real treat to see and hear him live. And then to top it off were the two jazz giants playing with him, none other than trumpeter Clifford Brown and tenor saxophonist Sonny Rollins. He could hardly believe his eyes and ears, feeling twice as high as birds can fly by the end of the first set. All the musicians knew Hi and came down to meet everyone on their way backstage. Tadd sat down with them exchanging up to date news with Hi while Monk just tuned in to the conversation. Then finally Tadd looked over at Monk exclaiming, 'Hi tells me that you play clarinet and you're itching to do some jamming. I must tell you that things are not at all the way they used to be and some clubs keep on changing their policies. Anyway, after Hi called me last night I made up a program of what's happening in most of the jazz spots I'm acquainted with and I hope it will help guide you through the coming week. Take a look at it and I'm sure you'll find something to turn you on. I've got to go back and play now but I'll be meeting you and Hi off and on through the week. Bells, man. Dig you later!'

They stayed on until 2 a.m. and a more swinging time Monk had never had in his life. Sleeping until noon the next day they awoke and after a generous brunch decided to improvise some duets together. Having practiced most of the afternoon they decided to lay off and decide what to do for the evening. As they put their horns away Hi looked over at Monk with a nodding smile.

'Man, you are in great shape. I can't wait until the session tomorrow.

We're going over the Minton's Playhouse where Thelonius Monk likes to play and Tadd will be there too. Tonight why don't we go down to 52nd Street. Tadd says there is a lot of action there now.'

Finishing an early dinner they listened to some of Uncle Louis' favorite records from the 1930s. Side after side they heard of the old 78 'pancakes' of Jelly Roll Morton, Louis Armstrong and early Duke Ellington, many of which Monk hardly knew existed. It really impressed him to feel the joyful spirit of those times and the utter conviction expressed in their playing. Soon it was time to depart and make the rounds of New York's 'Jazz Street'.

Taking the bus they hopped off a few blocks away from the leading clubs and started the evening at Jimmy Ryan's. As luck would have it Edmund Hall's quintet featuring Muggsy Spanier on trumpet and old 'Baby' Dodds on drums were playing like they were all right back home in New Orleans. After the first set Monk strode up to the stand to tell Hall what a privilege it was to hear him in person and the inspiration his records had given him for many years.

'Well, thanks, man. So you play clarinet too? Did you bring it with you?'

'No, Mr Hall, I'm just here to listen this evening.'

'Next time around you take it along. You can sit in and we'll blow together.'

Monk expressed his surprise at such an invitation to Hi, commenting that Hall had no idea about his ability to play with him. Hi explained with this opinion.

'There's a curious quality about truly great musicians like Edmund Hall. With so many years of experience and paying such heavy dues, they have learned to be generous and open minded especially toward younger musicians. His intuition is similar to extra-sensory perception. He simply knows that you are good enough. The really mature veterans in this business have a certain amount of humility and are ready to treat others as equals until proven otherwise. I hope we'll find time to come back so you can take him up on his invitation but there's more action so let's try a few more clubs.'

Ambling further down the block they ducked into the tiny cellar space of a famous club called the Three Deuces. They squeezed themselves between the tables and found a place in the far corner where they settled down to hear America's greatest jazz pianist, Art Tatum. Monk sat hypnotized while this musical shower bath of rich harmonic and rhythmic sounds flooded over him. He kept thinking, how is it possible to have so much to say and such a phenomenal technique to go with it? It's almost a whole world of jazz coming out of one piano. They were both spellbound and hardly said a word until they realized two hours had gone by and they hoped at least to have time for one more club before going home.

Their ears still ringing with the beautiful sounds of Tatum, they crossed the street to enter the Onyx Club where the jazz sounds nearly blew the door open for them as they climbed over wall to wall people to get a close look at Charlie Ventura's new group featuring clever arrangements in the bop groove and Babs Gonzales' style vocalizing in unison with the melody. Monk recalled several recordings of this combo and recognized the song they were playing as 'East of Suez'. It was mainstream bop with a happy sound that appealed to most average listeners and he thought that it filled a need for those who felt that bop was too intellectual. They stayed on until 1 a.m. enjoying the fun of it all. Time to go home and sleep until noon Sunday.

Late lunch and on over to Mintons Playhouse where the jam session started at 2 o'clock. Thelonius Monk happened to be standing at the doorway when they arrived. He greeted Hi immediately who in turn introduced Monk. Thelonius responded instantly to his name, exclaiming, 'Hey man, that's a gas. Sometimes they call me the loneliest Monk and you're a Monk who is a Free-man!' and he howled with laughter, patting Monk on the shoulder. 'Anyway you guys pull out your axes cuz we gonna start wailing soon!

They warmed up with a slow relaxed blues which made Monk feel at ease, especially when he realized that Percy Heath backed him on bass with Kenny Clark on drums. He kept thinking about Hi's advice: play just like you play back home, man. The next chorus after Hi finished was his. He drew a deep breath, coming in right on the beat, and blew ten choruses more inspired than he could ever remember with any group he had played with in the past. At the end he overheard Thelonius and Percy mutter, 'Yeah man, all right!' For about one hour and a half they played on nearly non-stop until more musicians gradually descended onto the stage anxious to play. During a pause Monk happened to hear Thelonius talking to Hi, asking, 'Wow, Hi, where did you get a hold of that clarinetist? Man, if he sticks around here for a while we can get plenty gigs for that cat!' They both listened to the other hornmen play for a while and were about to leave when Thelonius waved to Hi and Monk, asking them to join in on one last tune before they all broke up. Hi requested 'Bags Groove' which turned them all on with many lively choruses into a grand finale.

'Man you really wail,' exclaimed Thelonius. 'Hope we see you around again soon!'

'Many thanks to you, Mr Monk, I assure you it was all my pleasure!'

All the way back to Harlem Monk felt wound up and ready to play more, expressing relief to Hi that his college classical training hadn't ruined him as a jazz player.

'Well, as you know, Monk, I'm completely self-taught but I'm sure a little of your so called classical education would not have hurt me at all. One does gain some musical depth, technique and refinement which certainly comes out in your playing. Look and listen to that great jazz vibraharpist Milt Jackson, who recently finished his master's degree in Michigan. What would the Modern Jazz Quartet do without him?'

That evening they listened to more of Uncle Louis' records until Tadd Dameron called, reminding Hi that the clubs had no live music on Monday nights so why not come over to his place and do a little jamming. Hi told him what kind of compliments Monk had got from Thelonius at the Sunday session and Tadd answered, 'Well, then you must come on over. I want to hear him too.'

Sight-seeing all over the city Monday, they took a train out to Long Island that evening and had dinner with Tadd's family. Afterwards they jammed to his piano accompaniment until about eleven. Just before leaving Tadd praised Monk's playing and asked what his plans were for the fall.

When told he planned to study for his Master's at U of C in Berkley:

'Hey, man, that's the right idea and you're lucky too. It won't take you long to meet the greatest jazz clarinetist I know, a cat named Bill Smith who teaches composition there. The last time I heard him, he played with Brubeck. Look him up! Whenever you come back to New York again let me know in advance and I'll line up some gigs for you. Peace. And keep right on swinging!'

Now their days were numbered, with only a few more nights remaining to live it up in the New York jazz scene. Tuesday night they hit the Village Vanguard, arriving there at nine to get a good table up front where they were about to hear Quincy Jones' new big band featuring Peggy Lee on the vocals. What a sensational double feature, thought Monk. And he remembered long ago when he first heard her sing with Benny Goodman's band at the age of eighteen. Now being more mature and she as a mature woman he could appreciate better her intimate, sensuous style. The band itself consisted of top studio musicians who were inspired by Quincy's style of writing. The first three numbers revealed the fresh artistry of his arranging and the band was a powerhouse of driving rhythm. Just before Peggy Lee came on stage Hi nudged him, rolling his eyes toward the next table.

'Know who that guy is with the big round glasses?'

'He looks familiar, but I can't quite place him.'

'Why man, that's Dave Garroway. The host of the 'Today' show on TV. I remember hearing his all-night-radio program out of Chicago. He played the finest selection of jazz recordings I've ever heard and knew exactly what he was talking about too.'

'You're right, Hi. And I used to tune in to his program too. I think jazz lovers and musicians are going to miss him. He's highly intelligent, a beautiful personality and has a very special gift in communicating like no one else I've ever seen or heard. A man with a mature philosophy about his work. I really hope TV doesn't burn him out.'

Out came Peggy Lee and Monk broke out in goose pimples. When she started singing Alec Wilder's 'I'll Be Around' he found himself in outer space on the way to another planet. Gradually he became entranced as she sang through a potpourri of Wilder's songs. So spellbound was he that he sat perfectly still and couldn't touch his drink. At the end, suddenly Hi snapped his fingers, 'Hey, where are you, man?'

'Sorry Hi. I'm just coming in for a landing. When she sings I almost feel like I'm in bed with her. What's more, she's an artist and a musician.'

After thunderous applause for an encore, Peggy announced that she had spotted Ray Charles out in the audience. 'Come on up here, Ray. You can't hide any more. I want you to sing with me.'

Ray grabbed the keyboard and launched into one of his favorites, 'Georgia', both trading verses and singing out on the last half of the second chorus. It brought down the house. They couldn't leave the stage until they had done a 'command performance' of 'I Can't Stop Loving You'.

Finally the last tones died out at one thirty and Monk was emotionally exhausted by the whole phenomenal production. They decided to take a taxi home but got off a block from the apartment for a bite of fried chicken since they were both hungry.

'New York, New York, a fabulous city, isn't it, Hi?'

'Yeah, Monk, right now it really is. But you know something? My aunt knows very well from her work that this city is moving toward a social decline and may just go bankrupt in the near future.

Hi and Monk fell deeply into the arms of Morpheus that night and awoke realizing there were only two days left. At breakfast that morning they read an ad in the morning paper announcing that the new Gerry Mulligan quartet was appearing at a concert in Town Hall. Hi called the ticket office and they were lucky to get front row balcony seats. During the day they listened to a few Mulligan records which Uncle Louis had bought recently. Tuning in they picked up on the tunes and did some jamming together. Well prepared for the program that evening, they arrived early at Town Hall, took their seats and waited in eager anticipation. Suddenly the tall leprechaun figure of Mulligan pranced out on the stage followed by trumpeter Chet Baker, the bassist and the drummer but lacking a pianist which he preferred to do without. Pure flowing rhythmic lyricism, fresh contrapuntal duet playing, inspired solos built on a simple

25

bass line and the swinging pulse of brushwork drumming lifted them both into another realm for the entire evening.

On the way home Hi gave Monk his impression of the concert.

'You know, Mulligan is a rare bird in jazz. He's one of the few who has spontaneity and control of his ideas equally in balance at all times. There is thought and feeling behind every tone he plays. Besides that, he's one of our innovative composer-arrangers. And what a fresh new sound without that piano. He's right in a way. There are so few jazz pianists who really inspire a soloist. If you know the chords and your inner ear is working, all that's essential is a good bass man.'

Awakening early their last day they decided to stroll around downtown Manhattan, lunching with Tadd Dameron at a musicians' hangout and after a long farewell meandered on over to Central Park, passing by a poster reading, 'Jazz Concert Today – sponsored by the American Federation of Musicians Trust Fund at 2:00 p.m.' As they approached the band shell about twenty musicians were warming up behind music stands labelled 'New York City's AFM Band'.

'This is a small sample of what we were talking about the other night,' said Hi. 'Out of the ninety per cent of unemployed musician union members there are plenty of good ones who form their own groups for concerts which are paid for by recording royalties which go to the AFM. Of course none of them can make a living from a few union-supported gigs but it's a little consolation. Let's find out what they sound like.'

'Wow, they're as good as any Hollywood studio band I've ever heard,' exclaimed Monk as the concert ended and the musicians began to pack up.

'Man, you're right on, Monk. I'd sure like to blow with them!'

Looking at his watch he realized it was only five o'clock and the triple-header jazz program at the Royal Roost didn't start until nine.

'We've got plenty of time, Monk. Why don't we take it easy with a walk over to Times Square where I know of a neat little bar with good sandwiches and Michelob beer on tap. Let's try it and later on have a chicken dinner at the Royal Roost. OK?'

As they munched huge 'Dagwood' size sandwiches and guzzled mugs

26

of Michelob, Hi gave Monk a preview of the evening events.

'Monk, you told me once about your wonderful memories of the three-ring circuses? Well, let me tell you now that tonight you're going to see and hear a triple threat powerhouse of musicians that is unique in the annals of jazz club history. Outdoor jazz festivals are a completely different story. Here is an example of one all-star group – none other than Charlie Parker leading a quintet with Miles Davis (trumpet) and Max Roach (drums). Next are Lennie Tristano, Lee Konitz, Warne Marsh and Billie Bauer. You've heard a lot about this avant-garde combo. Sorry I don't know the bassists or drummers in either of these bands. And last but not least is the fine jazz singer Billy Eckstine with Jaki Byard on piano and Roy Haynes on drums. Not sure who the bassist is. I'm glad we don't have to take our bus home until late afternoon tomorrow because I'm sure we'll both want to stay until closing time. For a jazz club this kind of line-up is one for the *Guinness Book of Records* and what lucky timing for us!'

They arrived early at eight o'clock and were fortunate to be placed at a table right up front by the band-stand. The minimum charge for the evening was $1.75 each which incidentally covered the price of a chicken dinner! They spotted Thelonius Monk at the next table who greeted them with 'Bells, man! Tonight this is gonna be the coolest time ever. A real gone happening. Let's just sit here and let them blow us away,' bubbling over with a hilarious giggle.

In a specially built sound-proof studio sat New York's famous jazz disc-jockey 'Symphony Sid' who alternated between playing records and picking up on the live performance of the musicians.

No sooner had they finished their chicken and french fries than Parker's group kicked off with 'Ornithology', a swinging bop version of 'How High the Moon'. By the end of Parker's last chorus Monk felt as if he was flying toward the ceiling. His intense sound and the driving rhythm of the band seemed even more incredible than what he had heard on records. 'Bird' – his well known nickname – followed this with 'Confirmation', 'Chasing the Bird' and other favorites he had recorded earlier. Suddenly the forty-five minute set ended as though it had been a mere warming up.

27

Monk had only had two beers so far but was already intoxicated by the music.

The Lennie Tristano combo, known for its cool intellectual approach, excited Monk in a different kind of way. He realized that they were all exploring new scale possibilities slipping away into other keys and back again with a near atonal effect, a kind of lighter than air feeling. A master of a new theoretical concept in jazz, Lennie had impeccable technique but Monk found himself listening intently to Lee Konitz who he thought was an extraordinary alto sax player, finding a style all his own at a time when everyone wanted to imitate the giant innovator Charlie 'Bird' Parker.

Ex bandleader Billie Eckstine, a singer highly respected by many jazz musicians, came on stage for the third set with his trio. The previously unknown bassman turned out to be Ray Brown which pleased Hi and not least of all the audience. He sung several originals and some well known standard ballads while his trio was so superb that Monk concentrated more on listening to this background support than to Billie's singing. After a thunderous applause for his last song, suddenly Eckstine's eyes lit up and he shouted through the mike, 'Duke, I see you out there! Now you just come on up here and play something with me. You are so welcome.'

With a happy smile on his face Duke Ellington sauntered up on to the stage, grabbed the keyboard and whispered, 'Let's do "Lush Life", Billie.'

'Cool, man,' answered Billie, 'I can sing it in your original key too'.

By now it was near midnight but they stayed for another round of sets until three o'clock. On the way home in a taxi, Monk exclaimed, 'Hi, I knew that New York was a jazzman's Mecca, but for this last week I think I've been to heaven. It will take me another month to get back down to earth again.'

'Yeah, man, there's a lot to digest for me too. Tomorrow we can talk some more about it on the bus.'

They woke late that morning but had two hours before their bus left. Uncle Louis and Aunt Rebecca ate brunch with them while Monk and Hi reminisced over the week that was. Finally it was time to go. Hi spoke first saying, 'We've both had one of the best times in our lives here in

New York and we can never thank you folks enough for making it possible. Now I know you both have to work this afternoon so no problem, we'll just call a taxi and make it to the station on our own.' Monk expressed his thanks and there were hugs all around. A few minutes later they were waving through the cab windows and on their way to the Greyhound terminal.

7

Still wound up and digesting a rich musical menu of some of the world's great jazz they sat quietly contemplating the whole experience. As the bus rolled west along the Pennsylvania turnpike directly into a blazing summer sunset Monk turned to Hi, deeply concerned.

'Hi, let's hope your aunt's prediction about the decline of New York City is more wrong than right. If it's true, then musicians could well feel a depression as acute social problems arise. I really hope that we won't be the last generation to enjoy such easy access to jazz in a big city with so much variety.'

Then Hiawatha answered, 'Things are fairly swinging for the present but I'll tell you first hand that some very strange and peculiar things are going on which worry some of the leading studio musicians. For example, as I told you before, only ten per cent of the Union members have steady work to support themselves. Electronic industrialization of the music business is creeping in and it's not only recording which has its own monopoly. To put it simply, there is now an accelerating trend away from live music toward a new technology for any amateur who is cynically naive enough to believe that good popular music can be produced by push button methods. Already there are a few power elite recording companies exploiting this process and grinding out new 'stars' faster than Hollywood ever dreamed of. Soon you'll see a tiny staff of composer-arrangers and a mere handful of acoustic professionals left to cover and support the severe deficiencies of these musically illiterate amateurs. I'm not trying to be a gloom-doomer suffering from paranoia but realistically

29

I see this sound industry business killing the human spirit.

'Not long ago I talked with Roy Haynes, the most versatile jazz drummer of them all. He had just been honored in Copenhagen by receiving the highest international award ever granted to outstanding jazz musicians, a kind of jazz Nobel Prize if you will. In spite of this he was not at all optimistic about the music scene, when he told me quite frankly that today music is becoming synthetic push button sounds. Business is more important than music and all it takes to be a super star is a gimmick and a good manager. "It feels like I'm living a completely different life and it definitely is not pleasant," said Roy.

'Shortly after that encounter, I met Clark Terry, the finest New York studio trumpeter and a world jazz star as you well know. He had this to say about the whole situation. "Man, the scene here in Gotham is depression. There's no more steady work for big bands on television. Electronic synthesizers have taken over. As for the clubs, I can count the number featuring any mainstream or post-bop jazz."

'Already it's a catastrophe that factory workers are being replaced by robot computers, but it's another kind of tragedy when technology abolishes natural acoustic sounds which we have learned to hear and control with our inner ear. On the positive side, I want to believe that you and I are survivors. I really don't think either one of us is ready to sell out to these degenerate forces.'

'Hi, I'm afraid I could not agree with you more, but let's hope we're both wrong. During the past year I've been thinking deeply about where music is headed and why. As I see it, the dominant culture of our age is obviously science. These ego-tripping boys will not be happy until they have over-analyzed and mastered everything in our divine creation. Unfortunately music is no exception. For them nothing is untouchable nor holy. Musicians are faced with an army of overwhelming odds. Some of them refuse to fight and join them instead; the scientific approach, this new method of electronic technology is a wide open opportunity for some. They feel that this kind of compromise is an easy way out and pays well. Commercially it's a gigantic industry. Then there are those academic composers who impress their colleagues with new micro-tonal sound effects.

You know, really, it's my opinion that these egghead engineers must learn how to feel about what they think and stay out of areas like music which has never been their business and never was. On the other hand musicians who are the most abstract artists in controlling acoustic sounds in motion are keenly sensitive and have a need to think about how they feel in facing this age of scientism. Contemporary musicians should learn that technology is not necessarily a key to progress. Modern composers like Bartok and Vaughan-Williams went way back to the roots researching into ancient folk music. The electronic composer Stockhausen went into retreat to get fresh inspiration from ancient Japanese folk music. Instrumental soloists - jazz or classical - practicing in their studio have little need for electronic gear. Why can't we just all go off and blow in our own corner until we come up with something new? Anyway, Hi, this is why I've decided to concentrate my graduate work on research in both the philosophy of aesthetics and ethnomusicology. I hope I can begin to find a few answers to these problems we're going to face in the future.'

To all this Hi added a punch line ending the conversation.

'Was it Mark Twain who once said, "The future is not what it used to be!" Anyway, man, your constructive thinking for the future is about twenty years ahead of musicians I know. They are just not aware enough of what is happening and why, and I only hope they wake up before it's too late. Perhaps you are one guy who can provoke them. Lots of good luck with it!'

Then they went off to sleep and didn't awake until the bus entered the outskirts of Pittsburgh. As it pulled into the terminal Monk gave Hi a warm hug, thanked him for inviting him, adding, 'Remember, Hi, we're still survivors and we've got lots more wailing to do before we sleep. Let's keep in touch. We'll meet again soon. Peace!'

His parents were waiting inside in the main lobby of the station. Driving home to Sewickley he gave them a brief review of his New York adventure. They were happy for him that it had turned out to be so rewarding. He slept soundly that night dreaming of all his swinging times in 'Gotham', as musicians called it.

At breakfast next morning his father handed him his plane ticket to

San Francisco. Enclosed in the envelope was a generous check to cover all his expenses for the coming school year. Monk thanked him and promised to pay back this loan in the very near future. To confirm it he made out an IOU, keeping a copy for himself. Then he went downtown to shop for a few needed items to pack along with his clothes that evening. One large trunk had already been filled and would be shipped by train later on.

Two days later Monk made his farewells to his parents and boarded the plane for Chicago and on to San Francisco. He arrived a week before school started in order to get settled down well in advance. Finding his way to the address given him by the Dean he discovered his one-room efficiency apartment on Telegraph Avenue close to the campus in Berkley. It delighted him to know too that in thirty minutes he could be in downtown San Francisco. He registered immediately and made an appointment with the Dean of graduate studies to get advice on his double major in aesthetics and ethnomusicology. Monk decided to finish his master's in one year rather than become a half-time graduate assistant.

One day as he was practicing in his room he happened to hear the tones of another clarinetist across the street. Listening, it surprised him to hear such a modern concept of jazz playing and so very original. Intrigued he asked his landlord who it could possibly be.

'Oh, that's our neighbor, Bill Smith, a professor of composition at U of C.'

What luck, he thought. Tadd Dameron was right. I've got to get acquainted with him.

A week later, after attending his first day of classes, he read an ad in the paper announcing that Bill Smith would be featured with the Dave Brubeck quartet at the downtown Blackhawk jazz club that week-end. Friday night he arrived at the Blackhawk early to place himself up front near the bandstand. Bill Smith's playing astounded him, technically and artistically, easily surpassing any jazz clarinetist he had ever heard. Actually Bill and Dave had played together as kids and Brubeck had returned home after a long tour so it turned into a real reunion session inspiring each other throughout the evening. During a break Monk introduced himself to Bill and asked if he took on any pupils.

'Why sure, man, when I'm not teaching at the university.' Writing his number, he added, 'Just give me a ring or, since you live across the street, drop over and we can plan a time.'

Throughout the school year Monk managed to take two lessons each month. Occasionally Bill drove him downtown for Sunday afternoon jam sessions. Now and then other musicians offered him week-end gigs which gave him extra pocket money. Some of the best paying jobs were various private parties with Mexican bands where good times rolled with lots of food and drinks too. Once each month the Mexican-American Club held a dance in their private hall. Monk was a moderate drinker but on those occasions he abstained as the marijuana smoke made him feel twice as high as birds can fly even before they finished playing.

8

Throughout the week Monk stayed up half the night studying intensively. His aesthetics professor, Guido Bertolotto, assisted him as a mentor and recalled many stimulating times with Morris Weitz. Since Monk was required to write a thesis he advised him to decide which area, philosophy or ethnomusicology, to major in and to do his research on that subject alone. Monk preferred aesthetics and concentrated on gathering material to help prove his basic premise that a sensitivity and appreciation for the beautiful in art, life and nature can be related to one's conscience in making moral judgements. He felt strongly that there were strands of similarity between one's taste for 'good or bad' art and right and wrong decisions in ethics. There seemed to be a pattern that connected art and ethics which required a holistic world view. For Monk the most universal value must be the aesthetic value.

Until Wittgenstein died in 1951 world scholars proclaimed him a genius in the philosophy of mathematics. However he was critical about the limits of logic and all theories, both of which he despised. Instead he preferred to see within his lifetime a culture which treated music and art with the same seriousness and respect that society treats science. He hoped that the fear of the atomic bomb would turn society against any faith in the 'progress' of science. Wittgenstein truly believed that 'the age of science and technology is the beginning of the end for humanity, that the idea of great progress is an illusion, that there is nothing good or desirable about scientific knowledge and that mankind in seeking it is falling into a trap. Perhaps science and industry, having caused infinite misery in the process, will unite the world, condense it into a single unit, though one in which peace is the last thing that will find a home.' At the time he was convinced 'that the bomb offers a prospect of the end, the destruction of an evil, our disgusting soapy water science.' For him science and industry decided wars and the darkness of our times was due to the false idol worship of science. Wittgenstein was consistent in practicing what he preached especially as Monk discovered later to his pleasant surprise that Wittgenstein played excellent clarinet on a semi-professional level and upon request could whistle dozens of themes from major classical works.

The legendary Harvard professor, English-American philosopher Alfred North Whitehead, totally agreed with Wittgenstein that music is far superior to science, logic and mathematics. Whitehead, who had a comprehensive background in all three areas, once made this statement about 'sounds in motion': 'Music comes before religion as emotion comes before thought and sound before sense. Sound speaks to the emotions, the emotion then becomes thought and the thought action.' Subversive, alien and undoubtedly heretic ideas for the technology preachers of our times but scientists are deficient in understanding or respecting philosophical life values.

Upon further study of these two philosophers Monk felt inspired by their intellectual courage to penetrate and expose the falsehoods of our most omnipotent ideology, twentieth century scientism. Monk believed that unharnessed technological progress had been barreling full speed ahead on a one track for too many years relatively unchallenged. Again Monk reflected, wasn't it Socrates who said, 'The unquestioned life is not worth living'? Roundhouse thinking appealed to Monk more than linear railroads and besides there seemed to be a shortage of mavericks and dissidents in our squared off world. He looked forward to applying his philosophical reasoning toward a deep sense of aesthetics by establishing the point that some facts of life are irrefutable, and that there are essential elements in music that express aesthetic truths. Technical thinking is limited to figuring out how things work but reason is more demanding in that seeking a truth one must dig deep into the ground of being.

Monk planned to argue that there is much more to the spirit of music than what beats-the-feet or goes in one ear and out the other. He intended to show that musical tones do not simply exist as sound in the air but actually become qualities which the ear and the mind assimilate. The secret power of music lies in its spiritual qualities, not in its physical functions. Even the quality of a color cannot exist in the world outside of the mind. Instant hamburgers, short order restaurants and artificially processed foods cannot be expected to cultivate good taste. There will always be those who prefer to feed their face in the same way that they fill their ears with manufactured sounds. For example Monk believed that in choosing our food we want it to taste good and to nourish us. He felt strongly that if one is then consciously aware enough to demand quality in the music one 'tastes' then one is perceptive of a spiritual uplifting that empowers us with psychic energy that feeds our soul more than our bodies. This kind of listener knows what he likes as well as liking what he knows and through active listening becomes aware that music is a marvellous way to 'digest' time. Passive background music and electronic whipcracking sounds serve the functional level of instant gratification which is merely rudimentary and too often simply banal. And then there is the disturbing problem of lyricists dominating what used to be the art of popular song writing. Anyone can find words to any song using infantile rhythmic chants, repetitious bass-lines and ostinatos to deliver a message but whatever happened to the creative composers of melodies that often need no words? In all styles of music throughout history up to the present the majority of musicians, composers and the initiated public have placed fine quality melodies or themes as a priority. Besides, Monk was convinced that the personal human element inherent in acoustic music making demands an organic unity of rhythm, melody, harmony and various tone colors. Most of all he hoped to point out in his thesis that music reflects ethical ideals and aesthetic values which can never be processed into a commodity.

Chapter II

ON A CLEAR DAY YOU CAN SEE FOREVER

It takes many years to grow young
Pablo Picasso

It's never too late to start a happy childhood.
Woody Peacepiper

1

In our times it seems to be a common folk habit to classify other people based upon one's first impression and Monk was no exception to these collective notions. They found it quite easy to label Monk as some sort of ingenuous eccentric. When would he ever 'grow up' like the rest of them and settle for something they called 'reality'? As a lively free spirit, Monk was usually out of step with his more conventional companions, being driven by a beat-pulse-rhythm of some 'further out' drummer all his own. Most people who had lost their youthfulness by middle age naturally thought Monk was some sort of perennial adolescent. How in the world when he was searching for the real action in life could he seem to be enjoying all the benefits of maturity? For Monk the world was old and ever renewing itself.

Being aware of the dichotomy between idealism and realism, he was curious to research into the full definition of these terms whose original meanings had been wiped out by vulgarization. First of all he decided to ferret out a comprehensive definition of idealism. Exploring many reliable sources, he discovered that the mind, reason, consciousness and spiritual values are the most important factors in describing this concept. Even bad can be transcended to produce good. The only things that really exist are what we know, understand and perceive within our own individual minds. Idealism is opposed to materialism because mind is superior to matter especially if expressed in spirit. Applied to the arts this means that a mental image exists in the imagination and the pursuit of beauty, excellence and perfection then becomes an ideal in itself. For idealists, reality reveals its ultimate nature more faithfully in its highest qualities than in its lowest. Believers in idealism make room for the fact that over and above their own minds and ideas there are other minds and ideas from other people. Reality can only be understood as a totality that is spiritual in nature. Reason rises to truth that is timeless and universal. Idealists love to follow an argument wherever it leads, believing that eventually it will lead to some type of idealism. Holism (some wholes are more than the sums of their parts) is basic to the idealistic world view.

Now Monk was faced with checking out the meaning of 'realism'. To begin with he thought that our true reality is in our identity and unity with all of life. But mainly it is a realistic way of thinking as opposed to fantasy and demands actuality at all times, accepting the 'objective' existence of the way things are whether we like it or not, never a mere idea in our minds or imagination but an exact black and white conformance to facts only. There is a world of material things in space which do not depend for their existence on the fact that there is some mind aware of them. The objective procedures of the scientific method permit no speculations nor 'sentiments' like 'value judgements'.

Realistic thinkers embrace the idea that any object that can be perceived in general is real in its own right and exists independently outside of our minds. A photographic frame of mind and a microscopic attention to detail are essential for the realist. Reductionism - analysis and breaking things down into infinitesimal parts - is the ultimate goal for technical-minded realists. This twentieth century faith in realism was blessed by a latter day belief in utilitarianism (value is measured strictly by usefulness in things as well as people. Any action is right if it tends to promote happiness). As a result, idealism throughout the 1900s has been patronized with a large discount.

Monk concluded that idealism and realism coincide when strictly thought out but never liked to reason with people who make statements such as, 'Don't confuse me with your values. I only make decisions based strictly on objective facts.' Realists seem determined to wipe out everything of value that makes idealism possible. He recalled a prominent thinker who once said, 'We all march toward annihilation under the banner of realism.'

Monk considered himself to be a realistic-idealist but he had never thought about it in this way.

Starting an outline on his thesis, he filled in some notes on what he had learned up to this point. Then he put it aside and began to reflect over the unique privilege he had in developing his musical talents along with contemplating its spiritual values. In this time of disruption, the atomic age, the Cold War, McCarthyism, the Korean War, the booming military-industrial complex, the jet speed technological changes whipping everyone into the future, he felt even more grateful that his built-in gyroscope was centered down and guiding him in the right direction. And he kept in close touch with Cecilia who blessed him all the way. Other musicians described him as a clarinetist with *joie de vivre* and envied his exuberant spontaneity. He was consciously aware of this attribute especially when he observed in the world around him well trained technicians selling themselves out to 'defense plant' assembly lines such as the nearby Lawrence Livermore Laboratory. Most of these technicians had PhDs from the University of California and were employed in special areas of military technology.

This latter group of people were highly paid, enjoyed ideal working conditions and long term security but were among the most unhappy Monk had ever met. Occasionally he played at some of their private parties where he noticed a large number of them dispirited and depressed. He got the impression that they were deeply suspicious or even afraid of other people who might be getting more fun out of life than they were. Some appeared to be near alcoholics while others got drunk just to forget the macabre work of digging their own graves. Monk visualised more than a few of them conducting experiments in Nazi concentration camps. 'Perfect killjoys. Only alive because they are not dead. They'll never infect me even if the disease is becoming contagious,' thought Monk. After playing such gigs he could hardly wait to get back to the Mexican parties, enjoying the company of real people who thought it was a happy existence just to be alive. And what lively dancing and folk music they introduced him to! Recently the guitarist in the group he played with had been on a trip to Mexico and brought back several albums of old folk songs to present to Monk for his collection. Delighted, he offered to pay for these precious books but Carlos dismissed any thought of it, saying, 'The club is so grateful that you play with us so often that it really is a present from all of us.'

2

A better future consists of a large part of the past
Goethe

Monk dug into his assignment for ethnomusicology, covering the roots of 'sounds in motion', the ancient music history of primitive people. So far he had learned many fascinating facts about music in these early times. Long ago, when the world was less noisy than today, sounds and tones had deeper significant meanings for our forefathers. The actual language of primitive man was full of complex sounds, rising and falling tones, soft and loud, a certain tension-release which they used in imitating nature's noises at outdoor 'concerts'. When, according to Danish ethnomusicologist Otto Jespersen, primitive man spoke, he talked with more passion, color, spirit and tone quality than civilized voices while his inflections were more lyrical. In other words speech was literally sung. Only two known examples remain today, one being the Mongolian 'speech-singers' who are able to belt out vowels and consonants with an intense physical thrust from deep in the diaphragm, the sound resembling an

Oriental style yodel with a multi-phonic effect. The other is on Gomerra in the Canary Islands (off the north-west coast of Africa) where there is a whistle-talking tribe of Silbadores who whistle their language, Spanish, like birds from one hilltop to the next.

It amazed him to learn that the five-tone pentatonic scale was basic among primitive tribes all over the world as far back as thirty thousand years ago. Today the world famous Carl Orff pre-school music method is based on improvising pentatonic scales. In the Bible Monk read that Jubal invented music but ethnomusicologists claim that about eight thousand years ago a Chinaman named Ling Lun wrote the first laws for music theory. When China became established as a country about five thousand years later, the common people as well as the emperors actually worshipped music as the absolute highest value, ethically and scientifically. Sounds in motion unified all knowledge even beyond the wisdom of the universe. His research led him further to reveal that most of the great wise men representing highly developed cultures agreed that music is the one and only universal knowledge and without it one cannot penetrate the inner essence of anything.

Coincidentally and close to the same period, Egyptians borrowed the Phoenician music system and their priests gradually enshrined the principles of music in all holy places. The *status quo* lifestyle of the Egyptians placed a priority on security and they looked upon the Greeks as free spirited boyish adventurers. In his studies Monk was fascinated to read about the legendary hero Orpheus who later became a symbol for his philosophy. About 1500 BC Orpheus (meaning 'Luminous Medicine') left Greece to study music from the Egyptians. Returning home, he taught it to his fellow citizens and devised seven modal scales. Orpheus started a whole new era in Greek history, creating a magnificent mythology, uniting into a single cult twenty warring nations with various religious faiths, and rose to the rank of prophet and supreme pontiff in Greece. A revival of the Orphic cult occurred several hundred years before Christ and some of the early Christians saw Orpheus as a prototype for Christ, since both religions shared a promise of a divine life. However later, Christians destroyed the memory of the living Orpheus, wanting no competition, and only allowed him to be mentioned in the form of a childish fable. Monk discovered the real story of the living Orpheus after reading some research by the prominent French music historian Fabret D'Olivet, and confirmed later by psychiatrist Carl Jung.

In addition to this, the father of Western science, Francis Bacon, actually believed that the harp playing of Orpheus was a perfect example of the power of music in soothing the savage beasts and subduing the wilder nature of man. Bacon was convinced that Orpheus proved a point for all musicians to bear in mind: as long as the beauty of sounds in motion captured the attention of sympathetic, sensitive and active listeners then a society could remain at peace with the world. However, if the music stopped or was drowned out by louder noises or cacophony then we could only expect anarchy and confusion. Curious too for Monk to learn that the lyre (Greek harp) symbolized wisdom and moderation for the ancient Greeks and that Pericles, the great leader of Athens during the Golden Age, happened to be the finest lyre player in Greece. Along the way, he discovered the Greek word for music - '*mousika*'. Mousa and Ike together meant equality, fraternity and identity.

Nearly nine hundred years after the time of Orpheus, Pythagoras came back to Greece. He had spent many years studying in Asia and Egypt and eventually, upon his return home, devised a musical system according to mathematical laws. Pythagoras takes credit for being the pioneer digital thinker in that mathematics, the rule of numbers, became the only way of measurement for future scientific progress - digital computers etc.

He believed that reality is mathematical in nature and founded a religious brotherhood which believed in mystical wisdom. He established the first theory of measuring musical intervals and learned how it is possible to decide objectively the rules for composing melodies. Monk recalled even in our own times the Russian-American mathematical theorist Schillinger who taught George Gershwin. However, about 1500 years after Pythagoras's death (500 BC) a theorist named Aristoxenus feared that music was becoming a mathematical game rather than an art and established the ear as the primary guide to creating and performing music. He held that the notes of the scale should not be judged by mathematical ratio but by the ear. Aristonexus held ethics high in his sense of values and was convinced that the soul is related to the body just as harmony is to the overtones of a musical instrument.

About 404 BC Greek popular music degenerated into unmusical anarchy and promiscuous cleverness as instrumentalists turned into twisting, writhing creatures and singers sounded effeminate with their wavering, quivering voices. The criterion was not music but promiscuous cleverness and a spirit of law-breaking. One example of a 'born yesterday' pop super-star, Timotheus of Miletus, sang, 'I do not sing the old things because the new are the winners. Go to hell old dame music!' (Naturally unplugged!) This was typical of those times and reminded Monk of a recent record he had heard, Chuck Berry's 'Roll Over, Beethoven'. Nothing really new under the sun after all. As narcissism took over to flatter the egocentric passion of men rather than rebuilding their spirits the music industry in our time learned quickly how to manufacture a product to fulfil those infantile needs.

3

A real tradition is not the relic of a past that is irretrievably gone; it is a living force that animates and informs the present . . . What is modern is what is representative of its own time. In the past the term modernism was never used, was even unknown. Yet our predecessors were no more stupid than we are. Was the term a real discovery? Might it not rather be a sign of decadence in morality and taste? Here I strongly believe we must answer in the affirmative. *

Igor Stravinsky, *Poetics of Music*

Except for military bands the Romans contributed little to the progress of music. During the gradual decline of the Roman Empire the early Christians with their ignorance and contempt for all knowledge in the arts and sciences had an especially fanatic hatred for all music. Music was

---

* *No one could agree more with this statement than J.S. Bach who proved his point by first mastering medieval music to eventually create a new Baroque style for his own times.*

inspired by the devil and was the root of evil and depravity. Nearly all Greek culture inherited by the Romans was completely destroyed by these illiterate 'true believers'. Before the actual fall of Rome in AD 476 Bishop Ambrose planted the roots of Catholic music which took many years for Pope Gregory to accept. By finally eliminating several Greek modes and basic melodic structure, Gregorian chants were born. So popular were they that several hundred years later King Charlemagne imposed the practice of Gregorian chants and enforced it with the assistance of his army. But even before the reign of Charlemagne (AD 800) – during the Dark Ages – Christian humanist monks conducted research in their monasteries, collecting and assembling remaining fragments of Greek music. This intensive process of reconstruction and redevelopment continued for hundreds of years up to the time of the Renaissance. This intensive work established the very foundations of Western music and without this contribution the sounds of the Dark Ages would be inevitable.

About the year 1000 a dynamic turning point occurred in Western civilization. In northern Germany the birth of the Romanesque (uplifting the spirit with transcendental values) followed by Gothic church building (accent on the natural and humanism) created a new sense of wide open space. Not only architecture but later painting developed a concept of space and atmospheric perspective of light and shade. The mysterious compassion of early Medieval church rituals, rules and regulations along with the never ending sacrifice of the Holy Grail myth were followed by the Crusades. At the beginning of the second millennium the Germans had invented the mechanical clock which two hundred years later was placed on all church towers. Perhaps one might say that the common man's conscious awareness of both space and time was born shortly after the year 1000. Some historians call this period the birth of the 'Faustian mentality' which is still ingrained in our way of thinking today.

Whatever remained of the Apollonian spirit, with its Greek humanism, ethical ideas and aesthetic values, faded into a decline until a temporary revival came about during the Renaissance and the later Enlightenment. Even at the beginning of the twelfth century a whole series of social, political and intellectual transformations were set in motion which culminated in the Renaissance. One of the greatest musical events in history took place between the eleventh and fourteenth centuries when a group of musicians from French nobility descended from the mountains of southern France to bring civilization to a country full of ignorance and darkness. Up until that time people were living in a wasteland, never fulfilling what they wanted to do because of supernatural laws laid down upon them by the dictates of the church. Finally musical enlightenment came from the troubadours who sang the poetry of courtly love to protest against the church's commands that there was something sinful in the simple truth of the natural vitality of living. They were described as 'romantic' but certainly not the sentimental kind which is an echo of violence. The troubadours thought the rules of society were less important than spontaneous compassion, the opening of the human heart to another human being. Perhaps one could better describe them as realistic-idealists or humanists who had no other choice but to become dissident in their time.

At this point Monk realized that he had more material than he needed to prove his point. It seemed quite unnecessary to develop his argument further by analyzing the great contributions of composers like Palestrina, Bach, Mozart, Beethoven, Brahms, Stravinsky and Bartok. As music became more sophisticated, institutionalized and finally industrialized, his ethnomusicological research belonged more to the distant past than to recent music history.

Considering the human condition with all its peaks and declines and fickleness of tastes the basic principles of aesthetics were still intact and universal. He recalled Wittgenstein's motto about art and the good life viewed under the form of eternity, which further convinced him. Now it was time to complete an outline for his project. Seeing the pattern that connected and the strands of similarity between his subjects he decided that it was possible to make a synthesis of both areas. He entitled his thesis 'Music Aesthetics: From Ancient Civilization to Contemporary Society'. Dr Bertolotto approved of his research with some qualifications and thought it was a novel approach to both subjects. One month later Monk defended his dissertation verbally and prepared to graduate in

June. In retrospect Monk knew he had experienced the most exciting year of his life both musically and academically. He could only feel grateful for all his San Francisco memories, the joy of playing more jazz, lessons with Bill Smith, those hilarious Mexican party gigs, inspiration from his college teachers and the overall free swinging exotic atmosphere of this Golden Gate city with its cosmopolitan mix.

4

One Saturday night in May the leader of the Mexican band, Marcello Johnson, booked a party gig at the Swedish-American club. Marcello's father was Swedish and his mother Mexican. They had met in Mexico City where Mr Johnson had been assigned as cultural attaché. Now posted as consul general in San Francisco, he kept close contact with the local Swedish-Americans. For the past year Monk had been too occupied with his studies to have time for dates but suddenly at the party all these Swedish women looked very appealing. During a break Monk met Marcello's parents and his nineteen-year-old sister who had a 'click' in her eye for him. The family invited him home for dinner and later he dated their daughter Ingrid several times before graduation. Curious about Sweden, Monk asked all the right questions and, impressed by the lifestyle, promised himself to visit there some day.

Just after graduation he played his last gig with his Mexican friends. When one of them, José, heard that Monk had planned to take a train home through the south-west he persuaded him to stop over in Santa Fé – America's Shangri La – and visit his brother's family. José promised to call and tell them exactly what time he would be arriving. This was an irresistible invitation which worked out surprisingly well. José's brother Ruben met him at the station placed way out in a desert valley almost fifteen miles from the high dry mountain town of Santa Fé itself. His hosts were warm and friendly Spanish people whose ancestors had arrived there in 1610. Fortunately the family with two children had a summer vacation coming up and no special plans. They treated him royally and insisted that he stay for a week, giving him time for sightseeing, visiting various Indian tribes and taking trips to the mountains. At the end of the week he was so enthralled by this exotic small city that he knew he must return some day. Just before leaving he made the acquaintance of the professor of ethnomusicology, Dr Rudolf Eisenbach, at the College of Santa Fé, who suggested that he keep in touch as he had plans to hire an extra instructor in the near future. His parting words were, 'With your background you would appreciate the potential wealth of Spanish and Indian folk lore to be discovered in this territory.'

'Thank you, Dr Eisenbach, for your interest. When I arrive home I'll mail you my resumé and transcripts to keep on file. You'll receive a card of any new address changes.'

On the way to the station he expressed deepest thanks to his hosts for their gracious hospitality to which Ruben answered for them all, '*Mi casa es su casa. Adios, amigo. Vaya con Dios!* (Our house is your house. Farewell, friend. Go with God).'

Homeward bound he was at last, with plans to stop off in Chicago to treat himself to more jazz at the Bluenote Club. Once again he experienced the congenial atmosphere of the Pullman car and the refined, relaxed efficiency of the typically proud porter. Monk never realized that the days of this style of travelling were already numbered and would soon disappear forever.

5

While Monk was completing his master's degree his parents had bought a farm close to the famous author Louis Bromfield in north central Ohio. They planned to meet Monk in Columbus and drive him on up to their new home in the rolling hill and lake country of Richland county. It was mid September and except for some blushing leaves, autumn's chill had not yet cast its chameleon spell over northern Ohio's woodlands. His parents had never been happier initiating themselves into a new life as farmers in this part of Ohio which was well known for its unique landscape and natural beauty. One evening they were all invited for dinner with their neighbor, 'Mr B' as everyone called him. They did their best to dress up for the occasion and when they arrived at Malabar Farm Mr B greeted them from under a giant oak tree where he was sitting with his pack of eight boxer dogs. As he got up to welcome them they suddenly realized how over-dressed they were. A T-shirt, blue jeans – with an old rope for a belt – and sandals happened to be Mr B's standard uniform and he felt it quite unnecessary to dress formally for guests. But instead of embarrassment, in a short time they began to feel very relaxed and at ease with this 'old shoe' character. Here was a cosmopolitan celebrity with earthy roots, a cross between a philosophy professor and a retired wrestler, robust, muscular, with a broad-shouldered physique and blessed with a soft-spoken gentle manner spiced with good humor and charm along with deep insight into political and agricultural problems. Deceived by his middle-aged 'hippie' appearance, they learned that he was a pioneer in practicing and preaching dynamic organic farming practices which attracted international agronomists to his door. Mr B's secretary/manager, one George Hawkins, loved fine music and after dinner invited Monk to his room for some good listening. Some months later Bromfield's best friend Humphrey Bogart married his fiancée Lauren Bacall on Malabar Farm.

Feeling the need for a reunion with his parents in their new Ohio home, Monk helped his father with farm chores each day and postponed any plans for the future for a while. One day shortly after the daily mail delivery his mother handed him an official looking envelope. Bad news from his local draft board. America was once again going into the war business and Uncle Sam needed his nice young body. Welcome to Korea? Like hell! thought Monk. He knew his American history well enough to realize its built-in foundation of violence, its hundreds of interventions, and now this appeared to be another step toward building an imperial republic under the guise of 'making-the-world-safe-for-democracy'. He recalled the birth of the warfare state when the Pax-Americana strategy began with the Spanish-American War. When will it ever end? he wondered. At any rate it appeared that the Korean War was a perfect excuse to keep the military industrial complex booming. As a result of Monk's reading of US history he became a pacifist which for many Americans was the same as a radical dissident or a cowardly 'peace dove'. His feelings were further confirmed by America's second president, the arch-conservative John Adams, who once said, 'I study war and politics so that my sons may have the liberty to study mathematics and philosophy, in order to give their children a right to study painting, poetry and music.' It seemed obvious to Monk that America had evolved very little beyond Adams's first stage in 1797. Reading several historic opinions, Monk found that Adams was rated among the few American presidents with high intelligence and had been a realistic-idealist with vision.

But now what could Monk do? The plug-ugly killjoys were threatening to throw away his life just at the time when he was happy and well prepared in knowing what he wanted to contribute to the life, not the death, of a society. Being an agnostic-humanist and not a member of a devoutly pacifist religious denomination, he could not hope to be deferred from the draft. But what about the opportunities for a musician in the armed forces bearing a clarinet instead of a gun? A compromise but perhaps the only solution, thought Monk. He had to make a quick decision and soon discovered that the Navy offered the most promising conditions and treated their musicians better than the other armed forces. Monk applied immediately, took the physical, passed his audition in Washington, suffered three months of boot camp training and then went on to the Navy School of Music for six months of rather routine training. Here his greatest kicks were playing in a big jazz band under the leadership of Sam Donahue, a legendary saxophonist (arranger-bandleader) well known among Hollywood musicians.

Sam, a generous warm-hearted musician, always had extra time to help his students and Monk was highly inspired by the lessons he learned. Often after hours Monk and other band members would follow Sam to the enlisted man's club where they all guzzled mugs of beer listening to Sam's fascinating life experiences. During World War II Sam played solo tenor sax with Artie Shaw's famous Navy Band and his memories of this period were prize anecdotes in themselves.

6

All too soon 'Judgement Day' arrived along with his shipping orders transferring him to the ship's band aboard the aircraft carrier USS *Boxer*. He was granted thirty days leave and decided to spend half of it on his parents' farm and the other two weeks in San Francisco before meeting his ship in San Diego. The *Boxer* belonged to the Korean task force which cruised in the Sea of Japan close to Korea for eight months (spring and summer) then four months (early fall and late winter) back in California. Needless to say Monk did not look forward to playing a part in the action 'over there' but at any rate felt safer as a musician on a ship than joining the infantry in south Korea with orders to participate in the 'killing field'. His parents treated him royally, while he enjoyed country life at their farm home in Ohio. This idyllic vacation ended too soon and after tearful goodbyes he flew to Chicago and on to San Francisco. With only two weeks to go he wasted no time in meeting his Mexican friends and sitting in with Bill Smith at the Blackhawk. On several occasions he found his way to the Top of the Mark hotel where the great pianist-composer Walter Gross happened to be playing each evening. The second time around he felt more at home than ever before and so he savored every hour aware of a less happy adventure awaiting him.

Finally that day arrived and he caught a Navy seaplane flying to San Diego. Climbing aboard this giant 'floating flightdeck hotel', as the sailors described it, he reported to Chief Musician Glenn Raeburn who showed him to his division compartment where he met his fellow musicians piled up on their hammocks like so many sardines. The next day Monk warmed up with the band playing 'Anchors Aweigh' as the ship pulled out and headed for Hawaii. Four days later the *Boxer* weaved its way between sunken ships laid in their graves by the devastating Japanese attack in 1941. As the ship docked, the crew was pleasantly surprised by the strumming of ukuleles and the writhing bodies of four gorgeous Hawaiian girls in grass skirts and flower necklaces dancing out a native story from long ago. In response to this heart-warming welcome, the ship appeared to lean toward the dock as 2,000 sailors whistled and cheered for more. Honolulu at that time was a very enjoyable small city where the natives were unusually hospitable toward sailors. Their small division (quartermasters and musicians) held an exotic party at Nanakuli beach where nearly everyone got drowned in beer. Later Monk discovered a rather exclusive and intimate club which featured native Hawaiian music and dancers. There he got introduced to exotic rum drinks like the 'Pearl Diver' (after every third glass one found a real pearl at the bottom).

On the day of the ship's departure from Honolulu, the entire crew reported aboard promptly but for some strange reason the ship was delayed for over an hour. The band stood at attention playing farewell marches but no explanations were offered to solve the mystery. Suddenly the crew spotted a Cadillac convertible speeding down the dock toward the ship and who was that salty old man sitting in the back with two hula dancing girls but the Skipper himself. Red faced, clad in pink shorts and a flowery sport shirt, he scurried aboard to the accompaniment of the band playing his own 'Captain Gurney' march.

Now, Chief Musician Raeburn always made 'Brownie Points' writing new marches for each commanding officer to which he was assigned and the Navy School of Music printed them complete with the Captain's name. Recently he had written a self-appointed 'commissioned' march for the two-star Admiral now aboard the *Boxer*, the official flagship for the task force. On the long haul from Hawaii to Japan he hoped to give it a debut for the Admiral's approval. He thought that the most appropriate time for this première performance ought to be in the morning directly after the Admiral's breakfast. The master sergeant of the marine honor guard promised to notify him while the band stood by waiting each morning but unfortunately the Admiral chose to sleep late every day. Chief Raeburn then decided to postpone it until Admiral's inspection came up on the schedule. Otherwise the daily band schedule consisted of playing a noontime big band jazz concert on the hangar deck and twice weekly all day long when loading supplies. With such light duties the band often felt like luxury cargo but the main idea was to build morale with live music, an old Navy tradition aboard the largest ships. Not many years later this musical tradition disappeared because of whopping budget

51

cuts for increased military spending in other areas.

A week later the *Boxer* pulled into its home port in Japan, Yokosuka, where the crew had alternated liberty time for a week before sailing out to the combat zone off Korea. Monk thrived on the Japanese style of life and loved every minute of his free time with them. He managed to make a day trip to view the grandeur of Mount Fujiyama and to make a tour of Tokyo where he stopped at a music store to buy a huge volume of ancient Japanese folk music. On his last day of liberty he ate lunch at the enlisted men's club in Yokosuka accompanied by some of the ship's boatswains, mates who were enthusiastic fans of the band. Later they were joined by some sailors from the Thailand hospital ship who contributed their services to the Korean War. They insisted on buying everyone a beer and nearly succeeded but the *Boxer* crew took the initiative instead. After an hour of carousing together most of them left and just when Monk was about to leave in walked the executive officer of the *Boxer*, Commander Bengtsson. I didn't know officers felt welcome in our club, thought Monk. Maybe he's making sure we behave ourselves. Nonchalantly the commander bought a beer and took his place at Monk's table. He began to make some small talk, then suddenly asked, 'Aren't you the new band member on our ship?'

'Why, yes, sir. How did you recognize me so quickly?'

'Well, I keep my eyes and ears on the band because I'm a music lover and I think Chief Raeburn is doing a wonderful job.'

Delighted, Monk said he'd pass that on to the band master. Then, to carry on the conversation, he asked very discreetly if the commander had been assigned to the *Boxer* recently.

'Yes, I'm new on the ship too. My duty time terminated as military attaché in Stockholm and the Navy Department decided I needed some sea duty for a change.'

'You were in Sweden then. I'm seriously considering a trip there when I'm discharged. Maybe you could tell me a little about the country. What are the people like?'

Commander Bengtsson told him how impressed he was by their lifestyle, a highly organized democracy with very progressive ideas that worked

52

well for them and that he hoped to retire there some day. Being Swedish-American, he had distant relatives there.

'As a musician you might find work there quite easily too!' Monk thanked him for this information and began to consider Sweden more seriously.

The *Boxer* spent six months with the task force and just before the end of its tour of duty a fire broke out killing twenty-five sailors and causing such severe damage that it headed back to Yokosuka shipyards for repairs. These took six weeks which enabled Monk to do some travelling around Japan, this small island country with its 'cookie-cutter' contour terraced landscapes and so many gracious people everywhere. The scenery and the people he met he enjoyed immensely. Several times he was fortunate to tune in on some folk-lore ensemble concerts which were unforgettable.

The scuttlebutt aboard the *Boxer* were that the ship would soon make a goodwill visit to Hong Kong before going back to the States. Sure enough, the day arrived for the ship to head south to the East China Sea passing Taiwan and sailing into the harbour of Hong Kong. With his newly purchased binoculars Monk caught sight of dozens of fishing boats along the coastline and as the ship carved its way through the bay he observed hundreds of junks, sampans and odd sized houseboats where people lived their entire lives along with extended families. This exotic 'beehive' city was full of oriental contrasts: 'greed growing upward' skyscrapers surrounded by primitive ghetto living conditions. On a sightseeing tour the bus drove to the hilltop overlooking the city, the bay, the neighboring island of Macau and part of the coastline of mainland China. On the town he enjoyed the best Chinese food he had ever tasted and bought himself a tailor-made cashmere coat for much lower than the Stateside price. At a large international music store he picked up a book of ancient Chinese folk songs.

'Anchor's Aweigh' again, and off to Hawaii and California. The day after leaving Hong Kong Monk awoke one morning with what seemed like a heavy rash crawling all over his hands. Gradually they became swollen, making him unable to play his clarinet. He told Chief Raeburn who advised him to see the ship's doctor immediately. Monk was absolutely terrified. What if he had leprosy or one of those 'mouldy' incurable skin diseases? The doctor looked it over carefully and said it did not appear to be dangerous but gave him some salve and a powdered solution for dipping his hands twice daily. If there was no relief by the time they reached San Francisco then he would be sent to the Navy's top skin specialist at Oak Knoll Hospital. For the present he could play no more.

Over the waves and swells of the Pacific rolled the *Boxer* toward Honolulu and San Francisco while the band played 'California, Here I Come,' until they sang it in their sleep at night. Only a short stopover in Pearl Harbor this time but enough liberty for Monk to check out his favorite Hawaiian music club and indulge in a few 'Pearl Divers'. The leader of the group told him where he might buy some printed copies of authentic folk songs but said that there were very few published at that time. He purchased what he could find and added them to his collection.

The next day the ship pulled out and set its course for the Golden Gate. In spite of following the doctor's orders his hands were still quite swollen, occasionally sweaty and very itchy.

7

Jazz musicians are the unacknowledged healers of mankind.
Lee Lo

Immediately after pulling into port the doctor signed a medical 'chit' admitting Monk for examination at Oak Knoll Hospital where he had an appointment with Captain Gilman, the head dermatologist. Monk felt completely at ease as this sympathetic, warm-hearted doctor took one glance, touched his hand gently and diagnosed it as a case of neuro-dermatitis.

'This is nothing serious but simply a nervous reaction that breaks through the surface of your skin. Perhaps you're allergic to that ship and you've had enough of Korea, am I right? Well, we're going to keep you here for at least six weeks of treatment which should be sufficient and by that time I may consider recommending you for a medical discharge but I won't promise you that today. In the meantime, here is a special solution in which you must dip your hands three times daily. The nurse will help you and I'll be around to examine you each day.'

Dr Gilman was right. Monk had had his fill of the Navy: living in a giant floating sarcophagus, playing a few tunes each day, was an existence closer to limbo than life. Hopefully he would be eligible for a discharge so that he could go on living as a free individual for a change. Captain Gilman kept him under observation for ten days before allowing him to go on liberty. After three weeks his skin condition cleared up closer to normal so that he could take up playing his clarinet again. He found a room in the basement of the ward where he could practice freely until he felt he was ready to take lessons from Bill Smith again. Finally he called Bill who welcomed him home and gave him a time to meet the following Saturday morning. They had a great time playing together and Bill invited him to the session at the Blackhawk on Sunday afternoon. Both Dave Brubeck and Gerry Mulligan promised to be there too. That really turned Monk on. He arrived at the Blackhawk at two o'clock and had such a swinging time that he played on until late that evening.

It seemed like an old home week reunion to be back in the 'Frisco jazz scene again and Monk felt that he belonged and never wanted to leave. He called Marcello Johnson who invited him to play a party gig with the band the following weekend. In the meantime Captain Gilman called him in to his office and gave him the good news that they were processing his medical discharge and that he could prepare to leave within a week. The kind old doctor looked over his hands again, saying, 'They're completely normal and as long as you are out of the Navy it should never recur. If it does, this is the name of the medicine you can buy easily as it is prescription free. I'll be seeing you some more before you leave.' Monk nearly jumped out of his chair to kiss the old man but simply thanked him for all his sympathetic treatment.

One night he awoke from sleep hearing a voice behind him which sounded like Cecilia. 'Monk, I think you are playing with the idea of going to Sweden. And why don't you? It would be a great experience for you!'

Dear old Cecilia, thought Monk, she always knows what's best for me and that's exactly what I'm going to do. The next day he called Marcello Johnson's father Eric to ask for an appointment to meet him at the Consulate. Two days later they met and Monk told Eric of his plans. He listened carefully, saying nothing, but appeared to be making notes at his desk. When Monk was through, Eric handed him a long list of addresses of culture bureaucrats, organizations, schools, musicians' union and other contacts in Stockholm.

'You'll notice, he explained, 'that those names with asterisks are people I know personally to whom you can pass on my greetings. Lots of good luck, Monk. I'm sure you have something to contribute to Sweden's music life.'

Monk expressed his gratefulness for this valuable help and hoped to see him again at the Swedish-American Club before leaving.

Back at Oak Knoll Hospital he had befriended a black boatswain's mate from New York's Harlem. One day he asked Monk what he expected to do upon entering civilian life again. When Monk mentioned Sweden his eyes popped like two black marbles, prompting him to exclaim, 'Why I've been there. After the war (World War II) was over, our destroyer left England to make a goodwill visit to Gothenburg. We were there for two weeks and I'll never forget it.' Monk asked what he liked most about it.

His face took on a warm glow and a smile from ear to ear. 'My God, I felt just like I was in my mother's arms!'

Monk, like a contemporary Jonah, got discharged from the *Whale* on 15 March 1954, a day to remember for the rest of his life.

Released from the 'belly of the beast' he was now free to go on his way to a new adventure. Bidding farewell to all his San Francisco friends he boarded a United Airlines for Chicago then Columbus where his parents met him for a happy reunion on the farm. During the next three weeks he applied for a passport and booked his plane ticket to Stockholm. Using Eric's address list he wrote to several leading contacts, introducing himself and hoping for a reply before leaving. Three days before his departure he received answers from the Swedish musicians' union, the Folk Park Headquarters and the Workers' Educational Association (ABF). The directors welcomed his visit and looked forward to meeting him. Flying to Europe was not the most economical way to travel in the early 1950s but Monk had spent too much time on a ship already and his 'mustering out' pay covered the costs. Besides, his savings were sufficient to cover Swedish living costs for at least the next six months.

Deep inside Monk knew he needed a change and a chance to become acquainted with a more humane society which he hoped to discover in this far northern corner of the world. His inner compass pointed north and a current of energy made him go with the flow.

Chapter III

'DEAR OLD STOCKHOLM'

Originally an old Swedish folk song entitled 'Ack Värmland du Sköna',
made popular by jazz musicians Stan Getz and Miles Davis in the late
1950s

1

Arriving in Stockholm about the middle of April, Monk called first on the Folk Park administration. Here he learned that Sweden's unique folk parks have a long history which started when laborers in each town found a meeting place to discuss organizing the Social-Democratic party. After the meetings they held dances and hired entertainers to amuse them for the weekend. Since those early days they had evolved into amusement parks without all the mechanical rides. Summer was the high season but larger towns managed to keep their folk parks open all year round. Everyone, from opera singers to dramatic actors, comedians and small bands of musicians, were in demand most of the year. The director told Monk that at this moment many bands were being booked for the summer and he knew of several bandleaders who could use him. He passed on their names and telephone numbers, advising Monk to join the union and apply for a work permit the minute he was offered a contract.

Before calling these bandleaders he had to look for a reasonable place to live in or near the city. Eric had thoughtfully included on his list the address of the college of forestry which often had extra rooms in their dormitories for young foreigners who planned to stay for at least one year with or without studying. He took a taxi direct to the school office and asked to talk to the Dean of housing. There he was told that no rooms would be available until the end of the school year, the first week of June. In the meantime he was placed on a waiting list and given tips on landlords who took in boarders. Fortunately Monk found a kind old lady with an extra apartment room and took it immediately. Then he called a few of the bandleaders on the folk park list. Two of them were interested and asked him to come for an audition at their rehearsal studio the following week. One thing that puzzled him was that so many Swedes spoke nearly perfect English. This continued to astonish him until he learned that most of them study five years of English in grade school. Of course this made him feel more comfortable but he did plan to learn some Swedish too.

His landlady did not mind him practicing in his room so he prepared himself for the coming audition. Both 'try-outs' were scheduled for the same day, one in the morning and the other later in the afternoon. Finally the day arrived and Monk called a cab to make sure there would be no problem finding the place. As he stepped into the building he heard the strains of a rather mediocre Dixieland band warming up and as he was about to turn around and leave another musician with a trombone case followed behind him, exclaiming, 'Oh you must be the new clarinet player,' in perfect English.

'Well, not yet,' said Monk.

They entered the studio and Monk introduced himself to the leader and the other players. He was given a clarinet 'book' of arrangements to start with and they launched into 'King Porter Stomp' with each one taking a solo. After the romping final chorus, the leader cried out, 'Yeah, man, you've got the job! We want you if you want us. How about it?'

'Well, I'm not so sure. Dixieland style is not my bag. But just for curiosity, what are your terms?'

After carefully considering the conditions and comparing the facts he'd been given by the music union and folk park authorities, Monk knew he could do better and hopefully with a more modern style group.

He thanked them, wished them luck and went on his way to have lunch before his next audition. Monk had heard records and was well aware of Sweden's leading jazz musicians: 'Stan' Åke Hasselgård and Rolf Ericksson – then in Hollywood – along with the legendary Lars Gullin and Bengt Hallberg at home in Stockholm. These were the 'Big Name' stars but he soon discovered the large gap between these gifted artists and the average standard.

After lunch he took another taxi to his audition with band number two, a rather unique quartet with an excellent rhythm section and a leader who played a very swinging accordion reminding him of Joe Mooney and Ernie Felice in the US. They featured a male singer from India who was an almost perfect imitation of Frank Sinatra. Inspired by the swinging sound of the group and the fine block chord voicing (Glenn Miller blend) of the accordionist he thought this band would be fun to join. They tried three numbers together and finally the leader said, 'You're in. Would you like to play with us for the summer season? I'm not sure how the fall and winter bookings look yet but I'll know for sure in August. What do you say?'

They discussed the contract terms and it surprised Monk to find that his group was already booked at least four days per week from 1 May to the end of September. They had been organized for five years and apparently were popular all over the country. He was offered much better pay than he expected, so he could find no reason to resist signing the contract. Art Söderberg the leader helped him apply for a work permit and at the same time he joined the musicians' union.

It looked like a busy season touring Sweden and they had their first gig coming in one week. Rehearsals were underway each evening and in the meantime he found time to meet the director of the Workers' Education Association and the Superintendent of Education for Stockholm schools. From these discussions he learned that together they were working on long range plans to organize full time music schools and they needed advice and new ideas from Monk's American experience. Would he be interested in taking on a full time job as consultant starting in October? If so they asked him to apply not later than 1 June. Monk enjoyed playing more than teaching and bureaucracy but he seriously considered the proposition.

2

For the first two weeks of May they toured the rolling hill and lake country of Värmland, shuttling back and forth to Stockholm. During the last two weeks they played in the rich folklore province of Dalarna where the band was a big hit. Art took pride in the reviews as Dalarna had a reputation for producing some of the finest musicians in Sweden.

Back in Stockholm at the end of May, Monk had to make a decision on whether to apply for the music consultant position. He knew it would be impossible to tour with Art's group and hold down a five day a week job in Stockholm at the same time. As much as he preferred playing he was aware that he could carry on his research into Swedish folk music more easily by working in Stockholm. Access to libraries and contacts with academic colleagues were an obvious advantage. Considering time away and travelling, the salary nearly matched his pay as a musician. Besides, after a four month tour of Sweden he might well have seen and experienced enough of the country to stay in one place for a change. He talked it over with Art who sympathised with him and regretted his leaving in September but agreed to help him find a steady weekend gig in Stockholm so that he could keep on playing.

Monk applied for this new position and called the Dean of housing at the forestry college who assured him that he would reserve his room if he promised to move in before 15 June.

The first week of June found the band seated in their station wagon driving out of Stockholm, final destination Kiruna, north of the Arctic Circle. Monk studied the map in front of him and suddenly realized that Sweden is actually longer than the entire west coast of the United States. Art, seated beside him, remarked, 'This is the kind of trip we call "going upstairs" and it's such a long one that we can almost feel like it physically! We all take turns driving night and day. Two days away from Stockholm for three gigs but they pay us well for it.'

At this time of year the spectacular midnight sun rose up in this northern part of the world and the sun never left the horizon. What a fantastic phenomenon, thought Monk. For the entire time in Lappland, they were unaware of days or nights as the midnight sun rolled around high in the sky. Fortunately for Monk the hotel rooms were provided with special black curtains to permit undisturbed sleeping. One day Art drove him to a campsite where the Samer were herding in their reindeer and he took a whole roll full of pictures. Occasionally a few Samer appeared at the folk park dressed in the typically colorful red, blue and gold costumes. Before leaving, Monk dropped in at a tourist store to buy an authentic Samer chieftain's hat for a souvenir. Out of all his travelling in Sweden this trip to Lappland turned out to be the high point of it all.

During July and August the band toured mainly in the southern half of Sweden as far south as Helsingborg. The south central area around Sweden's two largest lakes, Vänern and Vättern, made a vivid impression on Monk and like two large eyes emerging from the earth they had a hypnotic beauty all their own. The gently rolling countryside of the deep south in the province of Skåne and the buttery, Danish-sounding dialect of its natives made him realize the diversity this country had to offer. In September Art Söderberg's quintet toured the major cities of Gothenberg, Malmo, Uppsala and Västerås, ending up in Stockholm where Art found a band that needed him for weekends playing at the popular dance hall 'Nalen'.

3

His application accepted, Monk started his new job promptly the morning of 1 October, meeting colleagues and conferring with them for most of the day. There was no problem communicating as they all spoke English fluently and one of them offered to serve as translator if any problems arose. The superintendent presented him with a carefully outlined agenda of questions and tentative proposals for organizing a comprehensive music school program to be launched within the next three years. For pre-school infants to eighteen-year-olds the department of education had already worked out a plan suggested by Swedish music educators but since American music training was more well established and required higher standards for their teachers they believed that Monk could offer them some new impulses. Assisting him were veteran music teachers with an open mind for improvements.

To begin with, Monk needed an extensive library of music educational material written by dynamic and progressive minded American educators. At the city library he found a copy of an American music educators' journal where he read that the New York State music teachers were holding a conference on Long Island in November. He wrote to the given address for an application and at the same time asked his superintendent if the budget would allow costs for such a trip along with a large order of new music and books on American music education. The superintendent liked the idea and did some quick calculations on the estimated costs, then asked Monk, 'How would you like to be accompanied by Professor Lindgren on this trip?'

Knowing Lindgren as a colleague and a well seasoned music educator, Monk answered, 'That's perfectly all right with me. In that way we could learn twice as much!'

At weekly conferences everyone discussed eagerly questions and problems they hoped Monk and Lindgren would take up with the New York teachers. Monk spent many hours in the library studying some of the few books and references covering American music education so that he would be well prepared to ask the right questions when he arrived in New York.

In the meantime the Nalen jazz combo he played with liked his playing and so did the dancers. They envied him his trip to New York and reminded him to visit all those jazz clubs they had heard so much about. To this he replied, 'You just name one I haven't been to or heard of and I'll buy one of you a ticket to fly over.' They said they would try to get a substitute and to hurry back soon as they were going to miss him.

Lindgren and Monk flew to New York the first week of November

63

and planned to stay six days at the conference with some time out for ordering literature at the large publishers in Manhattan. Their American colleagues were friendly and curious but most important for them was the stimulating exchange of information that went on continually at this momentous event. They browsed through new books and music, heard some excellent student concerts and joined in seminars which provoked new questions.

One of the most unforgettable lectures was delivered by the New York City supervisor for all science education in the high schools. She had a PhD in physics and was the chief organizer of a huge city-wide movement called 'Friends of Music'. Large numbers of parents and teachers were actively involved and gave their full support to this project. Naturally the loaded question arose from members of the conference: why she of all people should take such a dynamic initiative for music.

She answered simply, 'It is absolutely frightening for me to witness the pendulum swinging so far to the right for science. I believe that every student ought to have at least an equal amount of time participating in musical activities of some kind in order to become a whole, integrated and balanced person!'

Immediately everyone stood up to give her a resounding round of applause and many 'Bravos!'*

On the last day of the conference they had to leave early to shop at the music stores downtown. As they left, one of the officers for the state music teachers bade them farewell, saying, 'You've got a wonderful project going over there in Sweden. Keep in touch. I hope some day one of us can fly over there to see how things are going to help you out if we can. Good luck!'

With their Swedish list and tips from the conference they dropped in on four large music stores and ordered what seemed to be a truckload of books and music, beyond the budget limit. They agreed that they would pay for the overage themselves if the superintendent did not approve. That evening Monk called the New York City Jazz 'Hotline', only to

---

* *This incident actually occurred at the New York State Music Teachers Conference in 1962.*

discover that indeed the local jazz scene was in decline, and so they both went to bed early, waking up in time to take the noon plane to Stockholm the next day.

Back home again they met their boss Gunnar Sjöberg who was anxious to hear a full account of the trip. So enthused were they that they spent the whole morning convincing him what a worthwhile investment it had been and suggested it should be an annual event just to keep up to date. Superintendent Sjöberg was sufficiently impressed to approve the music order and requested that they write a report to pass on to higher authorities. The shipment of books and music arrived shortly before the Christmas vacation which prompted Monk to suggest at the last December conference that each member select a book to browse through over the holidays.

Between Christmas and New Year's the Nalen band Monk played with had several private party engagements around Stockholm. An A and R man from Metronome records expressed interest in recording them sometime in January. They made a date and began rehearsing for the session after New Year's.

When the holidays were over Monk met his colleagues at the education department, highly inspired about what they had learned from their reading. The written reports on the New York trip were printed and each member received copies but Professor Lindgren and Monk felt it necessary to discuss in detail, hoping to provoke some questions along the way. It turned into a seminar which took up most of the day. At the end of the day one colleague, a music educator who had written several books on the subject, proposed that they organize a committee to select some of the best ideas from these new American books, make a synthesis of those concepts most practical for Swedish use and translate them into a textbook for all Swedish music teachers.

'Great idea!' said Monk, 'now we're on the way. Let's just do it!'

4

During the long dark Swedish winter everyone involved in the project had a full time job to do. Monk's main task was to make up a comprehensive outline of methods for general, vocal and instrumental music programs open for everyone from the age of three to eighteen years. With the help of his new 'library' he conducted intensive research into the latest music education methods from Carl Orff, Kodály and eurhythmics, from elementary school pupils to progressive music appreciation techniques, choir training, concert bands and jazz ensembles for teenagers. As they all began to show some progress a surprise visit from the New York State music supervisor gave them a boost of encouragement. After presenting an informal lecture, he studied their program carefully, complimented them on the general plan adding suggestions and slight criticisms, and finally summed it up with this statement, 'America may have a longer history of public music education but you Swedes are fortunate in taking a short-cut around many of our mistakes. Now it looks to me like your dynamic approach will be most rewarding to everyone in the future. Keep up the fine work and good luck.'

Monk felt confident and had good reasons to believe that the project was progressing smoothly. He completed his comprehensive plan for all levels and they compared it with the earlier Swedish plan, finally synthesizing the best of both. Monk wrote a letter to his old clarinet teacher Dr McPherson at Ohio State University to keep him posted on what he was doing in Sweden. About the first week of April Monk received a letter from Dr McPherson thanking him for keeping in touch and adding that he had just got word of an opening to teach big band jazz and improvisation at the National Music Camp in Interlochen, Michigan. In case Monk was interested he enclosed the address and director's name, suggesting he apply before 15 April. Now, at the end of March, time was short and Monk as yet had no plans for the summer. He really liked Sweden and the jazz groups he had been playing with but he had seen enough of the country touring and his job would be terminated in June.

He remembered hearing many fine comments about the high music standard at Interlochen, the excellent teachers and guest soloists who trained some of the best young talent in America. Monk enjoyed teaching but needed more time for research. Except for his vast collection of Mexican, Japanese, Hawaiian and Swedish folk music he had devoted too little time for his special areas of ethnomusicology and aesthetics.

Until he found a college teaching position in these areas a practical compromise had to be made. Perhaps it was time to return to the US and get in tune with the rising young talent. He applied and to his surprise they accepted him, recommending he sign the enclosed contract and arrive at Interlochen on 15 June, several days before the start of classes, and finish teaching at the end of the term, 21 August.

By the end of May, Monk's project was completed and those who collaborated with him were more than satisfied. Gunnar Sjöberg, Kurt Lindgren and the entire music department decided to show their gratefulness by giving him a spectacular send-off party at Stockholm's Grand Hotel where everyone enjoyed a ballroom sized smörgåsbord complete with cocktails at the bar and exclusive wines on the table. At the end of the evening Monk felt as if he had to be poured into his room but he appreciated every moment with his colleagues and grew somewhat embarrassed listening to the many speeches praising him.

He picked up his last check at the cashier's office and went shopping for more Swedish folk songs which Professor Lindgren recommended. A large box of music and a trunk full of clothes were shipped back to his parents' farm in Ohio. Two days later he took the plane to New York where he would transfer to Columbus. All the way back over the Atlantic he felt wistful about his Swedish memories, the musical and research fun he had, the new friends he made and that special lifestyle and high standard of living which the majority of Swedes enjoyed. He had learned to be so much at home in Sweden - even becoming half fluent in their language - that strangely enough he sensed a culture shock awaiting him even before landing in the US. The Swedish experience gave him a new outlook on life which would never leave him.

Monk felt proud too that in a period of one year he had learned enough Swedish to serve his basic daily needs but the great challenge was understanding the mentality behind their language. Several of his acquaintances were professors at the University of Stockholm and had spent a few years studying in the US. During their discussions Monk often questioned them about the Swedish way of thinking. Combined with his observations and daily experiences he arrived at some interesting conclusions. He pulled out a notebook from his portfolio just to amuse himself about the Swedish 'mind-set'.

These were some of the items he described in his analysis. First of all he learned that in contrast to his Anglo-Saxon mentality the Swedes possess a Saxonic-Teutonic mind strongly influenced by the medieval period. They are clever at deducing theories and focusing intently on the core of a principle or a fact which they combine with an ability to observe, analyze and verbalize. Swedes assert a strong need to be right rather than unsure in seeking a truth and when convinced hold on to a belief stubbornly like a bitterender. Sophist rationalizations and deceptive reasoning play a part here too. Intuition and imagination are rather weak in this closed method of thinking when one frames systems out of a narrow round of ideas. The language is practical and lacks the nuances of English so that Swedes understand word meanings quite literally.

Psychologically it appeared that a majority are emotionally insecure. Except for all his musician colleagues, Monk felt disturbed by the predominance of faint-hearted spirits and an inability to envision and take initiatives to direct themselves into the future. His sociologist friend claimed that the Swedish mentality is a unique example of a 'low-context' culture, meaning people who are mainly introverted, slow to react emotionally, who think through a situation carefully, who keep to themselves with a need to be alone and left alone, who seldom argue or debate serious subjects. Finally, they insist on gathering at least ninety per cent of the facts before making a decision. Perhaps the main reason that the medieval mind set lingers on today is that as late as the sixteenth century, when continental Europe had already been heavily influenced by the Renaissance, King Gustav Vasa was keeping a tight 'iron curtain' around Sweden.

Naturally over the last four hundred years not only have continental ideas seeped through but since 1945 galloping 'Americanization' has moved in to stay. A veteran psychologist revealed to Monk that Swedes are relatively unaware of the medieval roots in their mentality, adding that college educated Swedes appear to be uninformed about the fourth dimensional way of thinking, 'I was partially right before and now I'm a little more partially right.'

Monk's political science friend pointed out that Sweden arose from a near Third World level in the 1930s to become a prosperous, progressive and pluralistic country, respected world-wide for its neutrality, but that Swedes have a marked tendency to wait for the world to change around them before making any decisions. As the world keeps on shrinking around Sweden, this academic friend detected degenerate forces challenging his country's image of integrity and independence. An international chamber of commerce regime was already breathing down its neck to join the 'Big Brotherhood' of Europe. If Sweden's politicians should decide to go the Quisling way and sell out to this gargantuan technocracy, this professor felt it would not only lose its unique identity but most of its political and economic power too.*

---

*In 1994 Swedish citizens were 'bulldozed' into voting 52-47 to join the European Union. Polls taken in 1996 reveal that 70% of Swedes now detest the EU and are demanding the democratic right of a new referendum. They are aware that the EU is a backward march to nowhere with its 20,000-man technocracy on top of fifteen other bureaucracies and today the push for single currency is being jammed down citizens' throats as a panacea.

Chapter IV

YOU CAN'T GO HOME AGAIN

1

In retrospect Monk felt lucky, and grateful that he survived and thrived well as a musician in this age of scientific materialism. In spite of the dominant 'culture' of scientism he knew deep inside that a fine sense of musical values was not only vital for living the good life but directed humanity upward toward a higher level of self-awareness. For many years Monk was puzzled about why neo-utilitarians ignored emotional and aesthetic values by making the measurement of inorganic matter and calculating stock prices their ultimate reality for the best of all possible worlds. Perhaps for those with stunted psychic growth, gullible followers of the latest trends and true believers in hard core values, this dwarfed stage of development is quite sufficient. For them outer space is a panacea, an escape hatch, while becoming consciously aware of their inner space is a challenge to be avoided. Monk believed that if we are to evolve any further then mankind must learn to have faith in the spirit within and pursue it with a passion until one is able to transcend beyond mere 'understanding'. Heaven on earth? Utopia? Well, if we are to survive then nothing less than Utopia will do, thought Monk, the realistic-idealist.

Kennedy Airport, New York and Monk could already feel the electric sparks flying in the atmosphere as he stepped off the plane and went through customs into the hysterical barking cacophony of the main lobby. Taxi to La Guardia where he transferred on to the next plane for Columbus. Having met his parents at the airport, they all drove north to the Lucas farm and suddenly he felt good about being home again. However his days at home were numbered as he had to book his plane and start work at Interlochen by 15 June. Breathing in the fresh country air he took this brief pause as a parenthesis before living the next chapter of his life.

2

Flying on to Traverse City, Michigan, Monk was met at the airport by a chauffeured limousine with two other passengers who were veteran teachers at National Music Camp. They introduced themselves and, Monk being a new teacher, they were naturally curious about his background. Arriving at the camp grounds after a twenty minute drive, Monk checked in at the main office, had lunch at the dining hall, got outfitted in the standard uniform - navy blue jeans and dungaree style blue shirt - worn by all teachers and students alike and spent the afternoon at a teachers' orientation meeting. Later the director informed him that the jazz program was a new experiment which he hoped would eventually serve as a model for many school music teachers all over the country. Then he introduced him to the head jazz teacher, Dr Jack Collins, a prominent pioneer in this area. Monk had read about Dr Collins and knew of his background as a New York studio trumpet soloist who now owned a publishing company specializing in jazz literature. He felt honored to have the privilege of working with him and relieved to know that there would be no shortage of rehearsal material.

Dividing the work between them, Monk took care of the saxophones, rhythm section and improvisation while Dr Collins trained the brass and the big band, the latter a select group of twenty advanced players. Since all these groups rehearsed daily they were expected to perform at a weekly concert. Both teachers were aware that although most students were good readers and technically proficient their jazz experience was limited. It didn't take Monk long to realise that except for a rare minority of scholarship pupils the majority of players enrolled at Interlochen came from upper-middle class families who could afford the expensive fees. Most of them were better than average musicians, more than a few quite spoiled and a small percentage were obviously highly gifted. He and Dr Collins developed a great deal of mutual respect for each other and were relatively satisfied with the progress their groups seemed to be making.

The unique natural environment of Interlochen with its massive forest and a huge lake as a centerpiece inspired everyone in their music making. The weekly jazz concerts were applauded enthusiastically by students and teachers involved with the various concert bands and string orchestras. Occasionally parents spent a weekend listening to their children play as members of different ensembles. One of Monk's saxophone players hailed from as far away as the British Virgin Islands and one week his father flew up for a visit. Mr Ramsey George happened to be Superintendent of Education for this tiny Commonwealth island territory. In describing his country to Monk, Bertrand George liked to point out that their nation was independent in spite of having a figurehead British governor. Bertrand once told Monk an anecdote from the newly appointed Winston Churchill. When asked by a young reporter, 'Mr Churchill, can you tell us where in the world the British Virgin Islands are?' 'Well sir,' answered Churchill, 'I cannot point them out on the map but I do know they lie a very long way from the Isle of Man!'

Mr Ramsey George was very proud of his son especially as he played clarinet and saxophone himself and had trained Bertrand as a small boy. Highly impressed with the jazz concert, he invited Monk out for lunch at the nearby bar one day and asked him about his plans for the fall. At that time he had no specific plans except to do some independent research in ethnomusicology.

'That sounds like a fascinating project. Did you ever think of collecting any folk music from the Caribbean?'

'No, but if I ever had the opportunity I'd like to do it,' said Monk.

'Well, Mr Freeman, I have a proposition for you that might make that possible,' answered Mr George. Then he went on to explain that his country of 10,000 people, the BVI as they called it, needed a music instructor with new ideas to initiate a general music program in the elementary school. If interested he could place Monk at the top of the BVI teachers' pay scale, offer him free housing and a much lower than average American tax rate, plus one free round trip plane ticket for annual vacation.

What an incredible offer, thought Monk, how could I possibly turn it down? 'You've got me, Mr George. Right now I cannot think of a better thing to do!'

'We'll be so very delighted to have you, Mr Freeman. Let's have a drink on that and from now on we use first names, right? – all right! We start school 7 September. Your contract will be mailed to your home address about the middle of August. If you want to order music and special rhythm instruments to be shipped by air I can grant you a 15,000 dollar budget to start with. In the meantime we're looking forward to having you join us. Good luck, Monk and see you soon!'

'Thank you, Ramsey. And I'll be there.' Incredible, he thought, it sounds like a dream offer.

Back at Interlochen he could not quite believe it. A little tropical island paradise in the north-east 'corner' of the West Indies where he could carry on some research, travelling around to other islands in his free time. His educational project in Sweden would now pay off in a practical way in his new position. Monk knew exactly what music to order and how to fulfil his secret ambition to teach the Carl Orff music method. This would also require buying special child size xylophones, metallophones and a large variety of rhythm instruments. He remembered several large music stores in Chicago where he planned to stop off on the way back to Ohio.

Now there were two more weeks left of the summer session at Interlochen. He and Dr Collins agreed that the next to last week's concert would include new music but that the final performance would be more or less a review of the best repertoire the groups had played at earlier concerts. The most pleasant surprise of the summer happened when the Count Basie Band and Sarah Vaughan appeared in concert at Interlochen's magnificent band shell-auditorium during the middle of the last week. A real breakthrough for jazz. As National Music Camp had long been a mid-western bastion for European classics and concert band repertoire. Now they were awakening to the need for promoting America's own original musical contribution to the world. The concert was a smashing success and Monk hoped that the summer jazz courses along with these kind of concerts would become part of a new tradition.

Three days later Dr Collins and Monk presented their young jazz musicians at a final performance. Although far from the Basie standard these players deserved high grades for the kind of jazz they produced in two months of training. Both the director and Collins were delighted with the results and expressed the hope that Monk would return the following summer. He thanked them, saying what a privilege it had been for him and promised to inform them of his new address.

3

Off to Chicago where he ordered reams of music and special Carl Orff instruments to be shipped by air to Tortola, British Virgin Islands. Then home to Ohio where he helped his father and Mr B harvest the wheat, followed by a few days of rest to prepare himself for the West Indian trip.

While relaxing on the farm Monk contemplated his plans to teach, research and tour as much of the Caribbean as his year there would allow. He thought it best to fly to Tortola two weeks early and get settled in the bungalow at Carrot Bay which Ramsey George promised him. Monk figured that the music and instruments might not arrive until a few days before school started so that would allow him time for a sample tour over the West Indies. In studying the map he had in mind four or five days in Jamaica in the far west then a swing way down south to Tobago. Perhaps on the way back he could stop off in neighboring St John, only a stone's throw from Tortola.

Shipping his huge trunk on ahead he booked the entire trip at a travel bureau in nearby Mansfield. On 22 August he boarded a plane in Columbus, headed for Atlanta, transferred to Miami, then on to Puerto Rico where he took a little fifteen-passenger 'prop' job over to Tortola.

Ramsey met him at the tiny airport and drove him to his new home on Carrot Bay about five miles over the hill from 'downtown'. He pointed out several school buildings along the way and the local car rental agency where the education department had leased a car for him. Monk was charmed by the cozy cottage with a panoramic view of the bay, a long sandy beach and hundreds of palm trees waving their greetings to him in the breeze. Eyes popping as he studied the scene, he exclaimed, 'Ramsey, I feel like a BVI native already. I could hardly dream of a more ideal setting!'

'That's good to hear,' said Ramsey, 'because if you're comfortable and your morale is high we know you'll do a fine job for us.'

Monk thanked him graciously and the next day picked up his car which he drove back to his bungalow. Sitting on his front porch enjoying a gin and lime he reflected over the past summer and the wise choice he had made in taking on this new project. Suddenly the soft voice of Cecilia whispered in his ear, 'Another example of your well deserved good fortune, Monk! You are a gifted musician well prepared to contribute to the dance of life while Philistines march in time to the beat of electronic sounds. For you the light at the end of this tunnel can only become brighter. Even though you're only a majority of one, ignore the zombies as you dance to your own tempo into the future. And believe me, these young island children will light up your life and swing with you.'

Chapter V

THE 'EVERYWHERE CALYPSO'

'Baps, him get de job cuz all God's chillun done got rydim.'
(West Indian language for 'Wow, he's hired because God's children
must have more rhythm.')

1

The next day Monk drove to the airport and boarded a plane for Jamaica via Puerto Rico. Landing at Kingston, he was rather unimpressed and a tourist guide advised him to take a bus north to Ocho Rios. Here he found a small seaside hotel with a nice beach for swimming where he stayed for a few days before making a complete tour of the island. Jamaica offered more natural beauty than he expected: gorgeous beaches, high mountain country, jungle rivers and waterfalls and happy people full of spontaneity and spirit. On the way back through Kingston he discovered a large music store featuring Jamaican folk songs and could not resist buying as many books as he could carry for his collection.

The following morning he flew to San Juan to make connections for his plane to Trinidad and on to Tobago, the tiny unspoiled tropical island he had read so much about. He recalled as a child that Robinson Crusoe landed here and met his man 'Friday' who guided him into one adventure after another. This trip from the far western Caribbean to the south-eastern tip near Venezuela would take almost four hours for a 1,400 mile flight including the stopover in San Juan.

The Boeing 747 started to dip down over Port of Spain airport, Trinidad, when suddenly it swooped up into the sky like a rocket ship. The pilot explained apologetically, 'Sorry, folks, but there was actually a fire-truck in the middle of my runway!' After a final smooth landing the passengers began to check in at the terminal, a nondescript warehouse-like building, where crude hand-printed signs guided people in all the wrong directions. After completing the customs procedure the same people reappeared at the gate until finally a businesslike gentleman protested loudly to the security guard, 'Is this an airport or a carnival funhouse?' Finally one of the guards guided the remaining passengers to the main exit.

According to his schedule Monk had to wait for an hour to take his plane to Tobago but for some reason it was delayed for three hours. While he waited in the main lobby, which resembled an old airplane hangar, he looked around at several clocks on the wall to check local time which should have indicated one hour ahead of Jamaica. Instead it surprised him to discover one clock set at 2½ hours ahead and the other three hours behind. He began to wonder what kind of timekeepers they had in Trinidad until he noticed two calendars behind the main desk, one a colorful view of Port of Spain in the month of June, the other an autumn scene of the famous tar-pits in October! 'What in the world is going on here,' wondered Monk. 'Their sense of time must be somewhere in outer space. When I arrive in Tobago I might just as well throw away my watch.' While waiting for his plane he observed the motley mixture of people coming and going, mostly Trinidadians at this time of year. It was fascinating to study the various racial types: Spanish, French, English, Indian, African, one polyglot on a small island. Finally his plane was ready to depart and he hopped aboard a little ten-seater wind-up prop job. This young native pilot in short pants and a T-shirt did little to bolster Monk's confidence in a safe trip but if all went well they would land in Tobago in thirty minutes.

Before Monk had time to browse through the tourist brochure on Tobago their Cessna cruised softly down the runway at Tobago airport, braking at a shack which served as a terminal. He thanked the pilot (and Cecilia too) for the smooth flight, grabbed his small suitcase and signalled a waiting cab, directing the driver to go to a hotel called Turtle Beach – expensive first class but the pictures shown him at the tourist agency tempted him to indulge. Besides, he could afford to live in high style for a few days. Pulling in the driveway he knew instantly that he had made a good choice. Hollywood movies could not have designed a more magnificent tropical garden laid out between the hotel complex and a generous sandy beach. From his sumptuous air conditioned bedroom he could pick bananas from a giant plant stretching up and over the edge of his balcony. Monk unpacked and spent the rest of the day sunning and swimming at the beach, enjoying a lavish lunch, getting acquainted with other guests and planting himself into this lush tropical ambience.

Waking up the next morning he devoured what the natives called a 'planters' breakfast on his balcony overlooking the garden. Upon finishing he ordered a taxi for a day trip around the island, telling the driver to take him to the large jungle area he had read about. There they parked for half the day while Monk zoomed in his binoculars on dozens of parrots, later telescoping his camera for a whole series of shots. In the meantime the wild monkeys strolled around begging for any kind of morsels or tidbits to be thrown their way. On the way out of the jungle they stopped at a tent where food and drinks were served to have lunch. Sightseeing the rest of the afternoon, Monk discovered that Tobago was a rugged little island consisting of high cliff views, valleys, lowlands, earthy folks and small villages scattered in the hills and along various beaches. The people of Tobago were pure homogenous African black in contrast to the heterogenous races of Trinidad. According to the taxi driver-guide, Tobagonians were so proud of their territory that few ever emigrated to the terrifying city of Port of Spain.

All along the road people recognized his driver 'Berty' and waved at him merrily with jovial smiles. It appeared to Monk that even Louis Armstrong's famous glowing face had little more to offer compared to the smiles of these happy Tobagonians.

Back at the hotel that evening the local steel band known as the 'Katzenjammers' were scheduled to play after dinner. This was a new experience for Monk and he was eager to hear what kind of musical sounds were possible from converted oil barrels. About nine o'clock he heard them warming up on the beach and from a distance the sound resembled metallic organ tones but the energy output was devastating. There was the whole family, soprano, alto, tenor and bass 'pans' consisting of carved out patterns on top lids of various sized metal oil barrels and struck with a variety of soft to hard rubber mallets. They played a repertoire of calypso and popular evergreen songs for dancers throughout the evening. At the intermission a native folk-lore group presented a performance of dances and songs dressed in old costumes from old times in Tobago. Highly impressed, Monk applauded enthusiastically, appreciating what a rare opportunity it was to witness such authentic folk art. Congratulating the director, he inquired where in Tobago or Trinidad he might purchase a collection of native folk songs. He wrote down the name of a music store in Port of Spain but warned Monk that much of this music remained to be published.

Monk slept well that night and in the morning, after another 'planters' breakfast, took a taxi to the airport and on to Port of Spain where he just had time to find the special folk music store. He relied on the owner's advice in choosing repertoire and packed a large bundle in his suitcase. He met his plane on time and flew to San Juan, Puerto Rico, transferring to a seaplane which took him over to the US National Park island of St John.

Splashing down in the middle of a fleet of sailboats in Cruz Bay the plane glided toward the dock. Monk stepped out and hopped into a taxi which drove him to the top of a hill where his hotel surveyed the entire bay. Renting a light weight Suzuki motorcycle he cruised over all the roads on St John. The landscape consisted mainly of high hill forest lands with dozens of pearly beaches strung like a necklace around the island. Because of its national park status only ten per cent of St John was populated. Monk stayed over only two days, knowing that he could return often on the commuter boat which took only forty minutes from Tortola.

With only four days left before he started teaching he hopped aboard the little boat headed for BVI. The route followed the coastline of St John, cutting in between several rocky islets covered with bushes and trees until they finally reached the long, fat, slithering lizard-shaped island of Tortola. Unfortunately his car was parked at the airport which meant a half hour taxi trip to the other end of the island. Arriving there he found the car in good shape and drove back to his bungalow on Carrot Bay. The shipment of instruments and note material had been delivered to the Department of Education and a janitor delivered it to the central elementary school. The plan called for Monk to conduct his innovative music training from Kindergarten to 6th grade level inviting in other classroom teachers to observe this experiment, hoping that they in turn would make use of these methods as a supplement in their daily teaching.

2

From the first day of school he got into action, hardly wasting a second of time. Tortola's black children were all surprisingly well behaved and needed little discipline. Good natured with happy dispositions, they fell into the body rhythm exercises so quickly that soon they were teaching Monk. They seemed to have a natural need for expressing themselves rhythmically, applying the Orff body motion of stomping, slapping the knees, hand clapping and snapping fingers in various combinations and rhythmic patterns. Monk kept the tempo beating away on his conga and bongo drums while later training some of the pupils to take over. Tambourines, maracas and claves soon joined in until it looked and sounded like a festive carnival.

The next stage involved teaching them to sing a collection of simple West Indian folk songs, keeping the percussion swinging and adding piano accompaniment. When he felt that they had sufficient confidence from several months of practicing this routine and adding new songs, then he introduced the sound of the Orff style xylophones and metallophones, teaching four pupils at a time (on soprano, alto, tenor and bass instruments) how to compose simple melodies 2,3,4, and 5 tones step by step. Everyone in the class took turns playing until Monk thought that they could play and sing the pentatonic (5-tone) scale backwards and forwards. When they had reached that level it was time for each pupil to play a five tone melody while Monk played a kind of 'seesaw' ostinato (repeated motif) line on the bass xylophone. Then he passed on the bass mallets to a pupil to play the same line while he made up a second part on the alto xylophone, inviting a pupil to do the same, and finally on to the third tenor part. This workout took several more months until each class mastered the basic routine. Finally the class voted on the melodies they thought were best, choosing six of them worthy of lyrics which they made up themselves as Monk stimulated them with suggestions. After these songs were composed complete with words there was nothing left to do but arrange a production out of it all: body rhythm 'dances', (stomping, clapping, snapping fingers) percussion section 'background', a four-part xylophone arrangement, and a choir of voices singing.

During the spring of the school year these 'jam sessions' rocked the entire school building like an earthquake. The visiting teachers were inspired by these performances and transferred some of the methods into their own classrooms. Ramsey George was delighted and highly impressed, exclaiming, 'I knew you were going to teach them to enjoy the value of good music-making in their lives but I had no idea that you would make them sound so professional. In all my years of education I've never seen a happier bunch of kids anywhere. If more kids participated in this kind of musical activity early on they'd laugh off teenage pop groups as deprived childhood exhibitionists. They're just as clever using the same musical devices but don't have to lean on the machinery of the electronic sound industry!'

Monk was gratified to hear his own opinions confirmed. He had already witnessed too many musically illiterate adolescents sucking on electronic technology to replace the inner living experience of music which they missed as infants. Repressed or deprived childhood? Poor things! Synthetic sounds are like magic, a deceptive power which creates an illusion.

If pop players ever grow up and out of it perhaps they might discover the natural joy of playing music acoustically. From this teaching experience Monk became convinced that creative music-making using natural acoustic sounds in early childhood builds a foundation to make more mature musical judgements in later years. In planting these musical 'seeds' Monk gave the children confidence in knowing that they could create and perform their own songs as a bulwark against all monoculture sounds.

Throughout this busy school year Monk found time to play weekends with a retired New York studio pianist at Tortola's luxury hotel Prospect Reef. Also a noted song-writer, Marty Clark was a 'Continental' showman in the Noel Coward-Victor Borge style, making their gig quite hilarious at times. Monk recalled one evening when the prime minister of this tiny country of 10,000 came in and seated himself close to Marty's piano. As Marty started to play the introduction to a song he left out a chord and missed a few tones which startled the audience until he shook his head, looked up into the microphone and bellowed, 'Oh Lord, forgive me. I always get so nervous when my Emperor is near!' Then he continued, playing better than ever as though nothing had happened. Another amusing event happened in December when many guests including single European and American women had flown in for Christmas vacation. Quite a few single black men around Tortola showed up at the hotel lounge to make themselves available. As they played 'White Christmas' Marty sang a chorus coming into the last four bars adding a new twist, 'And may all your mistresses be white!' Gazing out at all the single men he added, 'All my best wishes go to you local guys out there!'

Around the end of March Monk read an announcement in the *Ethnomusicology Journal* that their annual international meeting would take place the third week in June at the University in Barbados. From BVI he figured that was nearly a two-hour flight but if he flew to nearby St Vincent first he could include a three-day trip down through the Grenadines and take a short flight to Barbados later. Monk mailed his application and booked both the plane and the boat trip far in advance to assure good timing. Ramsey George offered him a contract for the following school year but Monk believed that he had proved his point for elementary music education and his collection of folk songs was more than adequate for the present. Besides, he still hoped that someday he might find a college teaching position in his major area.

During the last week of school each class from pre-school to grade 6 chose two pieces to perform in concert. By that time the local radio and newspaper had publicized the rehearsals in such a positive way that the whole community was curious to hear the results. Monk had rehearsed the children so well that the final performance took care of itself almost automatically with little need for conducting. At the end the audience applauded for five minutes non-stop and demanded an encore for which Monk led all the classes into a rousing rendition of 'Every Time I Feel the Spirit' - a West Indian classic folk spiritual. Many parents came forward and thanked him for his work, regretting that he could not stay on another year.

3

Now it was a hop to San Juan again and a long jump to the island of St Vincent where he boarded the mail boat for Grenada early one sunny morning. Grabbing his suitcase he found a cozy place forward on the forecastle and pulled out his binoculars as the boat got underway. The first stop was the beautiful but sparsely populated island of Bequia, a haven for many Caribbean sailors. Observing the passengers, he noticed a large gang of Rastafarians on the starboard side of the bow and on the port side a group of young people gathered around a middle aged man who appeared to be their leader. Upon leaving Bequia a much older Rastafarian with a head full of twisted curls crossed over to introduce himself to this white man. Shaking hands they each waved a black book in the other hand and sat down together to read. Quite spontaneously the black leader read aloud some verses from his bible version and while this was going on another young Rastafarian walked toward the white group holding high a huge portrait of Haile Selassie. When their leader finished reading the whole group of blacks shouted 'Amen!' Then the white leader started to read from the New Testament and as he finished the young people cried out 'Hallelujah!' This dialogue continued for nearly an hour until the boat pulled into a dock on the island of Canouan where the Christian group, waving goodbye, departed for their summer retreat. It turned out that this black congregation was headed for Palm Island, a meeting place for many West Indian Rastafarians. Marijuana smoking is a holy ritual for this Jamaican denomination so once again

Monk experienced getting high passively for the rest of the trip. All the way to Palm Island these Rastafarians serenaded the passengers chanting their reggae style hymns accompanied by two guitars, a conga, a bongo drum and several tambourines. Arriving at Palm Island the jam session broke up as this curly-locked group lined up at the gang-plank. A gang of fellow members greeted them from the dock and prepared to load them all into a large pick-up truck. Monk waved farewell, wistfully aware that the last part of the trip would be rather dull without them.

And indeed as they sailed on to Grenada he was not the only passenger to miss the exuberant Rastafarians and their joyful serenading. Other passengers included a mixed bag of inter-island traders, a few tourists and some medical students on their way back to school. Cruising into the main port of St George's Monk caught a whiff of spicy fragrance in the air. Then he recalled that Grenada is the nutmeg capital of the world.

As he stepped onto the dock he spotted a nice looking hotel only a block away. He walked over to inquire about a room and the clerk told him that he had arrived just in time.

'Yassuh yo sho is a lucky man. Fradie night, all the rooms done been booked foh weekend but someone just called and checked out on us.'

Tired from a long day's trip Monk slept early and woke up to enjoy another 'planters' style breakfast then signed up for a bus tour around the island. That evening the hotel featured a folk-lore show. An enthusiastic native audience gathered and packed the place, making Monk feel as if he was actually participating in a carnival. The spotlight centered on a popular Trinidad singer who had been King of the Calypso for two years in succession and Monk thought to himself what a privilege it was to take part in such an authentic performance. After the floor show everyone danced to the music of a local steel band that turned into a groovy production in itself. The free swinging hilarity became so infectious that Monk could not resist taking on several partners to join in the fun of it all.

4

The next morning, very reluctantly, he had to leave this cozy little spice island on the noon plane for Barbados. He arrived in Bridgetown a day before the conference began and took a taxi to the hotel where the meeting would be held. While walking through the lobby toward the main desk he bumped into his ethnomusicology professor from Berkley. Embracing each other, they had begun to exchange up to date news when suddenly the metallic rippling organ sound of a steel band broke through the conversation.

'Happy hours! Let's have a drink together!' said Monk.

They listened intently to the band and between tunes the long pauses allowed them to continue relating their experiences.

'It certainly is fascinating to hear what an adventurous time you've been having in exotic parts of the world. What are you up to next, Monk? Any plans?'

'Well after my Korean stint in the Navy I felt polarized by America's militarism but right now I miss the access to research in my special areas. Just for a change I'd like to drop back into the scene to discover what I might be missing.'

'I know exactly how you feel because I had to search and wait for too many years to get the right opening. And by now you know yourself how difficult it is to find those rare opportunities in our field. But Monk, from what I know about you, Lady Luck is always on your tail. You seem to be blessed with good fortune. I have a hunch it won't be long before you'll land a good position and this is definitely the right place to start!'

They were about to leave when suddenly an old familiar voice boomed through the lounge. 'Monk Freeman! And there's Donald Grove too! I see you're both acquainted.' Dr Eisenbach literally skipped over the dance floor to shake their hands.

'But first of all I want to ask Monk an important question. Did you ever receive my air mail letter sent to you in BVI sometime in April?'

'Very strange but I never got it. Occasionally the mail gets mixed up with inter-island deliveries. For all we know it may be lying in the USVI post office instead. But then they should have mailed it back to your address.'

'Oh well, I can understand that these things happen. The post office is not always perfect. But now let me give you the message. It's just this. You'll recall when we met two years ago in Santa Fé that we were making future plans to hire an assistant instructor in ethnomusicology as soon as our budget allowed. Six months ago we placed ads in several music journals that we had such an opening and received twenty applications. None were adequate for our needs. Fortunately you left copies of your transcripts and references with me which impressed our committee sufficiently that they asked me to notify you immediately. As of the time I left we have no one else in mind so let me ask you now, are you still interested?'

'You know very well that I'm enchanted by the ambience of Santa Fé and the potential opportunities for Spanish and Indian research but before I answer, let me ask what the terms and conditions are.'

'Right now I can only promise that your salary will amount to twice the pay of New Mexico high school teachers. You'll have a half time teaching schedule - about two classes daily - and half time research combined with field work and writing - hopefully for academic journals. Apartments are not always easy to come by but we'll find you one before you arrive. How does that sound so far?'

'My answer has to be a resounding YES! I can hardly wait to get started. During the summer I'll be staying at my parents' home in Ohio,' (writing the address). 'If you'll just mail it there I'll sign it and send it back immediately.'

'Congratulations, Monk. I know you've made a wise decision and we'll all be delighted to have you on the staff. Our committee chairman will be happy to hear the good news when I phone him which I'll do right now!'

As he left, Dr Grove nudged him, saying, 'My God, Monk, the very moment I mentioned Lady Luck your Muse connected you on the spot. I wish I knew her. Tell me, what's her name?'

'A guardian angel named Cecilia. But you can't have her. She's all mine!' Both of them laughed at the thought while Monk said a silent prayer – 'So very many thanks again, C.C.' This was followed by Dr Grove's comment:

'With a patron saint on your side it's no wonder you have such good fortune!'

Monk made copious notes at the four-day convention and enjoyed meeting colleagues from all over the US. The lectures were not only enlightening but gave him a feeling of 'welcome home' to his main interest. They brought him up to date on recent research and methods which he'd missed during his time in Sweden and the BVI. In turn more than a few of his colleagues were curious and a bit envious of his unique experiences.

The last night's festivities included a rum party and a steel band for dancing with many of the local women, waking up in time to prepare for the flight to Miami via Puerto Rico. Once aboard a plane Monk always got the feeling of gliding through time and space and while flying north-west over the Caribbean Sea the same sensation overwhelmed him. Here again he was making another leap, a geographical hop through space, as he reminisced over living, working and playing with the beautiful people of the West Indies: precious memories of an exotic time in his life – a high point which he would always remember with wistful regret.

5

From Miami he bade farewell to colleagues splitting off in all directions and flew on to Atlanta where he transferred to the Columbus plane to arrive home in time to help his father haul in the first clipping of new mown hay. On weekends he joined in jam sessions at nearby Ashland College hangouts. There he met a highly gifted jazz drummer, a Greek-American named Domitrius Karas whom Monk admired both musically and personally. 'Dom', as he was called, had booked a gig for the month of August at a resort on Lake Erie and the hotel owner requested some 'Dixieland' along with Goodman swing style. Having already lined up a sextet he needed a good clarinet man and asked Monk if he'd like to join them. Naturally Monk jumped at the chance. Dom explained that they were due to start 1 August with a contract to perform six nights per week for slightly higher than union scale along with free room and meals. The band consisted of string bass, piano, drums, trombone, trumpet and clarinet and after rehearsing intensively the last two weeks of July they felt rather good about playing together.

Pleased with their neat swinging sound and full of confidence, they packed up everything into three cars and arrived at the Hotel Madison Park the afternoon of 1 August. Their debut performance that evening was a great success and the owner seemed quite happy too. It was a swinging start for the band but the tempo of the days flew on at an accelerating pace and Monk grew restless waiting for his contract from Dr Eisenbach. Finally, toward the end of the month, the College of Santa Fé letter was forwarded to him by his parents. He read through the agreement carefully and, feeling secure that the terms were met, he signed the contract and mailed it. Then he called United Airlines to book his plane from Columbus to Chicago and on to Albuquerque on 7 September, which gave him a week to pack and a week after arrival to prepare for his teaching assignment. Monk wrote a short letter to Dr Eisenbach to thank him and remind him of his promise to find an apartment.

When the band finished playing that night Monk treated them all to a beer in celebration of his new job. They offered congratulations and wished him well but Dom could not resist quipping, 'Look out, man, you'd better get yourself a six-gun and horse to live in that cowboy and Indian country!'

Just as the band began to sound perfect enough to record or go on tour the gig was over. During the two hour drive home Dom and Monk talked over the contemporary music scene and arrived at the same conclusion: that the future for professional acoustic musicians appeared to be dismal and joining the amateurs in a music factory was simply too degrading and rudimentary for serious professionals to consider. Dom agreed that reconstructing a sense of aesthetics beyond the 'new sensibility' creed must be a priority. Perhaps Monk was on the right track, going back to the roots by researching and promoting folk music of which Afro-American jazz is an offshoot. And he envied Monk for his experience in training pre-school children with special music methods, feeling somewhat deprived by not having had that privilege as a child or a teacher. As they approached the family farmhouse Dom embraced Monk, wishing all the best.

6

Sitting down at dinner that evening with the family suddenly seemed like a special kind of reunion after being away so often so long and now preparing to travel again. While Monk pondered over all these midway house stopovers between trips his father looked over to ask with curiosity, 'You know, Monk, after all your travelling and living in foreign countries you ought to find time to sit down and write a book about it!'

'Well, frankly, Dad, I'm still digesting all this experience and until I can find my own permanent home somewhere in this chaotic world I'm not ready to organize my material. And now that I'm thirty years old it's certainly not too early to settle down. I'm looking forward to Santa Fé because all present signs point west and I may just discover my future there.'

The day before he left a letter came from the Dean of Housing in Santa Fé notifying him that they had found an apartment and including the address and telephone number of the landlord. It was heartening news to know that the welcome mat was laid out for him. Now all that he had to do was pack up his suitcase, get a good night's sleep and ride with his father to the Columbus airport the next morning.

As usual they got to the airport an hour in advance and after a long last farewell to both parents he boarded his plane for the first hop to Chicago. The stewardess started serving breakfast immediately when the plane levelled off but no sooner had he finished eating than they gradually descended to prepare for a landing. With only forty minutes to transfer to his Albuquerque plane he realized time was short when he stepped off into the 'suction tunnel' leading into a corridor. Hastening, he found his way to the proper flight gate, climbed aboard and settled down in a front seat with plenty of leg room. The plane took off on time and soon Monk's mind shifted into its usual three dimensional mood. However, this time he reflected over the fact that a new chapter in his life was about to begin. Philosophically it seemed that this passage might prove to be another stage demanding more maturity than ever on his part. At this point in time he considered himself a human being first and a musician second while being confined to a globe full of wandering pilgrims hopefully evolving into one world citizens. Then he recalled several aphorisms he had learned from Indian chiefs on his last visit to Santa Fé: 'The white man is always analyzing and exploiting nature. When times move too fast, slow up, contemplate and let your soul catch up with you.'

Indeed, these were thoughts for meditation which filled Monk with humility and at the same time prepared him for his future research. Indeed, perhaps it was time for him to devote more leisure moments for pure contemplation, an ancient Greek habit that is nearly obsolete in our age. This way of thinking is a waste of time for neo-utilitarian minds who have learned to replace such pleasures with second hand academic knowledge and 'info-tech' computers.

For thousands of years men were wise in knowing how to live with Mother Nature until the Western 'supermen' of science conquered her. These scientists are neither wise nor mature enough to control themselves. In fact some of them need their diapers changed before they turn our 'Big House' (Indian name for earth) into a planetary Augean stable. When will they switch their minds to another track and realize that superhuman reason along with a sense of ethics will be needed for mankind's survival?

Chapter VI

ALONG THE SANTA FÉ TRAIL

1

While ruminating over these thoughts Monk gradually drifted off to sleep until awakened by the announcement that the plane would be landing in Albuquerque in ten minutes. Looking out the window he recognized again the typical south-western sunbaked sandy landscape and the high rugged hills surrounding the city of Albuquerque. A smooth as velvet landing, off into the suction tunnel and hallway to find his luggage, then out the main door to wait for the next bus to Santa Fé. Fifteen minutes later he was rolling north into higher hill country toward the capital city. Arriving at the end of the line he got off the bus and found the telephone number of his landlord who happened to be home when he called. Pedro Gomez told him to wait and he would pick him up at the bus station to take him to the apartment. Almost within a few minutes Mr Gomez met him and together they drove to a high hill on the edge of town where he had a breathtaking view of the entire city from his balcony on the top floor.

'It's a beautiful layout,' exclaimed Monk. 'I feel like a lucky man,' thanking the landlord and paying his first month's rent.

Tired from the long flight but happy about his new apartment, he unpacked quickly, grabbed a chair and spent the rest of the evening sitting on the balcony enthralled by this city of enchantment, his Shangri-La. He slept deeply and well that night, awakening to radiant sunlight beaming through his bedroom window. Surprised in checking his watch that he had slept so late he jumped out of bed, initiated the bathroom with his morning routine, then sat down to make a list of practical details to be carried out: telephone service, groceries, leasing a car with option to buy later, and calling Dr Eisenbach. First he had to take a walk downtown, eat breakfast and look over the whole scene.

As he proceeded to leave his apartment building and start the long downhill trek to town he gazed upward at the Sangre de Cristo mountains only a few miles away. Monk was astonished to see such a huge belt of forests wrapped around these mountains in high dry semi-desert country where the sun shines 350 days of the year. But then he remembered that the snow-capped mountain tops are the main source of water supply for the trees as well as for the population. Coming into downtown he passed by sidewalk cafés where many local Spaniards were enjoying their morning coffee and continued on to the town square, passing through the Indian market which was opening up for the day. He stopped at a hotel restaurant to eat his breakfast and afterwards called Dr Eisenbach who was delighted to hear that he had arrived and hoped he liked his apartment. Monk was informed that the staff had scheduled the first teachers' meeting the following Monday morning at nine o'clock. He also got tips on where to lease a car and how to find the local shopping center. Spending the rest of the morning at a car dealer he finally decided on leasing a new model Volkswagen convertible which he thought was practical and sufficient for his needs. That afternoon he went shopping for groceries and other personal items. He bought a book on the history of Santa Fé along with a map and browsed through it when he arrived at home.

The next day, Saturday, he decided to take an all-day sightseeing trip through the vast mountain country surrounding the territory of Santa Fé. All along the route it amazed him to observe how nature laid out such contrasting landscapes between the desert and the mountains with no shortage of greenery. Sparse though they were, the desert still had its share of tiny bushes, trees and cactus, while the high hills and mountains abounded with forests. On the way home he passed through the nefarious birthplace of the atomic bomb, Los Alamos. Along the roadside he noticed red and white signs placed every 100 yards which read, 'Danger Explosives'. This puzzled him for several weeks until a well informed colleague later explained that when the atomic bomb was underway the scientists had no idea what to do with the nuclear waste so they simply buried it in landfill and even today no one knows how much radio activity is polluting the air and the ground water level. Then Monk reflected on such arrogant devastation, confirming his previous opinion about diaper changes for sloppy scientists who 'crap' freely everywhere using Mother Earth for an outhouse.

2

All day Sunday he engaged himself in some 'homework' by reading several books he had brought with him on south-west Spanish and Indian culture which were historically comprehensive but had little to offer for the music ethnographer. At any rate he needed them as an introduction and for further reference. After this intensive reading he mixed a tequila and orange drink and sat on his balcony contemplating the sunset glow over a myriad of hues blending the golden desert tan with the chocolate soda brown of typical Santa Fé haciendas.

Monday morning at nine he appeared at the college administration building, about to ask for directions when he met Dr Eisenbach on his way to the faculty meeting.

'Hello there, Monk! You don't know how happy I am to see you here at last. I hope you had a pleasant trip. Glad to hear you like your new apartment. I hope you're going to like it here as much as I do. And let me tell you right now that you won't have a chance to be bored because I've got some really exotic research adventures planned for us. Keep in mind that ethnomusicology is a relatively new major area here but the increasing enrolment means that we'll both share the teaching load. I hope that you might like to teach an extra course in aesthetics too. Anyway we can talk about all this later on. First let's go to the auditorium where I'll introduce you to our colleagues.'

During orientation week Monk kept busy organizing his schedule. As promised earlier he was given a two-year contract to teach twelve hours weekly and collaborate closely with Dr Eisenbach in his research projects. This included occasional excursions to local Indian tribes and visits to tiny Spanish towns in the countryside surrounding Santa Fé. It was also understood that he would contribute articles to academic journals each year and actively pursue his PhD at the University of New Mexico in order to secure tenure in the future.

Because of his education, background, maturity and experience as a professional musician Monk had little difficulty teaching his young college students. His most promising students were more philosophically inclined and enrolled in his aesthetics course while those in his ethnomusicology class had mixed motives: historical interest or an extra elective. However, there were a few studying ethnomusicology who proved to be outstanding and these students volunteered to follow with him on expeditions.

Dr Eisenbach and Monk devoted about six hours per week in the field and another six hours making reports on their findings. They alternated each week between the Spanish towns and the Indian communities. Both groups were usually cooperative, knowing their folklore was in good hands and would be preserved. The Spanish were outwardly warm, friendly and hospitable while the Indians showed a tendency to be detached until convinced of honest motives behind the project. In the long run Monk enjoyed working with the Indians because of their seasonal festivities which they celebrated throughout the year. At least twice a month various tribes invited them to non-stop day-long song and dance events that exploded in rhythm, color and brilliant pageantry.

A few tribes became so friendly that they broke tradition by inviting them to some of their intimate campfire meetings which have a deep spiritual as well as social significance for each tribe. They learned that this circle is a sacred symbol of creation which consists of a series of concentric circles beginning with the individual, then the family, followed by the tribe, the nation and finally the world institutions on the circumference. Each circle is responsible for protecting and caring for the other moving outward or inward as the situation demands. Every circle must be prepared to perish for the other until the whole becomes one life made up of individuals. From his earlier research Monk recalled that both Mahatma Gandhi and Albert Schweitzer advocated this concept too. Monk was impressed by this healthy way of living in a non-violent decentralized world, reversing the structure where a few world centers are autonomous and most people along with smaller countries are left out on the periphery. Sitting around these campfires they observed how well young and old respected each other in discussing various tribal matters. And nearly everyone joined in the singing, dancing and storytelling by participating or listening actively. It never seemed to occur to them that talent was becoming a monopoly of industrialized amateurs. 'Super-stars' were in abundance at these meetings.

With each visit Monk transcribed dozens of these Indian chants which were added to college archives. However, collecting the tribal music was only part of this uplifting experience, for Monk soon discovered that in spite of our arrogant world view of scientism there still exist earth people who have humility, wisdom and survival knowledge based on thousands of years of living, an eternal reverence for life that harmonizes with Mother Earth's own composition. Every time they called upon these tribes Monk learned a lesson in holistic thinking by witnessing people who appeared to be closely in touch with themselves as well as the earth. He felt empowered, inspired, and convinced that these so called primitive people are the true realists in being critically aware of the romantic illusions of scientific technique.

3

Day by day, as time passed, Monk began to feel that he really had found a new home. One day he called Marcello's brother Ruben who cordially invited him over for dinner to meet some of his Spanish friends. One of them was a folk singer who played excellent guitar and invited everyone to join in singing some of the familiar traditional songs. Monk felt a little embarrassed not knowing Spanish but promised himself to start learning soon. Throughout the evening his eyes were attracted to a vivacious and sultry young lady by the name of Anita Romero, one of Ruben's cousins. Small talk got them acquainted and he learned that she was the head librarian in Santa Fé and happened to be single. About a week later he called to invite her out for dinner at an exotic small restaurant in the desert far from town. As they sat at a table in the candlelight Monk was enthralled by her radiant beauty and subtle charm. From that time on there were many happy times together and a serious romance developed between them.

Monk had never been happier at any time in his life: a new love affair, a challenging job and finally settling down in the enchanting city of Santa Fé. Occasionally a sense of euphoria welled up in him that came close to a mystical or spiritual experience, almost like going to heaven and being born again. Entranced or a deep aesthetic response, he wondered. But whatever it is, perhaps it's time to meditate on Cecilia and express my gratefulness.

'I hear you calling, Monk, and you are simply fulfilling what I promised you. There's more to come but first look to the mountains!'

One afternoon after his last class he decided to drive up to the nearby Sangre de Christi mountains and investigate Cecilia's suggestion. After winding up the narrow mountain road he reached a dead end, parked and followed a path toward the top. It was late and the autumn sun gradually dipped toward the horizon. As clouds rolled by leaving their shadows on the desert below he recalled the local Indians saying that there was a time when even the sky had a voice but after the first atomic bomb test they have heard nothing but silence. The serene beauty of the desert scene filled him with the sudden rapture of being alive at this moment. Monk stood still like a Foucault pendulum on the equator and felt the earth revolve around him as though he were placed at a central point of the world where tranquillity is eternal and motion is time itself. Suddenly he realized that every second of his life was actually a moment of eternity and that this central point was where time and space intersect. Then he contemplated that perhaps the Great Spirit is centered deep within our minds while its power spreads throughout the universe beyond any peripheries. Envisioning the world from this 'central' mountain top enabled him to perceive a mystical kind of self-awareness growing deep within, a centering down which altogether made him feel as if it were possible to share this 'center' of the world with any other global citizen. As he focused his thoughts he felt positive energies centered deep within himself beginning to radiate and project outward toward any object he looked at. At the same time Monk sensed that an exchange of energies was taking place and perceived a kind of organic unity or oneness with the world.

He was aware that Cecilia had guided him here to awaken him to an intelligent sphere out there somewhere that wanted him to enjoy life but to find time for interludes to contemplate. His belief in the world as a sacred place and his faith in reverence for life was confirmed by this communion on the mountainside. The phenomenon of a centering experience raised waves deep within him sending ripples out to the horizon. Once again he was convinced of the limits of logic and the point where only mysticism can break through to provide answers. Later he would be astonished to discover that both Wittgenstein and Albert Schweitzer supported his view.

4

Anita and Monk hit it off beautifully together, taking turns having dinner in each other's apartments and occasionally eating out in their favorite restaurants. Toward the end of November Monk suddenly realised that his teaching assignments and dates with Anita were distracting him from clarinet playing so that now his 'chops' and fingers were beginning to itch. One evening they decided to try a hotel restaurant where they had never been before, dropping in toward the end of happy hour. An excellent pianist happened to be playing somewhat in the style of Walter Gross and they both listened attentively until it was time for his pause. Monk walked over to tell him how much he enjoyed his playing, adding that he was a clarinetist.

'Do you play jazz too?' inquired the pianist.

'Well, mainstream and post-bop is my bag,' answered Monk.

'You know something? I often get tired playing by myself all the time.

Why don't you bring your horn around next time and we'll do a little jamming just to shake things up in this joint. I'm here every weekend Friday through Saturday from seven till eleven. My name is Barry Stein.'

'I'm Monk Freeman. Thanks for the invitation. I'll be in soon again!'

The following weekend he took his clarinet along with Anita to the hotel restaurant during happy hour for a drink. As they sat down to order a glass of wine the pianist nodded and waved to him. During a pause he came over to greet them and noticing Monk's clarinet case exclaimed, 'I see you brought your axe along and I need a playmate. How about blowing a few choruses with me on the next set?'

'I'd be delighted, Barry. Here I come, ready or not!'

They warmed up by playing a blues, then launched into a potpourri of standard evergreen songs, followed by a few Fats Waller tunes and finishing up with Duke's 'Take the A Train'. Here was mainstream happy jazz for a crowd who showed their appreciation by clapping enthusiastically. Barry and Monk played on until closing time. Anita looked surprised and pleased to discover that Monk played so well.

'You play a fine clarinet, man! You know my wife sings with me on tour but how would you like to play weekend gigs with me when we're back in town?' asked Barry.

'I'd love to, Barry, as long as Anita doesn't get bored listening to me.'

'Oh, come on now, Monk,' Anita broke in. 'As long as you invite me to dinner I'll listen to you any time.'

'You hear that, Barry? I have to bribe her to come along! OK, see what you can do.'

Barry talked with the manager and called later to tell him that the hotel could promise the next four weekends. If business did well he could offer more gigs later on. Monk agreed and Anita looked forward to these live music sessions but decided a Friday night meal was quite adequate.

5

The following Sunday morning they attended a service at the Unitarian

Church where they heard a sermon on the topic, 'Compassion in the Human Spirit: Is it Obsolete?' This was a provocative subject in which the minister challenged the congregation by asking why we are not more shocked and scared about what's happening to our lack of feeling, sensitivity and compassion and about our dullness in spirit. Has our 'macho' society suppressed our ability to show pain and to be compassionate? It would appear that great technical and material power have been bought at the price of emotional and spiritual impoverishment. Not only a new way of thinking is required but more than equally a new way of feeling. The third millennium will demand more than square eggheads and emotional cripples.

On the way home after the service Anita asked Monk if he had ever read William Saroyan mentioning several of his books that inspired her, especially the play, *The Time of your Life.*

Then Monk replied, 'Actually he's one of my very favorite writers mainly because he expresses more human compassion than any other author I know of: the value of life, the basic goodness of people, the joy of living in spite of poverty. Although he insisted he was realistic in his writing too many readers labelled him an old sentimentalist.'

Monk explained further that 'those who describe his style as too sentimental are often typical American philistines who have vulgarized the word to mean mawkish or maudlin. They ignore that there are other nuances in defining this word which include emotional idealism, vision and refined feelings. Unfortunately, in our neo-utilitarian age, the most natural feelings of tenderness, happiness or even sorrow are likely to be called sentimental. Hard core realists with their ruthless "objectivity" are insensitive and unaware of this deeper meaning.'

Nodding her head in agreement, Anita asked, 'Do you think that Saroyan was trying to tell us that we should feel free to express our positive feelings spontaneously without being self conscious or sentimental in the conventional meaning?'

'Yes, he seemed to support the needs of sensitive people who were keenly aware of our dehumanized age. His readers shared with him the reality that human nature changes little in spite of living in the most brutal century in recorded history. Saroyan embarrassed the psychically numbed killjoys who tried to defend their view of the "real world", paradoxically the same ones who still believe in eternal progress.'

'Wasn't he saying that man can only know himself well by discovering his own inner life before analyzing the outer world of inorganic matter?'

'Of course. Without subjectivity or value judgements just how does anyone know who they are, where they are going or how to discover, invent or create anything? This absurd "scientific" striving after pure objectivity is suffocating and denies our own humanity. There is nothing better in life than to breathe the fresh air of happy human feelings as often as possible. A wise old man of the world once told me that humor, playing music and making love are all that really matter in life. Nothing else does. Realists need to be reminded that two of the greatest warriors down through the ages were incurable "romantics". Just recall Napoleon who established a popular military monarchy and actualized the present day European Union, a "Big Brother" economic organism which could well become a new Roman Empire during the third millennium. His early visions for Europe may yet come true. Perhaps these overzealous Orwellian technocrats are simply megalomaniac romantics attempting to bulldoze all of Europe into an impregnable fortress. However these highbrow civil slaves are merely small bully boys compared to the historic heroism of Aristotle's young protegé Alexander the Great, a military romantic who conquered a single world from Gibraltar to the Indian border before the age of thirty-three.

'In Sweden I met a prominent composer with two PhDs, one in music and the other in psychology. Upon reaching middle age he confessed to me that he knew Mozart's style only too well, had heard enough of Beethoven except for the later piano sonatas and his string quartets. But now he spent more time listening to nearly all of Robert Schumann's works which inspired him most. Then I recalled that philosopher Wittgenstein's favorite composer was Schubert and he loved to whistle any of his themes upon request. So one can only ask exactly who are these self-appointed critics and where do they get their aesthetic judgement when they continually condemn romanticism in literature or music? It appears to me that rumors of its death are highly over-dramatized.'

To this Anita replied, 'I've always believed that the means of thought is feeling, like the sense of touch, a thought can touch your feelings. While sight perceives things at a distance, feeling enjoys an immediate response of reality.'

'Now you're closing into my territory of aesthetics. What you said is true. Now let me fill you in on a few new psychological facts: the left and right hemispheres of the brain. I'm told that the left brain is very rational, logical, fitting together its information like a tailor and that this part of the mind sees black and white photos of reality. They say that the right half of the brain is intuitive, holistic, has a built-in music department, fine tunes its information and sees colored motion pictures of reality. Our contemporary education system teaches us to rely mainly on our left brain in most learning situations. A famous twentieth century philosopher named A.N. Whitehead tells us that people are ninety per cent emotional and only ten per cent intellectual. Since emotions, sentiment and even romance dominate human nature, the intellectual powers alone are inadequate. Academic people and scientists wear their intellect like a uniform to hide their feelings and turn into emotionally crippled nerds. A little more sensitivity and humor would serve them well.'

Chapter VII

BEWITCHED, BOTHERED AND BEWILDERED

(THE TURNING POINT)

Times have given way to a new age that seeks to reduce everything to uniformity in the realm of matter while it tends to shatter all universality in the realm of the spirit in deference to an anarchic individualism.

Igor Stravinsky, *Poetics of Music*

1

About two weeks before Christmas Anita announced that their whole family had been invited to visit relatives in San Diego for the holidays. That meant Monk would be alone for ten days.

The day after Anita flew off with her parents Barry invited Monk over for Sunday dinner. In the village of Tesuque on the outskirts of Santa Fé they lived in a typical brown Spanish style hacienda. Now that they were cultivating a personal acquaintance Monk was informed that Barry had been divorced five years ago before marrying his second wife. Neither of them had children but definitely planned on it before reaching middle age. By coincidence he learned that Barry's wife had flown off to visit her own parents in Boston for a week. It had been a whole year since she had seen them and she could postpone it no longer. So there was nothing for them to do except enjoy the holidays without their mates. Barry slipped on a record by Art Tatum and poured Monk a generous shot of Canadian Club with soda and a swimming pool of ice just the way he liked it. They sat quietly and listened for a while until Barry replaced it with an Oscar Petersson recording.

At the end Barry said, 'You can guess that they both are my favorite pianists for different reasons. Art is truly a great innovator, the first real concert jazz pianist, while Oscar is a brilliant technician but lacks the taste and harmonic sophistication of Art his idol. And of course I always admired Earl "Fathah" Hines and dear old Walter Gross, a great composer and the finest of cocktail lounge pianists. But let me ask you, who is your favorite clarinetist?'

'Well of course, Benny Goodman turned me on first but later I preferred his model Edmund Hall. At that time all the young clarinet players thought one could make lots of money playing clarinet but the problem was that Goodman made it all! But you know the great jazz impresario John Hammond was the real power behind the throne of the "King of Swing". What George Martin did for the Beatles Hammond did for Goodman. However Martin had a greater challenge turning common amateur street players into multi-millionaires while Goodman already had professional musicianship from the beginning. Time speaks a vulgar language today, doesn't it?'

'Unfortunately I could not agree with you more. Live acoustic musicians are facing a new dark age but I do see a few lights in the wilderness.'

'The clarinetist who inspired me most recently is Bill (W.O.) Smith. Have you heard of him?'

'I recall hearing one of his records with Dave Brubeck.'

'You're right. Bill grew up with Brubeck and they studied composition together under Darius Milhaud. Later in 1946 they formed an avant garde jazz octet three years before Miles Davis organized a similar group and made a big name for himself. Bill is the most innovative jazz clarinetist I've ever heard but his full time job is professor of composition at the University of Washington. He won several international prizes for his extended works and tours occasionally with Brubeck. I took lessons and played sessions with him when I did my grad work at University of California.'

'Wow, that's quite a résumé! I'd love to hear him. Do you have any of

103

his records?'

'Sure do. I'll play them for you next time we get together.'

Barry played several recordings of the Benny Goodman Sextet which pleased Monk, especially one tune entitled 'Pick A Rib'.

'Oh I do like that one. That's exceptionally fine Goodman!'

As Barry placed the record back in the rack, Monk's curiosity was aroused about his background.

'Barry, not long ago you told me that you were formerly a nuclear physicist at Los Alamos but never explained why you gave up such a fabulous career to go back into music full time. I hope you don't think I'm prying but most people would consider that kind of switch to be a risky gamble if not a sacrifice. Today's world of technology is the dominant culture while live music playing opportunities are fading away. For example, some top veteran jazz artists I know hardly earn more than an average bureaucrat and a good deal less than starting pay for technicians. Please don't blame me for being too curious but just what made you take such a leap?'

'I certainly don't mind trying to answer that question but it is a long story. Some day I might even write a book about it. First of all, it was an extremely difficult decision to make but I had to choose between prostituting my knowledge toward nihilistic ends and paying a moral price or investing in my musical talents to make myself and other people a little happier in these dismal times. There was nothing I could do to change the direction of destructive science except to leave and play no part in their madness. Fortunately and financially I could afford to take the leap and so I did. But now I'm getting philosophical about it. Do you really want to listen for a few hours while I try to boil it down concisely?'

'Barry, you are a rare individual, having experienced both worlds of music and science so intensively that you have a deep understanding of the dichotomy. You seem to have your head together in a way that enables you to view the world holistically. So go right ahead; I'm not only curious, I'm sure that I have something to learn.'

'OK, you asked for it, but first let me pour you a nice long stiff one and you just help yourself as I go along. We'll take it from the top first.

You want to know why I dumped my career as a scientist with all the prestige, security and high pay it offered to make a simple living as a pianist. Well, to begin with I had ten years of piano lessons before starting college. It was mainly classics but like you I spent a lot of time playing jazz, which I enjoyed most. My piano teacher knew that I had the talent to pass the audition for entrance into any college music school and he assured me that I could pass the tests in theory and harmony too. At the same time I found my high school courses in math and science "a piece of cake" as I managed to breeze through with straight "A"s. I suppose you were required to take these traditional courses for college entrance too?'

'Oh yes, three years of math and three years of science but my grades were probably not as high as yours.'

'Exactly. The ancient Aristotelian curriculum is still a priority in our high schools even though non-science majors never apply these subjects in later life.

'But at the same time you probably devoted more time and money to master your instrument and plan your musical career than I did. For admission to college music school you were expected to have better than average grades too. Do you realize that ninety per cent of my scientifically oriented classmates never had anything to do with music but took the same college preparatory courses you did. Their grades were no better than yours, I'm sure, but they were admitted to begin their science career "from scratch" so to say. Even pre-med students do not have such strict prerequisites as college music students. Another example occurred to me recently when I awoke to the fact that a musician reading a difficult piece of music for the first time goes through a similar mental process as a mathematics instructor working out a new problem. The musician translates rhythm patterns, melodic notation and harmonic symbols (jazz improvisation). Pianists master four to eight notes at a time and conductors up to ten parts simultaneously. The final musical "product" is sounds in motion while mathematical calculations merely reveal a solution in number form. Re-creating music on a professional level is highly abstract, demanding a certain precision allowing room for personal interpretation while the eyes, ears, fingers and body rhythm are all working simultaneously. Today's mathematicians are gradually discovering the limits of math and computers are beginning to master many of the problems of scientific measurement. So you see, the intellectual abilities of most scientists are vastly over-rated compared to the talent and skills needed for professional musicianship. Science is full of technicians and high class plumbers but of course scientists are too arrogant ever to admit this fact. Four hundred years ago the father of science, Francis Bacon, exposed these twentieth century ego trippers when he said, "Mere power and mere knowledge exalt human nature but do not bless it. We must gather from the whole store of things such as make most for the uses of life. There are clouds in the mind of man. I do not think ourselves yet learned or wise enough to wish reasonably for man." Most of all he hoped that a true scientist should be a man of both compassion and understanding. Unlike medical graduates who swear to the oath of Hippocrates scientists do not believe in such ethical creeds. Anyway, here I am beginning to digress from how I made my crucial decision. I'll take you back to my senior year in high school when I lacked both the confidence and the commitment to audition for a college music education. Considering that science was less challenging for me and offered more rewarding opportunities than a career in music I chose the easy way out and fell into the swamp of utilitarianism. Only years later did I realize that this lopsided accent on science at the expense of the humanities is absolutely disastrous.

'Before joining this army of philistines I spent eight bloody years of study, finally finishing my PhD at MIT where I graduated with honors. This achievement opened many doors and I accepted the best offer available, which happened to be Los Alamos Laboratories. Together with other Yuppie technicians I moved out to "Disneyland South-West" where they offered us an elite playground equipped with the latest toys including thirteen CRCY-1 computers, then the world's most powerful. By the way, here's a few hair-curling statistics for you. In the sacred name of "defense" our government now has 756 federal labs of this kind costing 76 billion dollars annually. That meant big loot to pay people like me but trivial compared to the world's yearly arms budget of one trillion dollars.

'America's military politicos have brainwashed us with that holy buzzword "defense" which is actually a multi-billion dollar protection racket for the military science industry. The president himself is chairman of the board of this "Pentagon Capitalism" and patriotism is measured in proportion to the blood money deducted from income taxes (52 per cent at present). This untouchable mob of parasites is cynically clever in selling a pitch using "Think Tank" jargon to intimidate gullible taxpayers. Americans are dependent on 137,000 companies offering "defense" jobs and numerous global interventions to reassure all Americans that their empire is on top of the world. Incredible as it sounds and whether or not we like it that's the present day reality of America's situation.

'Some of these statistics I gathered from retired Admiral Gene LaRocque, formerly assistant director for strategic plans in the Pentagon who resigned just before being promoted to organize his own Center for Defense Information. He was so disgusted and ashamed by America's accelerating militarism supported by a constant lying process, silent censorship and outrageous indoctrination that he decided to spend the rest of his life investigating and revealing the real truth behind America's permanent warfare state. If you're curious I'll be delighted to lend you some of his newsletters later on. Unleashed progress in military technology rushes on at its own momentum at an astronomic cost but what in hell does this have to do with Bacon's positively humanistic philosophy - "making the most for the uses of life"? As I settled down to this assembly line routine I began to miss my old girl friend back in Boston.

'However, that's another story which I'll explain later but let's hear some more music and have another drink before this begins to sound like some kind of lecture.'

'Have you ever heard one of the finest examples of Louis Armstrong's playing ever recorded - a piece called "Weatherbird" - a little duo with Earl Hines on piano? Let's put it on and listen.'

As Louis topped off a short coda with a high note at the end, Monk burst out laughing, joyfully exclaiming, 'What a beautiful and happy feeling they create together. It makes me feel glad to be alive. And such masterful musicianship too! For me Louis is the only musician I know who actually personifies the word "Jazz".'

'You said it! I've always felt that way too. His "West End Blues" is a great classic masterpiece but "Weatherbird" expressed such sheer joy that it's uplifting aesthetically.'

2

The idols of progress and the belief that technology will solve all our problems is profoundly wrong. Modern times are leading us into a new dark age.
Ludwig Wittgenstein

'You were starting to tell me about your lady friend in Boston. Let's hear the rest of the story.'

'Well, since you're interested I'll continue. Shirley and I dated often during my last year of graduate work and we always had great fun together. We met at a student party where she played guitar, singing mostly jazz and some folk songs. After moving to Santa Fé I really longed to see her again so I called and sent her a plane ticket to fly out for a visit. She stayed on for two weeks until I finally got up the nerve to propose. We got married immediately and found this nice house where we've lived quite comfortably for the past five years. We agreed not to have children until we were certain that Santa Fé would be the end of our trail. During the first two years social life for Shirley was somewhat disappointing compared to eastern seaboard style. As for me, the atmosphere of Los Alamos with its ingrown beehive full of boring egghead technicians became more suffocating day by day in spite of the praise and promotions I received. In this kind of environment Shirley began to make frequent flights back to Boston to see her friends and relatives. Then I got weekend gigs playing at the Hotel Estancia and I always looked forward to those as a celebration. Occasionally Shirley followed me and sang a few songs which she did surprisingly well too. Those weekends made my lab work a mere parenthesis.

'Then I began to become aware of my situation by doing research into

the history and philosophy of science, especially books by Loren Eiseley.*
I discovered that too many scientists are completely incapable of viewing
the world holistically and lack a perception of the deeper values of life.

'The prominent scientific philosopher Karl Popper states that science
is a world of preferences and biases which does not gather facts and
confirm theories as much as give imaginative explanations and test for
acceptance. Like Whitehead he criticized and questioned its fundamental
values. The Austrian-American physicist Fritjof Kapra in his *Tao of Physics*
attempts to educate his colleagues with his knowledge that eastern and
western philosophies have strands of similarities and by using this holistic
approach he hopes that science may yet reveal a human face. Of course
chemist-peace activist Linus Pauling (twice Nobel prize winner) and
theoretical physicist Stephen Hawking perceive these humane values more
readily than the majority of scientists. But over-specialized technicians
are alienated from the true spirit of science by lacking this drive for
childlike wonder and curiosity which are so necessary for innovative
discoveries to improve human lives.

'New techniques are easier to master and relatively unimportant
compared to the results of new discoveries. There is an illusion about
technical advances that make people believe that progress is being made
when actually its momentum is effete.

'Mediocre technicians have much in common with religious freaks
and locomotive engineers in that the one and only narrow way is the
only road to follow. This notion in turn is shared by contemporary
politicians who in a cynically naive way are steering us into a future
technocracy predicted in the early 1800s by the French thinker Saint-
Simon. About 160 years later a professor at the University of Bordeaux
wrote a book entitled *La Technique* where he proclaims that technology
has become so overpowering that other social phenomena such as politics
and economics have become situated in it rather than influenced by it. In

---

* *Eiseley, who died in 1977, was one of America's most prominent anthropologists, a science
historian and author. His accolades include thirty-five honorary doctors degrees and several
distinguished literary awards. Tap-dancing to his wife's ragtime piano playing happened to be his
favorite hobby.*

other words the individual is being forced to adapt to the technical environment rather than the other way around. Since 1954 the pontificating voices of "objectivity" from the forty-four year old Bilderberg Group, a top secret powerhouse of plutocratic technocrats planning a one world regime, is exactly the prototype I have in mind.

'But now, getting back to my boys with toys, it surprised me to find that the younger technicians are the real true believers and most dogmatic in their faith. The older secure veterans were slightly more flexible but unfortunately some of these old boys never grew up and out of their scientific adolescence. Now and then one of these fanatic characters would accuse me of deviating from the faith and going off on a tangent. It reminded me of the Russian communists denouncing all deviators as mystics or Senator McCarthy labelling me a red leftist for which I might well receive a dishonorable discharge from the whole Armageddon project. I'm quite sure that the CIA includes me on its subversive list. Oh well, boys will always be boys. It's most peculiar but military scientists appear to have contempt for colleagues who possess imagination and the vitality of joy. Not surprisingly I was classified as some kind of a maverick by my co-workers. I used to tell them that I cannot change their minds any more than I can change the world but I must seriously consider refusing to be a part of their plans for global suicide. Philosophical values are much too complicated to influence physicists whose interests are limited to means not ends. Myopia is a handicap that both scientists and politicians suffer from. Eventually of course I defected to the humanist side of life and have never been happier since.

'But before I took my leave let me tell you the events that occurred up to the final breaking point. One day in August about twenty Japanese Buddhist monks from Hiroshima stopped off to demonstrate a special kind of homage to Los Alamos, the birthplace of a bomb they will never forget. They did nothing but pray silently at the main gate of our "defense plant". A few of us stopped work for a moment to look out the window and contemplate the scene. Suddenly our foreman shouted, "Come on, you guys. We can't waste time staring at a bunch of yellow beatniks. We've got a deadline to meet!" I yelled back, "Oh yes, the final deadline and who is next on our list for annihilation?"

'One evening my Philistine cohorts showed up at the hotel to hear me play. One of them who appeared to be listening more actively than the others spoke up saying, "It sounds great, Barry. I like your playing but tell me something that's puzzling to non-musicians. Scientifically speaking, isn't it true that all pianists, jazz or classical, produce exactly the same tone as their fingers touch the keyboard? After all the finger pressure is the same and mechanically the hammers hit the strings the same way. How could there be any difference in the tone quality of any pianists playing the same keys on the same piano?"

Before I could figure out how to answer such an inane question one of his half-drunk companions belted out his comment, "Yeah, Barry. That sounds logical. And what about today's electronic instruments? Frankly I think they're a great improvement." Just as I was about to walk away from this vacuous babel, another nippy young "prepie" lunged out with, "Some day all music will be created and produced by computerized synthesizers. In fact progress in acoustical research is making it happen in laboratories today. Thanks to this kind of science technicians will replace musicians in the future."

'Of course, by now I was getting ready to climb the walls listening to such insolent irrationality so I had to let them have it full force. "Now I've heard enough of your absurd questions and comments. If you're all so insensitive that you are unable to discriminate the nuances between the artistry of acoustic musical performance and the mechanical-physical sounds of electronic instruments then you're doomed to spend your lives as reductionists in your own narrow philistine world. I'm ashamed and disgusted at your aural insensibilities. And as for our young whippersnapper over there: kid, you've been thoroughly brainwashed by a gang of nerds."

'This left them stunned and speechless as I stomped off to the bar to order a double Canadian Club and soda. I suppose these last two incidents were the catalyst which provoked me most in making my final decision. And finally Shirley got so restless living in Santa Fé that she took one of her flights back to Boston and stayed on for a whole month. This was time for making a crucial decision: to quit my job and follow her to Boston or try to get her interested in some community activity in Santa Fé. Alone for a month I spent every evening practicing, going through old fakebooks, Mehegan's advanced harmonic piano studies and Bill Evans' transcribed piano solos. Suddenly it dawned on me that only music making could ever make me happy and my life more meaningful. When Shirley returned I talked things over with her, explaining exactly how I felt. I told her that I was seriously considering launching a full time professional music career after five years imprisonment in a World War III defense plant. Already I had a considerable savings in the bank, decent dividends on my investments and the house was worth nearly twice as much as our buying price in case we had to sell it. If necessary we could sell it and move to an apartment to make ends meet. Other hotel managers in Albuquerque offered me gigs for three nights per week and I considered advertising for private parties. Several months before a Denver booking manager passing through Santa Fé had offered to be of service anytime I was interested. At last I asked Shirley the loaded question: if I made this decision would she be willing to sing with me and make it a duo? Reluctant to answer, we stopped discussing it until she thought it over for awhile. Occasionally we played and sang together after work. Gradually she began to listen to Peggy Lee and Sarah Vaughan records and soon I had her turned on to the point where she sat in more often at my weekend gigs. The manager of the Estancia liked our duo but perfectionist as Shirley is she decided to sit in for practice and work up a routine repertoire for private party gigs instead. That's one reason why there was an opening for you at the time we met. Now in about three months we'll be playing at a new hotel in Albuquerque for three nights per week at twice the Estancia pay and Sunday brunches here in Santa Fé. There are lots of private parties all over northern New Mexico where we have a name but most of them are planned for weekends. Fortunately the hotel managers free us for these gigs as long as we can get a substitute to fill in for us. So far the overall average is four parties each month where we earn at least four times as much as the hotel gigs. We take three months each year for longer hotel dates booked by our manager in Denver. But now I'm getting a little ahead of my story because we really

112

weren't earning enough to pay our basic living costs until the combination of hotel and party gigs were well secured. When that time arrived I marched into my supervisor's office to bid him farewell. He was not only shocked but jolted as though he were seated in an electric chair when he reacted to my announcement. Immediately he asked me to sit down and negotiate, promising me a promotion and a thirty per cent raise. To this I answered, "Sorry, but no thanks. Your parasites are sucking on taxpayers' billions to pay for your nuclear ego trip. What I want most is to enjoy my own ride, my way, swinging through life with a happy peace of mind. I'm sure you're not up to understanding that point of view, but that's all I have to say!" Since I made that final decision Shirley and I have never been happier. Not long afterwards my father died and left me enough inheritance to pay off the house mortgage, buy a new piano and a safari van for our travelling. Now for the first time we're truly enjoying living our lives and we've discovered that making live music is the only way to do it.

'Say, you know, I think it's about time for some more music. Now I'm going to give you a blindfold test on this one. All that I will tell you is that the leader of this group is one of my favorite old time pianists. Just listen.'

When the last tone faded away Monk exclaimed, 'Talk about beautiful happy jazz, there's only one band that sounds that groovy – Jelly Roll Morton's Red Hot Peppers. And did you know that critics credit him for being the first composer in jazz history? What's the name of the piece and the date of the recording?'

'Black Bottom Stomp, from 1926.'

'Wow! What fine musicians, spirit and originality for those times. It's really inspiring to know such great jazz artists existed in the 1920s. I'm familiar with some of Morton's history, his exceptional talent, eccentricities and the undeserved down periods in his musical life. He made his name during a transition phase somewhere between the end of ragtime and the beginning of New Orleans style jazz ensembles. Jelly Roll probably made more money gambling than he ever did as a composer-bandleader but like most musicians was hardened to the reality of roller coaster insecurity and refused to sell out for materialistic rewards.'

'Unlike Morton, I'm only sorry that I took a detour for so long before awakening to that moment of truth. Anyway, at thirty-two it was not too late to reach the right turning point in my life.'

3

The arts put man at the center of the universe, whether he belongs there or not. Military science on the other hand treats man as garbage – and his children and his cities too. Military science is probably right about the contemptibility of man in the vastness of the universe. Still I deny that contemptibility, and I beg you to deny it, through the creation and appreciation of art.
One of America's prominent authors, Kurt Vonnegut, in an
address at Bennington College in 1970.

'There is no doubt in my mind that your thoughts and feelings were in perfect balance when you arrived at this wise decision. But can you explain what historical events and degenerate forces contributed to indoctrinating the majority of Americans to pay up to fifty-one per cent of their income taxes to support a permanent warfare state?'

'Well, Monk, first of all I'm convinced that talk of a missile gap was a fraud and I'm one person who was never persuaded that the Russians were planning to attack the US some day.

'History shows that military technology served its purpose all too well throughout the nineteenth century period of colonialism. As early as 1898 America laid the foundation for its long term imperial ambitions by fighting the Spanish-American War. Wooden ships were becoming obsolete and most of the mainline railroads had been completed. The steel companies sold the government on building new naval vessels to keep them in business. These two events were the beginning of America's permanent warfare economy which prepared it to fight World War I followed by a depression that World War II rescued us from. In 1945 my old Los Alamos colleagues helped to vaporize 200,000 yellow people and the atomic age was underway. Sir Solly Zuckerman, a British scientist

114

who worked on this "Manhattan" project, identifies scientists as the driving force behind the arms race and not the men in the armed forces.

'The leading initiative is taken by these military technicians to maintain full production in their factories. For example, Dr Ed Teller was the head salesman who promoted the hydrogen bomb project. The Korean War in which you served was a catalyst in establishing the science-military-industrial complex into a booming business with the Pentagon as number one customer. Not many years later the US became the world's leading arms exporter. Of course there were spin-off effects like nuclear reactors built with a promise to make electricity cheaper than water, another one of hundreds of fairy tales big power science loves to tell us. The so called national "defense" bill keeps on rising into the trillions and it looks like the sky is the limit. Scientific military technicians never had it so good. So much for America's "defense" plan operations. I'd like to write a book on it but Professor Seymour Melman is the master economist on this subject and has exposed more than I'll ever know. In one final punch line let me just say that this entire defense industry is an incestuous mafioso, a juggernaut project with astronomic costs, and it's the most successful hard selling "con" job in the entire history of science.'

'And yet in spite of all you say still too many people believe that the overall progress of science has made giant strides in this century. What is your point of view on that?'

'To that I'll have to tell you right away that scientific progress cannot be proved because it is simply relativistic, subject to changing conditions and not absolute or universal. Old and new theories both lack a common basis of comparison in respect to a quality which needs comparison. And certainly science does not "progress" merely by collecting more truths. New theories continually replace old ones which prove to be false. Physics especially moves from one false theory to another. It reminds me of the old axiom, "facts are small theories and theories are big facts". One cannot help but wonder if facts and theories are entirely adequate. Occasionally science assumes theories which are impossible to prove and it resembles going through a religious ritual with holy incantations. And of course scientists are not miracle workers which the average layman wants to believe. However, some theoretical physicists claim to have a monopoly on the one and only scientific way to the truth. You know, it really shakes me up when someone tries to tell me that there is only one way to find a solution to anything. I break out in skin rash and start climbing the walls. Without trying to place myself into what the problem is, I tell myself this just has to be wrong. There are always more possibilities and alternatives but I will admit that there are occasions when theoretical physics may prove to be an exception to this rule. Ordinarily for every accepted theory there may be as many as seven or eight parallel theories, some of which may survive to replace the current theory.

'New technology is simply applying scientific knowledge to practical purposes like increasing production with more automatic robot machinery. "Progress" in this respect is step by step material improvement using well established scientific principles. The legendary sage Max Lerner tells us that "the great American achievement has been technological, less in science itself than in technology and engineering." America's Nobel Prize winning scientists are more often than not leaders of a well subsidized university team of laboratory workers with graduate students doing a large share of the research. What's more, several of these Nobel laureates have sold out their prize-winning ideas to industry for millions. If a genius among theoretical physicists is required, it's relatively easy to import one from Europe or Asia. Statistics reveal that half of the PhD "scientists" in the world are now working in military tech. industries. The other half are committed to humane research projects such as medicine. In comparison to the trillions spent to produce new weapons, medical researchers not employed by large pharmaceutical firms go begging for funds from charities. The advances of both science and technology have a long way to go to get in harmony with spiritual and moral development which requires more inner vision. Man's control of nature belongs to a lower level of investigation than gaining insight into the truth of our Being.

'Science is incapable of dealing with real problems of life and the human level of Being. Visible things – inorganic matter – are obvious and temporal. Invisible things are eternal and lead to insight.

'Incidentally, are you aware that the whole idea of progress for western civilization was introduced by a Christian humanist monk named Abbé Saint Pierre in 1713 in his book *The Project for Perpetual Peace*? Several thousand years earlier the old Chinese philosopher Lau-Tzu reminded us, "He who knows others is wise but he who knows himself is enlightened." Good advice for everyone but not least of all for scientists deficient in self awareness and self control.

'As long as we are discussing progress how can we avoid the problem of time? Space can be classified, measured, understood and analyzed easily by scientists but they have much to learn as they investigate the element of time.

'And now that science is venturing into outer space it will prove nothing unless it somehow coincides with our interior universe, our inner space which is always growing and expanding. The inward skies of man will accompany him across the galaxies and stay with him until the end of time.

'Some scientists believe that the universe is always beginning in the present and that there is nothing to stop us from accepting any new idea if it's useful in the present. So why is there any need to study the past or understand any philosophical or ethical meanings? For them utilitarianism is the way to go and the future is now.

'Concerning concepts of space and time, there is agreement on their relationship but they disagree on how it comes about. Although we are all consciously aware of space we can only become equally aware of past, present and future by contemplating deeply until we gradually suspect that we ourselves are actually time as we live our lives. Time appears to have an organic quality that is tied to the present in such a way that we cannot retrieve the past. Even language is limited in revealing how we feel at the sound of the word "time". However, here is where only music can clearly express it: sounds in motion, music moving in time. Active listening to music is one of the best ways to digest time.

'Oh man, when I find myself talking like this I just want to leave heavy gravity behind and take off into space. Pres! Wherefore art thou? Please save my savage egghead soul by flying me to the moon. Now is the time!'

Barry slipped on an old recording of Lester Young playing his great classic 'Lester Leaps In'. Monk nodded in time, almost conducting the rhythm of the phrases up until the end when he exclaimed, 'The immortal president of all tenor saxophone players, dear old Pres, and how refreshing he sounds today! Pres knew all about swinging freely in space stretching out his phrases to the horizon and beyond. He was free as a bird, with all the room in the world for swinging out his own way. Musicians credit him for founding the cool school whose style consisted of a laid back pulse and a phenomenal spatial concept of driving rhythmic phrasing. 'Pres' was not only a unique artist but one of the few real innovators in jazz history. Of him one can truly say that he found the patterns that connect time and space in jazz improvisation.

'And where would Stan Getz have found a model without Lester Young? That was 1939, wasn't it? My God, you know my old musician friend old Hiawatha Edmundson back in Ohio transcribed almost every solo that Pres ever recorded!'

'Since we're discussing tenor sax players, I read recently about a New York tenorman who released a new album named "Exact Science". Do you think he's one of those musicians who still has an inferiority complex about the omnipotent powers of science? Either he needs our support or hopefully he is merely paying a sarcastic musical tribute to the mob.'

4

Philosophical inquiry began long before scientific experimentation and it will also continue long after we have reached our limits of experimental knowledge . . . It is philosophy, not science, which should be uppermost in any culture or civilization, simply because the questions it can answer are more important for human life. The more science we possess, the more we need philosophy because the more power we have, the more we need direction.
Dr Mortimer J. Adler, Director of the Institute
for Philosophical Research

'Now that we're shifting the subject back into science, I'd like to hear a comprehensive definition of the "scientific method". I can't recall that any of my high school science teachers ever stated it in a clear and sensible manner.'

'Monk, your question goes straight to the heart of the problem. Today's purely technological progress is so busy overleaping itself with "pie in the sky" ambitions that both technicians and teachers have a born yesterday attitude in their assumptions, so much so that they overlook root causes and basic principles. Science teachers are so often preoccupied with teaching dogmatic principles that young students are seldom stimulated to ask questions about what they are learning. In fact, as they move on into college studies too many of them remain passive, taking in only the practical information with little or no inquiry. This presumptuous attitude does little to encourage curiosity or wonder of scientific methods.

'A textbook definition of scientific methods might be something like this: a process of establishing a scientific law through inductive methods (arriving at a conclusion by reasoning from the particular to the general) but this is only a conventional view. Often enough inspired guessing (intuition if you will) helps form a theory which is gradually confirmed or supported by evidence and then relates the premise to a final conclusion. But then where does deduction come into the process? Aristotle, the Greek genius who mastered logic, mathematics and sciences, started with inductive reasoning to establish his basic premise then a minor premise followed by a conclusion through syllogistic deduction (general to particular).

The roots of this deductive system of mathematics inspired Descartes over two thousand years later. He revived deductive reasoning and promoted rationalism where reason above all is the source of knowledge while mathematics is its inspiration. Rationalists stress the superiority of deductive methods and they see reality as having an inherent rational structure. However Aristotle had a more holistic view believing that all sciences were inter-related while Descartes promoted the concept of dualism ("split-level thinking") which later gave birth to specialization of all sciences. There are good reasons for disputing Cartesian thinking today and critical holistic thinkers are increasing in number. Only four hundred years ago and nearly two generations before the birth of Descartes, the father of "modern" western science, Francis Bacon, was born. He promoted the inductive method which is the basis of scientific thinking today. Inductive reasoning provided general premises upon which deduction had to be based. Deduction resulted in laws which had to be tested by inductive procedures. So by now we can say that the scientific method begins with induction which develops into deductive logic and finally mathematics verifies the final conclusion, fundamentally Aristotelian but certainly not the whole story for our times. In a more general way we could say that the basic aim of science is to discover what is permanent, what continually changes and finally what kind of scientific law (principle) we can get from what is specific. Then we have to try to find the simplest explanation for complex facts.

'The ancient Greeks, who made such phenomenal contributions to the arts, sciences and philosophy before and during the Golden Age, applied a holistic perception of the world around them. They searched for root causes, and were never satisfied with second hand facts or effects and had no use nor need for our scientific way of thinking. The Greeks had a way of observing nature and explaining her laws and purposes in a practical manner. For example here is a small but vital difference: if a child asked, "Why does it rain?" a Greek teacher answered, "To help the flowers and plants grow." Today our "more scientific" answer would be, "There is water in the clouds." Both are equally correct but I prefer earthy scientific explanations to lofty abstract descriptions.

'Scientism demands black and white facts and nothing else, reducing mind and spirit to the quantitative categories of physics. They claim that scientific knowledge is the only kind of factual knowledge and philosophical ideas are rejected as meaningless. Of course this is a cynically naive dogma by "bully-boys" who intimidate the laymen and assert a patronizing attitude toward any other way of thinking. As a mature scientist I'll never be convinced that scientific knowledge is the only kind of factual knowledge. Analyzing matter while measuring every word has now become the disease of the modern mind. This type of mind set is a left-over from Vienna in the 1920s, logical positivism: entirely too logical and not very positive!

'Although science deems personal experience to be unimportant compared to experimental verification, physics often bases itself on experiences which are shallow and superficial. This extreme concentration on science and reductionism can only lead to disaster. Presently this trend is underway as science marshals all its forces into the world spotlight while believing that they have a monopoly on strictly objective knowledge. For them subjectivity is simply unscientific or in fact not quite rational. But after all, isn't all knowledge relatively subjective as long as we react, respond and reflect experiments and experience through our eyes and minds where subjectivity must exist. And just how could we invent, create or discover anything without first making some kind of value judgement? What makes us think that scientific proof is the only way to understand something? You know, sometimes even science can actually be irrational, illogical and downright dishonest in its findings. Why is the linear view considered to be so superior to holistic perceptions?

'And why are scientists so reluctant to admit their reliance on intuitions? Isn't it rather pretentious to deny the possibility of arriving at direct knowledge or certainty without rational thought or reasoned conclusions? Perhaps it's humiliating for them to confess that instinct or divining empathy can offer insight into reality. The history of science points to abundant examples of intuition being the mother of invention.

'It appears to me too that the old Newton-Cartesian mechanistic scene is becoming obsolete as we pick up the fragmented remnants of its limited view in knowing nature. In addition to this, science must learn to play it cool by avoiding pushing reason too far and too fast. Otherwise they will get a whipcracking backlash attempting to jump into an instant future. Most of all, it is high time for technicians and scientists to start criticizing the foundations of their hypothesis with some humility and contemplate positive ends for humanity. The key to all this may lie in finding the pattern that connects the surprises waiting for us in this unexpected universe.

'Oh my God, Monk. In preaching about this ideology of scientism it makes me feel as dry as a prune and thirsty as a camel. It's time for a nice tall drink and a cool piece by Duke Ellington. How about

121

"Transblucency" sub-titled "A Blue Fog You Can Almost See Through". If I were a disc jockey I'd dedicate this to all my fog bottom colleagues. All of Ellington's works are masterpieces but this one in particular is unique for its clarinet and vocal duo. Remember Kay Davis and Jimmy Hamilton back in 1946?'

'Yes, this is definitely one of my favorite pieces of Duke's and dear old Jimmy Hamilton has the most gorgeous tone and finest taste of any jazz clarinetist I've ever heard. I remember at one time in the early 1940s *Downbeat* readers jazz poll rated him number one, over Benny Goodman, Artie Shaw and others. This is the kind of Ellington that's worthy of deep contemplation. Let's hear it!'

A long pause after the last note and finally Monk said, 'Ellington was the greatest of all big band composer-arrangers and he had a genius for blending tone colors and inspiring his soloists like no other bandleader. Duke's band seemed to grow organically as if inspired by Claude Monet's impressionistic garden paintings. It's been said that prominent Hollywood arrangers met occasionally to hear various recordings of famous big bands and after hearing each one different arrangers would take turns analyzing the style, methods and techniques used in creating the unique sound of these bands. Typical comments were, "Oh there he goes again, up to his same old tricks, those mixed voicings in the brass and clarinet lead in the saxophone section!" Then they listened to a new Duke Ellington release. All they could do was scratch their heads and throw up their hands wondering, "What in hell is going on here? I never heard anything like it before. Where does he get those exotic voicings?" etc. For me his extended compositions were colorful rhapsodies which became timeless works of art even after several generations. From his band in the twenties take "East St Louis Toodle-oo" for example. You know, when I'm at home and undecided what jazz record I want to hear, I reach for some Ellington and I'm never disappointed. I can enjoy him for hours. By the way a moment ago you made a crack about philistine fog bottom technicians who are unable to relax their reasoning powers to truly appreciate an Ellington piece like "Transblucency". What kind of world do these people live in? What sort of mind set or temperament are they stuck with that inhibits their senses and emotions? Some macho men are emotionally crippled in this way too.'

5

I was walking about in Cambridge and passed a bookshop and in the window were portraits of Russell (Bertrand) Freud and Einstein. A little further on, in a music shop, I saw portraits of Beethoven, Schubert and Chopin. Comparing these portraits I felt intensely the terrible degeneration that had come over the human spirit in the course of only a hundred years.
Ludwig Wittgenstein

'Well, Monk, I warned you when we started that this could be a long story. At the same time, perhaps it's good therapy for me to reveal the truth of my life's experience to a sympathetic listener like yourself. You know the old cliché "old too soon" and too late smart in waking up to the reality of it all. When I discussed this with Shirley she found it incredible that such a powerful negative animus prevailed among my colleagues.

'Unfortunately, scientific man carries an air of detachment striving for pure "objectivity" in his life. By playing this role he keeps his objects under control more easily. It's not uncommon for them to have a restrained sterile attitude toward life that suggests Puritan inhibitions. In seeking a truth they abstain from any feeling that has the slightest spark of spontaneity. Interesting too that Einstein himself claims that this value neutrality (an evil sin to make value judgements) is the result of a slow development peculiar to western thought. Prominent psychiatrists know that these types of men often show little interest in life, persons, nature, ideas or anything alive. In fact they observe a trend among them which reveals the loss of their human capacities of reasoning, seeing, hearing, tasting and loving. Only the logic of technique determines their lives, lives with no goal nor plan. For them the next stage of evolution would make man a robot. More than a few of these nerds are evolving that way already.

Devastating, isn't it? To imagine that such schizoids exist with calloused thoughts and a total lack of feelings. No wonder that critics accuse the scientific mind of being so obsessed with death. So exasperated was Francis Bacon with his sixteenth-century colleagues that he confessed, "I have lost much time with this age. I would be glad to recover it with posterity."

'Anyway, let me tell you a story about some real killers, the martinet scientists of Nazi Germany. Pure logic and a highly structured organization made the holocaust possible. The Nazis were in fact quite proud of their skills, techniques and scientific methods which they applied with perfect precision to this new genocide industry. It is said from reliable sources that the director of annihilations at one of the leading concentration camps loved classical music and played his favorite recordings all day long over the camp loudspeaker system. The music of Wagner continued non-stop except for intermittent announcements such as, "*Achtung*, Sergeant Muller, you now have exactly ten minutes to march your workers from Barracks number 21 to the main shower room" (code word for the final solution). Undoubtedly Nazi psychologists considered Wagner's music to be an appropriate accompaniment for the extermination of "non-Super-Race" people. A perfectly logical process, all in a day's work at the death factory. In checking the records of these scientific executioners investigators found that many of these men were exemplary fathers and husbands simply doing a good job by following orders. Today we have more sophisticated death factories managed by nuclear physicists filling multi-billion dollar orders for the latest model nuclear missiles. In their narcissistic frame of mind the threat of global suicide and blowing Mother Earth to smithereens is dismissed as something that could never happen to Americans.

'You know, considering the outright contempt and alienation that these schizoids show towards our "Big House" (the world and nature), I can think of only two words to describe them - "Cosmic Orphans". As the North American Indians would tell us, they no longer belong to Mother Earth nor Father Sky and there is no one at home out there in our galaxy who will have anything to do with them. Now in order to get things in perspective we must see the right proportion in the time dimension. In the more constructive sciences such as geology we are told that the earth is about five billion years old and anthropology informs us that man is approximately two million years old.

'Western science is only a four hundred year old baby preoccupied with its immediate needs and merely a tiny infant unable to perceive its ends. Mother Earth is chiding, in fact crying out to, this new born babe to start wearing its diapers because it's polluting her Big House and needs to be trained. If Mother Earth is willing she may wait for our "baby" to get its shit together and evolve out of this mollycoddling stage. When science and technology really mature then Bacon's dreams and visions for humanity might be fulfilled. In the meantime the common layman own good reasons for criticizing these high class plumbers. The average person is oversold and well bribed by certain alleged benefits of technology but at the same time suspects that there is something rather superficial about the scientific mind. The well informed see science as a recently invented institution which requires a special kind of indoctrination to be learned and practiced. In studying this subject area all feelings and desires are discounted and anything to do with our practical daily lives on earth is irrelevant. Thinking in this way is completely foreign and unnatural for the great majority of mankind. Why should man have any interest or inclination for science when he is much happier with his own uninhibited dreams and fantasies? Indeed scientists forbid such frivolous attitudes! Actually most scientific projects can be carried out by well trained but second rate men with nippy young minds and utilitarian values. Overspecialized and having a keyhole view of the universe, they are able to follow assigned procedures within a limited field but lack creativity. Their achievement may wear the look of originality yet be so limited that it may not represent one thousandth of real experience.

'You know, life is actually larger than logic, math or science and this lockstep approach is strictly for goosestepping eggheads.

'I hope I'm not boring you by explaining the scientific mentality in detail but presently I have good reasons and a need to flush away the excrement of these holy priests of scientism. Let me add too that I'm capable of refuting most of their arguments as pure rationalizations. Now it's time again for more important things in life like listening to good music. What would you like to hear?'

'Well, there's one genius we haven't heard from yet, the man who will influence all jazz players for many generations to come - alto saxophonist Charles "Yardbird" Parker. Lyrically, rhythmically and harmonically he covered it all until his tragic death at the age of thirty-five. From outer space he zipped down on us like a comet and his musical gift burned intensively every moment until the end of his short life. Three of his pieces are my favorites. Do you happen to have "Ko-Ko", the original "Cool Blues" and "K.C. Blues?"'

'Man, are you lucky! I just happen to have all three recorded on old 78 "pancakes" but they're still audible. "Bird" was the great innovator among jazz artists and always had something new to say - a beautiful sound and a driving swinger. Here they are, let's dig!'

Monk listened intently to each one as though they were a three-movement suite, then said, 'This musician has inspired me so much in my playing and yet I feel so humble every time I hear him that I know I'm still a beginner. And he's such a lovely person too. I met and heard him in New York about ten years ago when he had an all star rhythm section, Roy Haynes, Red Mitchell and Walter Bishop Jr., and they backed him up beautifully. However I got the distinct feeling that Bird was on top and leading them on all the way. My opinion was confirmed when Parker left the stand during a pause and I overheard Red say to Roy, "You know, Bird is the only musician I ever played with who actually swings me!" Roy answered, "You're right, man. Me too!" In spirit and musically "Bird" will be flying over us for a long time to come.'

6

Imagination is more important than knowledge.
Albert Einstein

'I wonder why it is that we musicians, jazz and especially classically trained performers, have a deeper sense of their own history than college educated scientists.'

'I must admit that you're correct in saying that. In all my eight years of college studies I had only one course in the history of science which I chose as an elective. Of course my professor referred to the leading scientific geniuses from the past but there were no course requirements in this area. I can only assume that today's technicians are riding too high into the future to take time to check their roots or pay any tribute to their scientific ancestors. Old Mark Twain had less of this born yesterday attitude when he stated, "My forefathers have stolen all my best ideas!" Lack of humility, contempt for the past, always breeds arrogance. I am grateful to dozens of books and my own research for what I know about the history of science.'

'I'd really be delighted if you would continue enlightening me with what you've learned. If, as you say, scientists neglect their history then you can be sure that I'm one representative for millions of other laymen who are entirely ignorant in this subject. And in this new age of technology, if so few of us know where we've been then how do we have any idea where we're going?'

'OK, you asked for it, but first I'll have to say that there are hundreds of books covering this area and I'm no expert. All I can do is draw a sketchy map and briefly give you some road signs to follow. I'll start with an outline and point out essential facts as we go along.

'As far as I know, the Chinese were the world's first inventors, philosophers and worshippers of music. Some historians tell us that each of their eight greatest dynasties contributed as much to the human progress of those periods as the Greek Golden Age.

'During the lifetime of Pythagoras the thrust of Greece's Golden Age was already underway. Pythagoras embraced a mystical view of science that was integrated with art and religion while seriously concerned with ethical ideals and moral values. Copernicus actually gives him credit for discovering that the earth and other planets rotate around the sun. Within a period of 150 years (600-450 BC) the Greeks had discovered and classified practically all of our present day arts and sciences including theories of atomic energy! Our scientific age has not yet matched that rate of

127

"progress". The legacy of Pythagoras influenced medieval European thought and his astronomical concepts were even acknowledged by Copernicus. But it's fascinating, isn't it, that all the ancient Chinese, Egyptian and Greek sages placed such great importance on music?

'As a teenager in Macedonia, Alexander the Great had the privilege of being taught by probably the greatest Greek intellectual figure, Aristotle. Whitehead rates him a better scientist than a philosopher, but he did extensive medical and biological research, organized colleges and actively pursued all areas of human knowledge.

'He believed deeply that rational human beings were able to develop to the highest level by learning to use knowledge for the benefit of positive human progress. In other words, reason and ethics are inseparable.

'Aristotle died 322 BC and Archimedes was born forty years later in Syracuse, Sicily, to become the most famous mathematician and inventor in what was then ancient Greece. He knew as much mathematics as was known at any time up until AD 1300. By 250 BC all the principles needed for development of today's science already existed. And just like our twentieth century scientists, Archimedes sought to control nature through prediction and experimentation. Archimedes is remembered for his famous statement, "Give me a place to stand and I will move the earth!"

'Although the Romans boasted some outstanding scholars and lawmakers, monumental architecture and ingenious plumbing facilities, practically all their arts and sciences were inherited from the Greeks. Incidentally the Romans contributed even less to the development of music except for the invention of the organ. After the fall of Rome (AD 485) Muslim intellectuals from the Arab world made magnificent strides in mathematics, science and medicine. Then toward the end of the Medieval period in the late 1400s we can recall the genius of all the arts and sciences, the epitome of the Renaissance humanist ideal, Leonardo Da Vinci. But did you know that few people realize that the height of his ambition was to trace a map of the universe and show the possibility of man becoming a God possessing all sources of truth?

'From the last half of the sixteenth century to the first quarter of the eighteenth century, four of the most prominent men of science lived.

Francis Bacon, whom I mentioned earlier, came first and still deserves credit for being named the father of western science. However, I must add that he was ignored as some kind of maverick during his lifetime and was somewhat controversial among contemporary scientists mainly because of misunderstandings and often flagrant distortions about the man himself. Nuclear physicists especially have good reason to fear Bacon's condemnations for contributing to an Armageddon with their sophisticated military technology. Bacon's basic creed was – science for human welfare and nothing else. His visions for science were purely humanistic and four hundred years later far from fulfilled.

'Now I have something more to tell you about René Descartes who opened the door to the Age of Enlightenment and understanding the world strictly through mathematical analysis. From his dualism he divided mind and matter, body and soul, subject and object, always with a mechanistic view of the universe. Parts and means were most important in order to impose his will over matter while experimenting to gain more knowledge. He solved problems systematically by analyzing them part by part proceeding from the simple to the complex. Using this quantitative approach science became identified with methods of isolating factors and observing them from a supposedly detached base. This "Cartesian split" is very much alive in present day scientific thinking with its reductionism and obsession for technique and has forced reason itself into a technique.

'Shortly before Bacon's death, Blaise Pascal, the eminent French mathematician, physicist, religious philosopher and writer who discovered the theory of probabilities, was born. He also discovered the law of pressure, the principle of the hydraulic press and invented the first digital calculator. On top of that his literary talents helped him to create the beginnings of modern French prose. A deeply spiritual and religious person, he spent the latter part of his life doing good works for mankind. Pascal believed that the "heart has reasons that the mind will never know".

'And finally, Isaac Newton, born nineteen years before Pascal died. As a physicist and mathematician he laid the foundation of calculus, extended the understanding of color and light, examined the mechanics of planetary motion, and derived the inverse square law which later supported his theory of gravitation. Incidentally, when the logic of his scientific method revealed no solution to a problem he simply resigned to the faith that from now on only God himself knew the answer. Nevertheless, Newton always believed in a mechanical universe and that our earth was something like a global clock. Two hundred years later Albert Einstein, basically a Cartesian, discovered his theory of relativity, a mathematical structure in which curved space and warped time are used to describe gravitation. This dynamic breakthrough upset many well established laws of physics. And of course we know that his genius as a theoretical physicist did not interfere with his hobby of playing the violin.

'The true men of science have a philosophic world view far above the mere over-specialized technicians of our age. Granted that we are all children of our times, but some children become more spoiled, complacent and even stunted in their psychic growth when their talents or skills are over-rated.

'And now it's enough of this lecturing for awhile. Let's swing on into some higher realms where all God's children got rhythm! I just bought a new recording of that fabulous trumpet player, Clark Terry, performing live at the Newport Jazz Festival. He has one helluva lot of fun playing that old time standard "Bye, Bye, Blackbird". Let's hear it.'

Monk chuckled with pleasure all the way through to the end, then commented, 'You know this is one of my favorite tunes which I play often myself. Not long ago John Coletrane and Miles Davis produced a beautiful recording of this song. However Terry sounds fresh, and inspired just as though he were playing it for the first time and making it all his own. Here is a professional artist with umpteen years of big band and New York studio experience plus teaching young students to play jazz. There is no finer all-round jazz trumpeter in the business than Clark Terry and he's never afraid to be an entertainer or a showman. Perhaps he learned these lessons from his old colleagues Louis Armstrong and Dizzy Gillespie. Training and practice for a jazz musician is very serious work but performing for a public must express pure fun and joy. One should have the attitude that you belong to the people when you're playing. It's your responsibility to show them a good time. That's an important tradition in jazz to let your feelings go and have fun. Playing jazz has nothing to do with conducting an experiment in a laboratory or brain surgery. There is a unique spontaneity in Terry's solos that comes right through on the recording.'

'I heard Clark Terry the first time in person at the Albuquerque Jazz Festival when he played and sung his famous "Mumbles" song and he got more applause and encores than any of the other top soloists. I noticed too that his happy spirit infects the musicians as well as the audience.'

'He's such a refreshing change from the typical post-bop-avant-garde jazz players who take themselves and their music entirely too seriously, almost academically. And yet he can make himself right at home playing with the most far out modern musicians too.'

'When I see and hear Terry I sometimes wonder if he and others like him are born gifted or possess powerful genes which guide them in the right direction and gradually become part of their nature. Anyway there is something like an organic unity about Terry and his trumpet that is completely natural.'

7

Experimental science has progressed - thanks in great part to the work of men astoundingly mediocre, and even less than mediocre.
Ortega Y Gasset (Spain's leading 20th century philosopher)

'In other words Clark Terry seems to have a natural talent that has become part of his nature. And that brings up another question. As a scientist how would you define nature?'

'Nature is mainly matter in motion or a flow of physical energy and our entire universe is always changing by this process of "becomings". Both Plato and Goethe were deeply aware of this concept which also includes an accent on intuition. I feel that if one desires to learn nature's secrets then one must first become more humane than others. That means a lot less arrogance and a good share of humility. Science is so very smug, uprighteous and cynically naive in believing it is working in the service of civilization when actually it possesses only an idea of reality with a halo of civilization around it. We must always keep in mind that science is not and never will be the ultimate reality no matter what they try to tell us.'

'All right, so far I can't help but agree with your criticism of scientism as a new religion but isn't there a strong case for the positive benefits of technological progress?'

'Of course there is. Foremost in medicine which receives only meager support compared to military technology. However, universities and pharmaceutical laboratories do compensate for some of this deficiency. One cannot overlook the areas of communication, transportation and other basic living comforts and essentials. No one wants to go back to the days of the caveman. That kind of alternative is not at all relevant to my discussion. What I propose is an attitude of healthy skepticism by daring to question the authorities of science and technology. To begin with I am not easily persuaded that this new generation of technologies will ever deliver us a utopian future. This is a romantic delusion being promoted by multi-billion dollar advertising budgets. Peculiar, isn't it, how people tend to be too skeptical about man's ability to develop higher humane values but less critical in accepting all ideas and products blessed by scientists.

'I manage to protect myself against all this bombastic bullshit by maintaining a consistent attitude of suspicion toward all technology. I am critical of all their claims; guilty until proven innocent. There is no such thing as "value free" technology because there is always a built-in price to pay for its social and environmental consequences. I ignore the flashy appeal of new technology knowing that it takes time for negative effects to develop. Just because one of these tools may benefit me I ask first who does it benefit the most? And toward what end? Next I strongly suspect that a particular piece of technology is part of a giant web leading to "megatechnology". How does this small part fit into the larger whole? Also I try to distinguish between the technologies that are useful for the individual or the community (solar energy for example) and those that function on a larger scale beyond community control (nuclear energy). Some people argue that technological progress is good in the long run in spite of destructive effects (pollution, etc.) but this kind of progress I prefer to call sheer bribery. Unemployment, suicides, violent crime, alienation, narcotics and slime mold cities are all side effects of accelerating technology. Others tell me that it's impossible and too late to reject technology but I say that this attitude is too passive and makes one become a victim of its madness. I think and accent the negative in these technological times. That's the only way to be positive!'

'Barry, you positively amaze me. It appears to me that you've done enough intensive research on this subject to write another PhD dissertation. It's provocative for some and most enlightening for others including myself.'

8

Nothing impedes freedom of thought like faith in progress.
Leo Tolstoy

The life principle is spirit; this spirit is inherent in all men, it goes beyond the confines of space and time and those who live in the spirit achieve immortality.
Leo Tolstoy

'Monk, before you wind me up and place me on a soap box again I want you to hear a brand new recording which my musical nephew just sent me. The leader of the group is a gifted young guitarist named John McLaughlin who is working on a synthesis of post-bop jazz and refined rock sounds, a style which he calls Fusion. I won't say anything more. Just listen and give me your opinion.'

As the last overtones of the guitar dissolved into the air Monk's eyes popped as he exclaimed, 'This guy is absolutely astounding and the rest of the band is really beautiful. This is professional musicianship that the amateur superstars lack making it necessary for their "Godfather A and R" men to hire teachers, arrangers and studio musicians in order to make a recording. For a young musician he is already a mature artist and sounds like he's had a lot of fine experience. Tell me where's he coming from?'

'Well, to start with, he's made all the rounds in New York scene and played several years with Miles Davis and John Coletrane. Not only that but this Fusion concept has inspired him to organize a new band featuring more collective improvisation. My teenage nephew idolizes McLaughlin and found out that the name of the new group will be the Mahavishnu Orchestra. He thinks that the Beatles are still infants in Kindergarden in comparison and hopes that his classmates will soon wean themselves away from sucking on the industrialized pop trend to hear this kind of mature music for a new age. He's only sixteen and plays guitar but believe it or not those were his words, not mine! As for me, I'm convinced that McLaughlin is converging intelligently in the right direction. What's more, I'm sure we'll hear lots more great new sounds from him in the near future.'

'I'm delighted to admit that in this Neo-Dadaism era of electronic sound industries McLaughlin is like a fresh wind blowing over a garbage dump. And you know, if he thinks philosophically as well as he plays musically you can be sure that he is consciously aware of the same values we've been discussing. For example the nature of being natural. Isn't it the nature of life that there is a subjective personal life we live full of craziness and fantasy. One could never be an artistic jazz soloist without those last two elements. And yet today we are all victims of a peculiar kind of consciousness dictated by society, which makes us conform by being rational, logical, and intellectualizing to the point of over-specialized eggheadedness. Some people pretend to be orderly and sane in a lunatic world while creative musicians appear to be deranged only to contribute pleasure to the community. They have the ability to perceive that both the music and the world are madness. It's a miracle for them to enjoy the daily experience of being alive and that's more amazing than logical. In this meantime society buys technological power at the price of spiritual and emotional poverty. Applying sensitivity and intuition musicians in the spirit of Orpheus express their need to get in tune and in touch with the natural world of sounds in motion. By liberating their subconscious mind they are able to transform reality and transcend to another state of consciousness where they can cry out against the world of high tech.'

'You have keen insight into the psychology of music, Monk. You know too that good professional musicians always control the four Ts – Tone, Time, Taste and Technique. And naturally musicians trained early on to handle acoustic instruments have sensitive touch and better tone control. Often electronic performers can hardly control themselves but in their muscular playing they are deceived by the sound power of explosive energies artificially reproduced. As the sound of music reflects society and its environment the sound pressures of louder than life electronic groups are portents of a syndrome physicists call entropy. This term is usually defined in terms of matter (the second law of thermodynamics) but has also been applied in such fields as economics. One could describe it simply as a vacuum where energy builds up, levels off and finally remains useless for man or machine. More specifically it is a quantity that is the measure of the amount of energy in a system which is not available for doing work and it is the ultimate state reached in the degradation of the matter and energy in the universe. Experts say that entropy is increasing as there is less and less energy available for conversion into mechanical work and its potential goes to waste because it is neither converted nor recycled. However the energy that is useful reaches a point of inactivity unless outside forces act upon it. Finally this wasted energy slowly deteriorates irreversibly toward disorder. Even a society can wind down from its own pressures and complexities so that opposing forces are choked into a static balance, a uniform state, a center of indifference. Astronomers too might agree that even the universe is wearing out as they see signs of old age in the black holes of our galaxy. At any rate back here on earth social problems grow out of control, resources become scarce, capital expensive and cheap energy no longer available. In our times the potential energies of highly educated Baconian humanistic scientists as well as the musicians and artists are gradually going into decline along with an economy infected by entropy. Increasingly employers in all areas are

135

inclined to invest in sophisticated technology to replace employees which in turn replaces personal service, the human communication element. This raises the loaded question of why do we need more "technological progress" when we're falling into that kind of trap?

'Well let's have no more of this gloom-doom talk. Wasn't it Thoreau who said, "When I hear music, I fear no danger. I am invulnerable. I see no foe. I am related to the earliest times and to the latest." Just for a change, what do you say about listening to some authentic folk music from Ireland? Not long ago I happened to visit Dublin and heard a concert of the Chieftains, the leading Irish folk ensemble. Do you know anything about them?'

'You bet I do, Barry. And as a musician and ethnographer I have only the greatest respect and admiration for their artistic contribution to Irish music. Play anything at all from their repertoire. I love everything they've recorded.'

After hearing several songs Monk's eyes were misty as he confessed, 'I'll have to admit, Barry, that I'm part Irish and those guys make me a little homesick. But what's more important, they are really a musical phenomenon. The Chieftain ensemble was born about the same time as the volcanic eruption of the Beatles. In spite of our era of electronic pop rock this purely acoustic Irish folkgroup has cut dozens of records and toured the world. Moreover they do scholarly research for repertoire, their professional musicianship is impeccable, and they maintain a relaxed earthy folk sound interpreting these songs. From what I've read I understand that they have inspired a revival of Irish folk music and since the 1980s publishers are meeting the demand by printing over six thousand authentic folk songs. New editions of O'Neill's Collection, the *Complete Works* of O'Carolan and several volumes of the musicologist Breandan Breathnach are now selling like never before. Actually Ireland is not alone in awakening to this Renaissance of folk music. Some countries, particularly in eastern Europe, are training professional folk dancers and recording folk musicians for international distribution. Of course it's no secret that many great classical composers lifted folk melodies to develop further in their extended works. Apparently today it's becoming more popular to go back to our musical roots.

'Say, by the way, I just happen to have with me a 45 EP recording of some Swedish folk music that you might like to hear. It's in my jacket pocket there on your coathanger. Here, let me pick out the song I want you to hear. This is a recording by one of Sweden's finest jazz pianists, Jan Johansson, who specializes in interpreting folk songs in his own style. The name of this is "Kullerullvisan" from the province of Dalarna.'

As the last strains faded away, Barry commented, 'That's a very clever way to play an old folk song using slightly jazzy rhythmic phrasing but with respect and refined taste too. Very original and I like his style of playing piano.'

Then Monk added, 'Johansson recently cut an entire volume of Swedish folk songs and now is collecting songs from all over Europe. And there's a music ethnography group in Sweden called "Big Sounds From Small Countries" which is sponsored by the government. Every year they spend several months in various countries with folklore traditions which are drowning in the flood of industrialized sound products. In contacting government, private, media and tourist interest groups they discuss and eventually persuade them to promote and distribute more of their own native music to domestic consumers as well as to the rest of the world. Meanwhile back home Sweden lives up to its fine reputation in Europe for actively preserving its folklore. Each province has well organized folk dance and music groups. During my work in Stockholm I travelled all over Sweden and had the pleasure of seeing these ensembles in action. Aesthetically it was a beautiful experience. I'd like to go back any time and relive it again.

'By the way we've covered some samples of fine jazz tonight but just out of curiosity I wonder if you have any classical recordings in your repertoire?'

'I'm glad you asked me, Monk. A few of my favorites right now are Wilhelm Kempff playing Beethoven's last sonatas, Martha Argerich's Schumann and Alfred Brendel's versions of Schubert. And what precious works of art they all are!'

9

The world view of modern science is misleading and has deficiencies which have a decisive significance for individuals and society's well-being. This can have a negative effect on the ability of human civilization to survive. William Harman, Director of the Institute of Noetics (noetics - pure abstract reasoning and the logical laws of thought)

'You'll recall a while back when I dropped the term "web", the buzzword for technology? Now think of technology as a giant Godlike spider weaving its net all over the globe and we imagine artists as flylike intruders continually tapping spokes of this web until the vibrations awaken the spider. As these vibrations gradually slow down, the spider fingers the guidelines for signs of a struggle and is puzzled living as it does in a world of spider ideas. One must then realize that everything outside is irrational or merely useful raw material for our spider. Artists simply do not exist or at best are persistent little frills existing on the outer fringes of the web. Now we must ask the loaded question: Is it possible that these spider-like minds are caught in their own trap? We are all aware that man is the only highly specialized animal who evolved with a brain to escape from an over-specialized programmed existence but not to be trapped into it. In my opinion this is the real truth that must eventually liberate man and free his creative imagination for living with the natural world constructively, not destructively. However, man will continue to spin his web and perhaps it is his nature, but if he continues playing this role his brain may become a new version of an old trap. Nature has always laid many traps for the animal who never learns.

'But you know, I often wonder just how far mankind has developed during the past 2,500 years. When one reflects on the dynamic achievements of the Greeks in a brief period of 150 years we need to be a little less arrogant about how we use the word "progress". A small portion of humility might serve us well by granting a realistic perspective enabling us to perceive the "benefits" of materialistic utilitarianism as a mirage. For example, if we take a look at the last 150 years of human development in western civilization we see more downers than uppers from slavery to egocentric capitalism. Other "ism" ideologies of our time include communism (more dead than alive), fascism (recent revival), militarism, scientism, retrogressive religious fundamentalism, anti-humanism, the megalomania of solipsism, and finally the forces of "economism" where people are less important than economics itself. Add to this a century and a half of the scourge of wars – twenty-five annually since World War II – while seventy per cent of the world is fading into oblivion one might be tempted to ask whether the clouds of dehumanization have overshadowed any rational notion of human progress. In fact it appears that reason and ethics are hiding somewhere on another planet. In the meantime hundreds of jet-setting "organization men" have found a career in saving the world for technocracy.

'Now, please don't laugh at my idea but I have a proposal that is no crazier than some that those barnstorming bureaucrats dream up. I think it's about time to recruit some devoted realistic-idealists for full time work as "Peace Pilgrims". In using their fantasy and imagination they could improvise and dramatise scenes concerning current critical issues at unexpected times in different places. Now there are thousands of creative people in this country who have seldom had the opportunity to express how they feel about present day problems. Bring in the clowns, dancers, comedians, actors and even poets. Last but not least perhaps hundreds of unemployed professional musicians (rock and pop players need not be invited to commercially exploit this generous idea. This will not be a trendy thing for television cameras to zoom in on narcissistic megalomaniacs) and thousands of young music students might lend their talents to such a project. This kind of support could build morale, uplift the spirits and make some big band noises that might be heard by the power elite political leaders. The repertoire ought to include generous portions of jazz and folk music. Just recall old Joshua who fought the battle of Jericho and those walls came tumbling down. Of course the media would call such a suggestion absurd and ridiculous. But now I am convinced that if creative human beings never voluntarily marshall their forces behind such a thrust, the hard core realists, those cynical bad guys, will keep right on winning. And today the highways are well paved for those marching killjoys in stomping boots. Dancing shoes are the real winners in the long run. Now in considering all this what bothers me most about the future is the next few generations as we move into the third millennium. For me the meaning of life is the vitality and adventure of playing with new ideas – the joy of improvisation. And of course jazz is the best example. Any rigid systems are dangerous for mankind's psychic evolution and can only lead to the decay of a society.'

Monk glanced at his watch and exclaimed, 'My God, Barry, it's already the wee small hours of the morning and I'm half-smashed. Before you pour me out the door I may have to sack out for a while on this sofa. Do you mind putting up with me?'

'You're very welcome. You're not only my guest but a new-found friend. But before Morpheus embraces you let me tell you a little bedtime story, a coda for this over-extended opus.

'If this "Dark Age" trend continues it's quite possible that man might reach the height of his intellectual powers and go into deterioration that could last for thousands of years. The momentum of independent thought is so easy to lose. Men might sink into a mere routine repetition of habits, acts, instincts and functional social patterns at a fairly low level, almost brainless as computers and robots take over. It's a biological fact that certain insects can run a very stable society without any brains. Our computerized world is already contributing to this kind of existence. If all these patterns I've mentioned begin to connect then we will have to learn to live in a state of entropy governed by a global technocracy. If we surrender to this whirlpool of degenerate forces, what poor creatures we'll have become. Imprisoned in this maelstrom will there be any room for creative imagination or artistic expression? Or will science have covered that outlet for us too? If so then we are indeed an endangered species threatened with losing our humanity. I'm not really afraid of man having no future because of nuclear war and our extinction. What frightens me now is the nature of our future. As these spiders weave their web over the arts – computerized music as well as painting – perhaps man will eventually have little use or even contempt for art. Art has made man what he is and man as we know him. We may survive catastrophes but what joy is there when we become strangers to the idea of art which once contributed to sharing our common humanity. And what a devastatingly tragic irony if this were to occur because any realistic-idealist knows that deep inside us there is a natural heartfelt need for right and good self-feelings which include ethical ideals and aesthetic values. There is something incredibly sterile and destructive about any science when it is directed toward dominating and manipulating man. It appears to kill those natural needs for joyful feelings, beauty and wonder.

'When western science was born about four hundred years ago an unknown author wrote a classic tale about a wizard skilled in the occult sciences of alchemy and astrology. This particular wise man was dissatisfied with the limits of mere human knowledge and sold his soul to the devil to gain more worldly knowledge, power and the pleasures to go with it. Dr Faust was tormented by an insatiable striving for mastering all knowledge and ended up sacrificing spiritual values for material rewards. Seeking absolute knowledge and power is a dangerous game when we must confront this instinct of annihilation common to mankind. This Faustian spirit of omnivorous scientific inquiry is very much alive today.

'I'm sorry for finishing my last "chorus" on a dissonant chord, Monk, but look, it's sunrise, a new day, tomorrow is already here and nature's own overtones may yet resolve it. Go ahead and sleep well, dear friend.'

Chapter VIII

TWO PALEFACES AT AN INDIAN POW-WOW

1

Monk and Barry continued to meet and jam together for the rest of Christmas week until Shirley arrived home the day before New Year's Eve. Monk picked up Anita at the Albuquerque airport the next day. Barry and Monk were booked to play for the big hotel celebrations that evening and their wives tagged along to join the fun. Shirley 'sat in' intermittently to sing and the full packed dining room guests were in high spirits all evening. A small dance floor attracted too many dancers while the listeners showed their appreciation with grateful applause after each tune. The evening was such a success that they were asked to play until 2:00 a.m. for which the manager paid them double for overtime. Anita and Monk finally got to bed about an hour later.

Awaking Sunday morning at high noon they drank a cup of coffee, dressed hastily and drove to the hotel for a New Year's Day brunch. While they ate Anita described in detail all the Christmas fun she had had with her Spanish and Mexican relatives. It was a gregarious family reunion that seemed to go on non stop for four days and nights. Many of them she had not seen for years and she enjoyed brushing up on her Spanish with those who had turned up from Mexico. As Monk listened intently he felt almost envious of her happy family relationships.

'Anita, I really think you're so lucky to have such warm, lovable relatives. I wish I could say the same about mine.'

'Oh Monk, I can't believe that you came from an unhappy family. Surely you must have some good memories?'

'Well, typical middle class Anglo-American families like ours tend to be duty driven and certainly less amiable than yours.'

'Some day I'd like to meet your parents and I hope you'll meet my San Diego relatives too. In the meantime you and I are having a happy life together, aren't we?'

Suddenly Monk felt a verbal nudge as if she were expecting a future commitment. Although they were as close as lovers could be he knew it was not the time nor place to make any proposals. Instead he simply replied, 'We have nothing but fun all the time we are together. And speaking of good times, we still have four more days of vacation left. Why don't we take a long break driving out to the mountain country? We could start off in the Jemez area where I know of a bed and breakfast place run by my Indian friends. And I'm quite sure there is at least one ceremonial dance festival going on about this time. I'll check my calendar to confirm it. By the way, did you know too that I'm so well acquainted with these tribes from my research projects that I've been honored by being given an Indian name? You'll find out what it is when we visit them. What about it? Do you want to join me?'

'Monk, I can hardly wait. Let's go!'

He called his Indian friends and confirmed a room for three nights and was informed that the annual tribal deer dance ceremony would take place on the last day of their visit. Early the next morning they set off in Monk's VW convertible heading west for the Jemez mountains. On this fifty-mile drive they cut through the boundaries of several Indian tribes along the way, among them the Santo Domingos, the Cochitas and the Zias. While passing through these territories several Indians walking along the road recognized Monk immediately and waved shouting, 'Hi there, Peacepiper, see ya comin!'

Looking over at Anita Monk smiled, saying, 'Well, now you heard it. That's my Indian name and I do feel proud of it!'

'I must say that I do agree with them. It's very appropriate,' replied Anita. 'And I'm beginning to think this will be an exciting adventure. The first and only time I visited a reservation was fifteen years ago as a high school student. I'm willing to bet that tourists and other Anglos are more well informed about them than I am. In your work you certainly know more about them. I think it's remarkable that they respect you so much by giving you a special name.'

'The respect is mutual but my respect for them is even greater. I admire these people highly for their profound wisdom, deep psychological insight, reverence for life and spiritual relationship to Mother Earth. Once upon a time we too had these prehistoric "first world" qualities, a mastery of the essential facts of life which we are now sacrificing for a jet speed way of living. The more I learn the more humble I become, knowing that for thousands of years they knew the art of survival. It's incredible to think that these early Americans emigrated from southern Mongolia over the Bering Strait to Alaska from 60,000-10,000 BC, then wandered down to north, central and south America to settle down. Many thousands of years later Chinese dynasties arose and declined, followed by Egyptian civilization, the Greek Golden Age, and five hundred years of the Roman Empire. Another thousand years passed before the Calvanist Pilgrims established their "City of God" on the shores of Massachusetts where the Indians befriended them from the moment they landed. For this the true believing Puritans deliberately infected them with incurable diseases and massacres. Under the Indian Removal Act of 1830, ninety per cent of those who remained were herded west into desolated territories until gold and oil were discovered by the white man. Even the kings of Europe could never afford to purchase all the land which the white warriors ripped off for next to nothing. History is full of wars and violence but for America this was its first consciously planned genocide.

'Historians estimate that out of 40 million Indians living in North America in 1600 only 200,000 remained after 1900. These peaceful food gatherers who had lived for nearly sixty millennia in America had expressed their willingness to teach us the facts of life and the art of survival in this new country. Instead our armies forced them out of their homes and fenced them into desert lands. They had established a living style in perfect harmony with Mother Earth, practicing the first natural laws of sustained development which we desperately need to learn today. The Indians knew better than we about how fragile and limited the earth's carrying capacity actually is. Are you familiar with the penetrating environmental prophesy that the legendary Chief Seattle wrote to America's president in 1852? It is said that they represented the last generation of the upper Palaeolithic-Stone-Age-Indian moral order. Another example: were you ever taught that in the late 1700s our founding fathers actually visited the Onandaga tribe in upstate New York to study their ideal democratic society? And what amazes me too is the Indians' high level of artistic creativity, an outgrowth of the basic human need to record, recreate and reproduce elements in the environment. Unique handicraft designs and literally earth moving song and dance ceremonies are further evidence of their deep sense of aesthetics. Indian festival music may sound primitive and monotonous to our ears but for them every repetitive chant and drum beat takes on spiritual meaning for all participants. What's more the entire community has an endurance which is incredible. I've witnessed these day-long marathons with hundreds of half bare bodies stomping around in the rain and snowy weather. Incidentally, they believe that upon death one's spirit becomes a cloud and bringer of rain. Sometimes I nearly pray that when we reach the end of our "technological progress" epoch enough Indians remain to teach us "Palefaces" how to survive. I'm sure we'll need their wisdom. You know, old Chief Seattle was right. It's simply an honor and a privilege to work with them. I do hope you will like them all as much as I do. Anyway we're going to have some fun, I promise you that.'

'Don't misunderstand me, Monk, as I appreciate the useful information you're giving me, but sometimes you sound like a typical teacher. Oh look, there's a sign telling us we are now entering the Jemez reservation. We'd better keep our eyes open for the B and B house.'

Then Monk spotted them. 'There they are, sitting on the front porch just as though they were expecting us.'

Suddenly, wrinkled leather-faced Chief Red-Eye leaped down to greet them as they drove in to park the car.

'How! Peacepiper. Yo! So good to see you again. I hope you brought your long black stick to blow some warm winds for our Deer Dance. And who is your companion? Wow, you have beautiful taste, man,' as they

145

introduced themselves. 'Well, you're both so welcome so step right in. My house is your house, as they say in Sante Fé. And here is my wife, Little Fawn. You remember Peacepiper and this is his lady friend, Anita!' Then he turned to both of them saying, 'I'm glad you'll be staying for three days. As I've mentioned before, we're busy preparing for the ceremonies Thursday and now you'll learn how we get things organized. Meanwhile maybe Peacepiper can warm up his stick and practice on the chants we're going to sing.'

They unpacked and ate a lunch of corn meal pancakes and vegetable soup with chunks of rabbit meat. The rest of the afternoon they spent driving around the reservation.

Monk visited Jemez often for his research work but each time he came it seemed like a reunion of old friends. As they drove by many of the local folks greeted him with a friendly smile and exclaimed, 'Peacepiper's back!' They enjoyed his clarinet playing and felt he was one of them. As for his performing at the actual dance rituals, they were a sacred tradition and he was restricted to improvising on the chants before and after the ceremonies.

Driving back in the early evening they gazed at the sunset sliding down over the high woodland hills and approaching Red-Eye's house they listened to drum rhythm patterns and a chanting choir rehearsing the deer dance repertoire.

2

After dinner they slept soundly and awoke in the morning to a far off rooster crowing. While eating breakfast Red Eye invited them to spend the day watching the rehearsal for the final production.

About ten o'clock enormous waves of people from the entire reservation gathered on a broad open plain to sing chants to the accompaniment of six thundering drummers. Gradually a dance consisting of writhing and gentle stomping gripped this mass of Indians as though they were caught up in a hypnotic trance. At lunchtime everyone took a two hour break before returning to the afternoon session. As they began streaming back, Monk took out his 'long black stick' and, recalling the pentatonic motifs he had learned earlier, started to improvise on the chants.

As they gathered in procession Monk noticed that children as young as eight were proudly participating while parents coached them. After several more hours of this routine they finished just before dinner. Anita and Monk went for a long walk through the woods and part way up a nearby mountainside to watch the sunset.

When they returned for dinner Chief Red-Eye welcomed them to a campfire meeting at eight o'clock. This was story telling night when various natives volunteered to relate their dreams and visions. Monk remembered reading that the famous Swiss psychiatrist Carl Jung attended some of these sessions and was both fascinated and inspired by what he had learned. Chief Red-Eye started off describing a dream he had had the night before, followed by the medicine man, the elders and finishing with parents and children. More than a few of them weaved a nearly hypnotic spell dramatizing the stories with the help of songs and gestures. Everyone listened in silence and rapt attention. Naturally these stories were told in their own tribal language while the medicine man's teenage daughter did her best to translate the essential contents.

The next day the community planned to rehearse dramatic details of the deer dance. Anita and Monk preferred to wait for the final performance and decided to tour the surrounding tribal communities. Leaving early after breakfast, they drove south through some of the same reservations they had crossed through on the way to Jemez, the Santa Domingos, Cochitas and the Zias on to the Laguna and Canoncito which were originally Navaho tribes. Along the way Monk pointed out, 'It's surprising but true that New Mexico has more Indian reservations than any other state or any province in Canada, exactly twenty-two.'

Then Anita interjected, 'And as we look around at these "ghetto retreats" supervised by the Bureau of Indian Affairs I recall several points from my college studies in American history which you touched on earlier. I'd just like to elaborate on that Indian Removal Act. Most of the Indians have known nothing but violence by the white man as his superior forces destroyed and isolated what was originally their home country. The whites were obviously dominant and treated them finally as small colonies of troublesome squatters. Remember too that those who were not massacred bought guns and "firewater" from white pioneer hustlers. Now today uninformed Americans wonder why the Indians have such acute alcohol and suicide problems.'

'Yes, Anita, and let me add to what I said earlier, that America's Calvinist Pilgrims had such a frozen image of the past in believing that all human history started with Christ and that only some chosen few were elected to be saved. Like the ancient Hebrews they thought that God created the world from out there somewhere all at once. Then God selected these 'true believers' to organize all Christians to prepare for a flight heavenward here on earth. Meeting other human beings who had found their own way of living for thousands of years before Calvinism was a shocking challenge to the pilgrims' faith. Showing little willingness to learn they simply labelled them pagan savages and went about "saving" the gullible few. Not only were they anti-intellectual Philistines but the pilgrims hated all music. Calvinist Christians possessed the one and only superior dogma.

'Contrary to Indian philosophy Christianity eliminated God from nature and promoted man to dominate and control the created world. This same type of conservative "true believers" in our day belongs to the creed of scientism. This fellowship actively promotes the idea that technological progress is eternal and the one and only path to the ultimate reality. Ironically there is now a reactionary twist of new fundamentalists who are drifting toward a brand of Christian Fascism. Coincidentally, our father of science Francis Bacon died only a few years after the Pilgrims' landing in Plymouth, Massachusetts. For nearly the last four hundred years both Puritanism and scientism have contributed to the negation of the Palaeolithic human spirit which contemporary anthropologists are beginning to re-evaluate. In this mean-time our first Americans are still looked upon as enemy images in old Hollywood films.'

Anita interrupted with her comment, 'It's appalling that school textbooks do not inform pupils about these vital facts in our early history. This subtle kind of silent censorship is sponsored by the power-elite who sell the "American dream" to those who prefer to deny reality. But you know, I have a hunch there could well be a backlash among our Indians just as is happening among the blacks nowadays. The Bureau of Indian Affairs has a long history of keeping these native Americans in their place "in the back of the bus".'

Then Monk answered, 'Not long ago I read about a case of cynical exploitation where uranium was discovered in Navaho territory. The Indians were paid off by giving them jobs working in the mines and today their cancer rate is soaring.'

Driving around the Jemez Canyon reservoir toward the Santa Ana reservation, Anita remarked, 'How refreshing it is to see this long body of water in the middle of all this desert country. It's like a huge eye in the earth. Reassuring to know that it's a water supply for thousands of thirsty people. If the south-west ever begins to dry up like a sunbaked Sahara desert as climatologists predict, soon after the year 2000 we'll need all the dams we can build.'

Just before they arrived at the Santa Ana community they turned around to follow the reservoir road back to meet the route going north to Jemez Springs, a charming village perched alongside the Jemez riverbank. As they approached the town Monk glanced at Anita, saying, 'There are more forests in this high hill country than I expected. Lovely green glens and groves too. I'll have to drive over this way more often.'

The later afternoon sun reminded them it was time to return for dinner. After a leisurely half hour drive they met Red-Eye as they stepped out of the car. He greeted them with, 'Howdy folks. I hope you've had a good day touring. I just want to tell you that our deer dancer is a real star. As you know the big production is tomorrow and I'm glad you're staying over to join us. Tonight Peacepiper is welcome to attend the Peacepipe ritual.'

'Thanks, Red-Eye, I'll be there.'

On the way to their room Monk informed Anita, 'As you can see this ceremony is reserved for men and it's obvious I cannot afford to miss it. Even if I don't smoke this is a special exception to the rule.'

When dinner was over Chief Red-Eye guided Monk to an old wigwam where the medicine man and the elders were sitting in a circle in total silence. Everyone appeared completely relaxed as the smoking pipe was passed on from hand to hand.

This was not the first time Monk had attended this ceremony and he was quite familiar with most of the symbolic meaning behind the rituals. The pipe is like a portable sacred altar which represents the universe where all nations are united. The stone or clay bowl symbolizes the earth elements and the female energies. The wooden stem represents the male and the plant kingdom and is decorated with feathers and fur to symbolize the animal kingdom. At the beginning of the rituals the pipe is filled with tobacco in the following way: pinches are offered to the Earth Mother, the Great Spirit and the four directions, the four kinds of animal creatures, the four elements (earth, fire, water and air), the water beings, the spirit keepers and any other meaningful purpose. In lighting the pipe each of the four directions receives a puff of smoke and at the same time the smoke sends out prayers into the universe. As they inhale they believe that the breath of the Great Spirit is in the smoke. Then they pray for understanding, healing and unity. The group of twenty men sat contemplating for nearly an hour. Finally Chief Red-Eye pointed the pipe in all directions uttering a short phrase in English for Monk – 'Go in Peace, brothers.'

When Monk returned to their room Anita remarked, 'You smell like charcoaled hickory smoked ham!' to which Monk replied, 'I'm sure that I do. I don't think you would have enjoyed it. It's such a rich aromatic blend of tobacco and I feel so high after inhaling it that sometimes I think they spike the mix with marijuana.'

3

The following morning Little Fawn knocked on the door to awaken them in time for breakfast and mentioned that Red-Eye looked forward to guiding them during the Deer Dance. Eating breakfast Red-Eye explained the spiritual significance of the ceremony.

'You see, our rituals reflect the way we look at the world and even the universe including life on other planets. Every person, plant, animal and supernatural being has meaning for our lifestyle. We expect the active participation of every individual in the group because without them all we believe that the cosmic order might break down. For example, we not only respect our older people highly but they are obligated to advise us and we really do listen to them seriously. We give older women a great deal of power because they decide who the Chief will be. And of course we encourage and stimulate children to speak out freely at some of our campfire meetings. In the Deer Dance today you'll see what I mean when you understand that we consider the deer like all animals to be holy. When we kill one for meat we pray for forgiveness to its spirit. The deer dancer dresses up and acts like a deer having studied carefully all its movements. This ritual is dedicated to all deer with both reverence and sorrow.'

Suddenly they heard choirlike voices singing a chant far away but gradually coming closer. Chief Red-Eye explained further.

'You hear those voices? They are singing for power. We believe that the power of music expressed by individuals singing together can actually heal people and make them whole. For us, praying, chanting, dancing, drumming and rattling as part of our ceremonies are the most powerful means we know for feeling more relaxed, at one with the way things are, recharging the earth and all her children with life energy that will circulate around the planet. Our medicine men have practiced this well known therapy for thousands of years. What's more, this music brings harmony to the individual, the group, nature and the spirits we call supernatural. Now it's time to go out and enjoy the ceremony.'

Monk and Anita followed Red-Eye out to the stomping grounds. Observing the procession carefully they noticed their soft, sensitive walking style as they seemed to feel the earth itself with each footstep. The hypnotic drum rhythms and the vigorous, forceful voices enchanted them while they stood perfectly still listening intently.

Suddenly Chief Red-Eye pointed out a figure taking up the rear of the parade, exclaiming, 'Look, folks, there is our sacred clown who appears especially during the first week of the New Year. Watch him dancing madly and notice his obscene gestures as the participants hurl insults at him. Actually he represents chaos in the universe, long before the creation of our world.'

The gesticulating clown took over the show with his wild dancing style. Behind him paraded a white hooded dancer with the head of a deer tied to his own head stalking proudly through the procession. Bare chested, wearing a long blue and black skirt and bells on his legs, he shook two king size maracas to announce the beginning of the drama. The deer dancer began his story by acting out the start of the hunt, walking slowly, eyes alert, looking in all directions, finally spotting the animal, stretching his bow and aiming for the heart, approaching the deer with sorrow and a prayer, placing it over his shoulders and returning to the reservation where all were overjoyed. This ritual went on for nearly an hour while the dancer slowly and gradually built up dramatic suspense. At the grand finale the whole community broke out into song accompanied by the drummers and danced out in the same way that they arrived.

Anita and Monk were enchanted by the whole performance and delighted to have gone through two films for future memories. That evening after dinner they paid Little Fawn and thanked Chief Red-Eye graciously for his hospitality, to which he answered, 'Peacepiper, you and Anita will always be welcome here at any time.'

Driving home in the glow of the desert sunset they were both enraptured but somewhat wistful too. Monk spoke, breaking the silence.

'What an exotic extravaganza! Those wild, vibrant energies really shook me up. As primitive as their dancing appears to us, one should never underestimate the artistic abilities of the exceptionally gifted Indians. In fact history tells us that two of the very finest ballet dancers in American history were full blooded Indians from Oklahoma. Marjorie Tallchief became a star ballerina with the Ballet Russe de Monte Carlo and guest artist with the Paris Opera, the American Ballet Theater and New York City Ballet. In fact she was considered one of the top ballerinas in the world until she went into semi-retirement to help her ballerina sister Maria organize the Chicago City Ballet.'

'They are all such wise and beautiful people,' Anita replied, 'and what a false notion we have of human progress when we stop to consider that innocent babies speak the truth while ancient primitive tribes have wisdom but cynically naive contemporary minds place their faith in computerized knowledge. And for Sante Fé natives, they are our neighbors whom we take entirely too much for granted. I'm really delighted that I followed with you and I've learned something from this visit. You're lucky that you can see them so often. I hope we can return again soon.'

They slept deeply that night, dreaming of the enchanting days in Jemez with bronze skinned early Americans from a prehistoric culture. The last day of their holiday vacation dawned all too soon upon them and they decided to relax to digest the past two weeks' events. At breakfast Monk felt that it was time to talk things over.

'All in all we've had some rather fantastic vacation days, haven't we? San Diego, New Year's Eve, and the Jemez Indian community really topped it off. I'm glad you had a great time in San Diego but now let me tell you how I got better acquainted with our friend Barry while you were gone. I've never met a man who had such gumption to act on his convictions. He faced a turning point which was just phenomenal. This guy studied eight years for his PhD in nuclear physics, landed a top military science lab job, then threw it all away to find his real happiness as a professional musician, but now I'll fill you in on the incredible details.'

Monk summarized briefly the high points and the painful awakening to the destructive course Barry's life was taking until he made this leap. Anita thought for a moment then asked, 'I understand why you admire him for all this but what does it really mean for you?'

'You see, Barry stimulated me into reflecting more deeply about what I'm achieving in my own work - teaching music. I've had some beautiful adventures as a musician both teaching and playing. However, as we mature in our chosen area we may feel content but if we are self-critical we inquire about what difference it is making for humanity. Now Barry realized he was collaborating in global suicide, the inhuman condition of mutually assured destruction, until his Muse awakened him to the fact that making music was more important than anything else in the world. In making his decision it was a matter of ethical ideals and a sense of aesthetic values which prevailed. For him the solution was obvious. As for me, I'm looking for an opportunity to contribute my talents to the community beyond my daily work routine. Fortunately I made the right decision from the beginning but I'm qualified by education and experience to develop my musical ideas further. This means that rather than simply making a living in what I like to do I'm prepared to make a commitment to share my talents in a project with those whose music is becoming an endangered species. Barry suggested a few creative ideas which I'm considering quite seriously for the future.'

'You're sounding like Don Quixote preparing for battle against the evil forces of our times. Or perhaps it's a mouse fighting an elephant. Can you explain to me what kinds of music are in danger and why?'

'As a professional musician who has studied, seen and heard the contemporary scene I'm convinced that for the last forty years music has lost its way. The king size "six pack" of electronic sound industries with their huge assembly line productions are processing musically illiterate amateurs into superstars. Sound pollution is the name of their game. What's happening to our ears? Why is some of the world's most valuable jazz and folk music continually being threatened by synthetic monocultural sounds?'

'I agree and understand what you mean,' answered Anita, 'but if you feel so strongly, what do you propose to do about it?'

'Before answering that directly it's necessary for me to fill in a little background for you. I remember what a feeling of great joy I had when I played new music for the first time. In those days genuine folk music was more available and I picked up many songs by ear. Later on I started listening to big band jazz which excited and thrilled me. Seeing the world as it is today and now that I'm somewhat mature in my profession I've become philosophical. I consider myself a human being first and a musician second. Social solidarity is essential in guiding musicians because it not only enriches one's talent but helps turn people into better human beings. Now of course it's much too late to reach perennial adolescents who are so zapped and addicted to electronic pop that they can never be weaned. Sometimes I think these kinds of people need their neurons rewired. Perhaps their nerve cells are so calloused that they have lost their ability to communicate impulses actively and spontaneously. Just think that once upon a springtime nearly two hundred years ago a greater part of humanity lived a frontier life with nature as culture, a grass roots lifestyle, independent, confident, maturing, growing from within and folklore traditions were well cultivated. A living nature and wonder were the highest values. In the 1700s in Europe there was actually and effectively a culture of music that flowed and spread over all of life. This kind of culture-man lived inwards while civilization-man lived outwards into spatial thinking among bodies and "facts". The first type learns to accept natural conditions as they are and the latter person is the materialist who can only understand life as a linkage between cause and effect. Then technology becomes the basis for civilization. As men moved to the artificial soil of the cities the order of society inevitably broke down while the "civilization-landscape" gradually evolved into an inorganic slime mold. Even styles of art were invented to replace the "elitism" of great masterpieces which could no longer be matched in quality.

'As we move into the future the populations of the world's cities will increase by multi-millions so we can be sure of an increased production of monoculture for the masses as music reflects this decline. Meanwhile Santa Fé still has some of the richest folklore in America with its indigenous Spanish and Indian cultures. Young people from pre-school onwards must have these native seeds of tradition planted like a tree of culture which will take root and grow throughout their lives. And those young Anglos who no longer suck on their electronic security blankets are growing up to listen and play jazz. They ought to be given the chance to cultivate America's only original art form. Now I hope you see what I'm driving at. I'd really love to see young folklore and jazz ensembles have the opportunity to do their thing their own way without having to be ground up in electronic soundmaking machinery. One might call it cultural confidence building by stimulating a sense of aesthetics to defend the beauty of their own culture against the tide of manufactured sounds. You see I'm already planning ahead for a post-technological music era. Anyway,

155

I've said enough about this for the moment. Let's just think about it. If you have any suggestions please pass them on to me when the time comes.'

Chapter IX

ALL THE THINGS YOU ARE

You are your greatest composition,
The one folks hear when they hear your name.
You are your spirit's own physician,
The one who heals your soul as a daily game.
You can't create yourself; that job's been done.
You can compose yourself; it's kind of fun.
You are the people you have turned to,
And you are the one who does what you do.
Your greatest work of art is you!

(The late Red Mitchell's* lyrics to
Jerome Kern's song)

1

Monk's professor in the philosophy of aesthetics once told his class after their final exam, 'Now I want you all to go out into the world and try to make your own lives a work of art!' On a trip to the north-eastern corner of neighboring Arizona Monk heard a similar message from the wise old Hopi Indians: 'Man is an artist who continually creates himself from deep within.'

Contemplating this Monk arose early the next morning to prepare an

---

* *The legendary studio jazz bassist Red Mitchell spent the last twenty-five years of his life living in Sweden.*

outline for his first day of classes. Anita joined him for breakfast while he made his last minute notes before leaving.

'Looks like it's time to face the music once again,' as he embraced her on the way out the door. After an unusually long goodbye kiss a second thought occurred to him. 'You know, it's about time you moved in with me. What do I have to do to make that happen?'

'Only time will tell,' she said. 'See you at my place tonight. So long for now.'

While his ethnomusicology class remained at the same level Monk was surprised at the increased enrolment in his aesthetics course. This made him curious to find out what stimulated this sudden interest. But first of all he had to get acquainted with these new students and learn about their backgrounds.

'I'm delighted to see such a large number of students interested in studying aesthetics this coming semester. Unfortunately it's a subject that's often overlooked in college philosophy curriculums so it's a privilege for me to teach it and I hope you'll appreciate this unique opportunity as much as I do. Please remember now that you're all college students and we're all here to learn together. As a matter of fact, I plan to learn a lot myself just from the questions you'll be asking me. I want you all to feel free to inquire about anything concerning the course that puzzles you. Before you all start firing away let me begin by pointing out that just as there are facts of life one must know in growing up to adulthood, so there are also facts one must learn about the elements of art in order to respond aesthetically. First let me explain the difference between ordinary taste and aesthetic judgement. Taste is simply a matter of personal opinion, limited as it may be but can never be argued. Now on the other hand aesthetic judgement must be cultivated for years to develop sympathetic detachment. Then there are occasions when words can never express how deeply we feel so we must remain silent. Now I'll try to define literally the term aesthetics and some of the problems we'll be investigating as we pursue the course. The Greek word "aisthesis" is the root for our word aesthetics and basically means "sense of perception" or to become consciously aware of one's feelings and thoughts in order to appreciate beauty. It's the philosophy of art where we study certain states of mind, attitudes and emotions involved in an aesthetic experience or response. We try to understand and evaluate beauty as it is revealed in art. With this knowledge we attempt to cultivate artistic taste by becoming more sensitive to beauty in man's creations as well as in nature itself. We must always bear in mind that we can never demand that a work of art delivers us a message, offers information, serves a practical purpose or has a special function or use. Great art is opposed to such utilitarian thinking. And while we're at it let me explain that we are all victims of utilitarianism today. Most of us believe more or less that the only value of any object or person is its usefulness for us in the short or long run.

'The father of utilitarianism was the English philosopher Jeremy Bentham who arrived at this concept about two hundred years ago. His thinking was not all as rigid and severe as it sounds because there were many nuances and degrees in his philosophy that were easily misinterpreted. Fundamentally one could describe him as a liberal humanist with utopian visions. However, the old Victorians succeeded in distorting his views into strictly hard core materialistic values for the industrial revolution and now we are stuck with them in today's technological world. Add to this our American heritage which gave us a Philistine streak of Puritanism from the Calvinist pilgrims who actually detested music and the arts as something satanic. They in turn shared this with the ignorant barbarians who destroyed all the Roman works of art. For these historical reasons many of us are inhibited from our ability to relax our reasoning in order to enjoy a profound aesthetic response.

'By the way, I cannot over-emphasize the fact that art and history are inseparable. For example, some historians hold the opinion that music has the power to direct the course of civilization. Learning to cultivate an aesthetic response teaches one to develop the art of contemplation which for the Golden Age Greeks was the ultimate goal of philosophy. In covering the elements of aesthetics we'll discover the nature of the work of arts existence, a pattern of words, sounds in motion, patches of color or even a physical thing. Most important of all we will try to find the relationship between aesthetic and ethical values. In a way they are married; neither

159

one can do without the other. Aesthetics today is expanding into such problems as its nature of style, the viability of the history of art, relationship to evaluating culture and the areas of Freudian psychology, sociology, ethnology and the place of aesthetic judgement in practical reasoning in the conduct of daily affairs. As you must be aware, any politician or businessman with a sense of aesthetics is a rare bird indeed.

'Finally, we'll discuss the question of whether great art can be said to deal with simple subjects freshly in the light of contemporary life. Is it possible that fine masterpieces can be created by primitive or naive people who can take old things and be innovative by making them new?

'Let's open the floor for questions. It's your turn to take over. Out of my own curiosity may I ask only one question first? What was it that motivated your interest in signing up for this course?'

One freshman girl held up her hand and explained: 'Recently a local and prominent art dealer was interviewed by a reporter friend of mine and asked for his definition of aesthetics. This highly successful gallery owner was utterly speechless and could not even come up with a rudimentary answer. The journalist thought he was joking but not at all, he simply did not know. Shortly afterwards I read a full page ad in a leading national newspaper placed by a multi-billion dollar electronics company which boasted that their top design engineer had an intimate understanding of the aesthetics of most countries in the world. Then I knew that something drastic had occurred when such a philosophic term could be twisted by an Orwellian minded advertising promoter. Going through the college catalog I discovered that this course was available. I feel enlightened already by your articulate definition.'

'Well, I'm delighted to have one student with such an eager attitude to learn but I'm sure there are more in the class who feel the same way. Now for those questions on what you expect to learn, I won't have all the answers but we're going to discover them together. I'm going to make notes of your questions and I suggest that you all do the same so that none of them will be overlooked along the way. As you know the required textbook is *Problems in Aesthetics* by Morris Weitz. There are plenty of copies in the college book store so I urge you to buy one soon. As I look over my student list I see that most of you are philosophy, art history, literature and music majors. Aesthetics has something to offer in all these areas so please feel free to ask any question about our subject no matter how foolish you think it is. I may sound foolish when I try to answer it, so now's the time, fire away!'

A long-haired Beatnik-looking student arose to ask, 'As an art history student I'm well aware that all the fine arts reflect contemporary society in one way or another but in my studies I can't help but notice a real contrast in painting during the first half of our century and what's happened since the end of World War II. What can you tell us about that?'

'That's a very keen observation you've made. Please make a note of that, everyone. It's a loaded one and for now I'll try to answer it as concisely as possible. We must realize what a dehumanized century we're living in, having survived two world wars and hundreds of conflicts and interventions all over the globe. No one can argue that World Wars I and II have not influenced all the arts very significantly. There were also two great geniuses who were not artists but nevertheless changed the direction of art. Freud gave birth to surrealism for which Salvador Dali is an outstanding example. Einstein introduced the concepts of space which then inspired Picasso's cubism. World War I was supposed to be the war that ended all wars and people thought that in spite of those horrors something good had to come out of it all. About that time Dadaism broke through to deny everything rational because we had not yet become physically numbed to all that killing as we are today. Not much later came innovations with Picasso's cubism and various other styles which dominated the first half of the century.

'The greatest influence in the last half of our century came from Marcel Duchamp, a highly intellectual, unemotional, witty, nihilistic, minimalist who stopped painting in 1923 at the age of twenty-five. This "painter's painter" reacted early on against the current which later re-discovered him. Ironically that is exactly where modern art is today. At the end of World War II, exiled Max Ernst made surrealism popular followed by the abstract impressionism of America's Jackson Pollock. Incidentally, one

161

of the world's greatest art connoisseurs, Peggy Guggenheim, lost interest in all modern works since the early death of Pollock and began collecting primitive African art.

'Since about 1950 the abstract impressionists have been the real pioneers: spontaneous, highly personal, very emotional, innovative but perhaps not so humorous as one might expect. Concerning some of the latest art production, I know of art critics who are shocked at the number of popular artists who are completely unable to draw a line and express only anger and brutality with lots of messy smearing. Not only that but some of these critics are bored to death by the regimentation and feeble technique exhibited by these contemporary painters. Right now you might feel that this information is opinionated but in our class we shall study how these prominent critics have arrived at their conclusions. And at the same time we will expose the aesthetically uneducated art journalists and cynically naive museum directors who really ought to know better. By the way, one standard principle to remember is that a competent art critic always attempts to place himself midway between the artist and public before making his judgement. This naturally requires a profound sense of aesthetics. You can understand that this topic is almost a separate course in itself but I promise you that we'll discuss it more comprehensively during this semester. How about some more questions?'

'You mention the problem of judging but how do any of us laymen begin to evaluate or even decide that an object is truly beautiful?' asked a scholarly looking young lady in the front row.

'Great! We're beginning to ask all the right questions. That's another good one. Well, I would start by saying that one must first establish an ideal and by understanding why an object is thought to be beautiful one is able to distinguish passing or fleeting "ideals" from those that spring up from more fundamental feelings that are comparatively permanent and universal. My own aesthetics professor used to suggest that after viewing the first five thousand paintings or hearing the first hundred concerts one then has a highly developed sense of personal taste. By that time you will certainly be qualified to discriminate between pop commodities and a work of art. One must consider too that all human

162

beings are predominantly emotional so that we respond first with our feelings and later analyze art intellectually. Again this is only a brief answer to your question and there will be more to discuss later on.'

At the back of the classroom a hand shot up with the following question: 'I understand what you mean by the primary emotional response but what part does reason play in making aesthetic judgements?'

'Content appeals to our feelings and later we analyze the form. Form always measures and analyzes after the fact and the artist is usually aware of the form he or she is creating. Imagination, expression and emotions are the real contents. Cézanne was aware of the search for form when he stated that nature consisted of triangles, cylinders and cones. Modern film makers are often obsessed with form. Emotionally uninhibited primitive people have no demands for form but respond spontaneously with a natural sense of aesthetics which is astounding for those of us who study the subject. Of course we must not become slaves to unreasoning feelings that explode in such a way that it is beyond all proportion to our will and intelligence and is unworthy of the human mind. Then we lose self control, a factor that is deficient in our jet speed world of technological progress. For example music, sounds in motion, is the most abstract of all the arts. It is said that the great composer Berlioz always responded with deep feelings the first time he listened to a beautiful piece being performed. However, when one of his own compositions was being played he followed his score with a magnifying glass. If you can read notes and listen often to favorite recorded symphonic works at home you can purchase pocket scores in the music store and study what you are listening to. Otherwise you trust only your feelings in responding. In looking at a new painting take in the whole composition, emotional lines and color without any pre-judgements and if you approve then view more of the same artist's paintings. Then read about their background, personality and training which helps you understand the style. Will that help you for the present?'

A philosophy student speaking in a shy half-whispering voice inquired, 'What did Socrates and Plato have to say about aesthetics?'

'Offhand I can start by offering you a quote from one of Socrates' prayers. Let's see if I can remember it. Oh yes, it goes like this. "Beloved Pan and all you other gods who haunt this place, give me beauty in the inward soul and may the outward and the inward become one." Of course he had music in mind when he included that lusty old Greek piper Pan but his view of aesthetics was holistic, an integration of the outer natural world with our own inner nature; a perfect harmony, an organic unity one might say where we come into balance centered down. Plato, who often distrusted artists, reluctantly proclaimed, "The Gods endowed us with vision, the Muses gave us hearing and harmony so that we could use them intelligently in developing our inner soul while restoring it to order and concord with itself." Plato believed that the masses were foolish and deceived themselves into thinking that there was no right or wrong in music, that anyone could judge it good or bad simply by the pleasure it gave, adding that music lost its finest values when mass entertainment became a popularity contest. He was convinced that the majority of the public react with impulsiveness and capriciousness but seldom respond with good judgement or knowledge. For those of you who are studying philosophy this is an appropriate time to point out Kierkegaard's definition of a modern public when he said that it is not a real community nor does it consist of real persons but is simply an abstract collection of individuals. At the moments when they are nothing that is when they are acting like everyone else. And we are all supposed to conform to the will and opinion of this so called modern public: collective tastes and group ethics. Kierkegaarde might add to this that today if we do not join this other directed crowd we would be labelled snobs or undemocratic. We will learn that just as there are facts of life we must know as we mature and face reality there are also essential elements about art which express an aesthetic truth to broaden our enjoyment of life.'

A music student asked, 'The title of our textbook is *Problems in Aesthetics* but it seems to me that all the fine arts in our times are suffering from many problems not least of all music which I plan on for a career. How do you perceive this syndrome that we artists are now facing?'

'Now you're driving right down my alley because I've been a professional musician most of my life before entering college teaching. To quote a

164

hackneyed phrase, "Let's face the music!" Technology is the dominant culture and driving force in our society today. We are over-accenting science at the expense of the humanities which in turn places the fine arts low on the list as a breadwinner. Besides this musicians live in a noisy world where people are now conditioned to react to sound bites whether it emanates from pop, rock or television commercials. This means that the attention span for an average audience has been reduced to three minutes and it's getting shorter all the time. For example, the sound pressure from electronically powered pop bands pound at the listener hard and fast so that loudness larger than life becomes an instant success formula but eventually can cause the incurable ear-ringing disease of tinnitus. Such pyrotechnical productions cripple the progress of serious art which depends less on rudimentary physical reactions. It might surprise some of you to know that without electronic equipment the Carl Orff music method teaches pre-school infants how to use these elementary pop band devices in making their own music. Moreover, these children learn early on that there are such things as discipline, concentration and patience involved in intelligent music making. Society as a whole needs these values if we are to develop new ideas and meaningful feelings. Otherwise we are destined to fall into the trap of utilitarian materialism. I hope I can help you all discover that humanity has infinite possibilities for cultural enjoyment which have hardly been explored yet. Creativity, the vitality of joy, the pleasure of contemplating new ideas, is an adventure which gives life meaning and stimulates the imagination more than the utilitarian pursuit of hard core technology. Nineteenth-century wise men offer us this thought to contemplate, "Music expresses that which cannot be said and on which it is impossible to be silent. Where words leave off music begins." And so there is nothing more I can say for the moment.

'Before I tack on a coda to our discussion we'll take time for one more question. I see a hand from that gentleman in the third row.'

'From an aesthetic point of view how seriously should one consider trendy fashions?'

'If I have a problem with this one perhaps some of you women can help me. Fashion and cosmetics obviously belong in the field of aesthetics.

Women of all generations, all cultures and all periods in history have always made an effort to look beautiful. And of course hair styles, make-up and a wardrobe are necessary accoutrements. It's not just vanity but part of human nature. Also men like fine clothes, hair styles and exotic deodorants as we all know. What women don't know is that beauty has very little to do with fashion or style. Our mothers' pictures, old movie stars, make us laugh until the fashion industry sells us on imitating them or until we take time to study their faces carefully. It is not faces that change over time but fashions. Like the frame around a painting the appearance of the painting may be altered slightly but not essentially. You'll know better what I mean if you take a close look at the "Mona Lisa" and contemplate her serene beauty. There is also a universal recognition of beauty that transcends national and ethical differences as well as time which renders consideration of trendy fashions irrelevant. Cleopatra is still an example of Egyptian classical beauty that has been universal for over two thousand years. Naturally some degree of symmetry is a common denominator in the faces of beautiful women but there are also subtle spiritual dimensions. Physical beauty ought to reflect a peaceful or integrated frame of mind. And, oh yes, there have been furious beauties but they exist on the margin of calm integrity.

'Now, you ladies may correct me but aren't there too many contemporary women who are obviously in the vise-like grip of a fashion called "neo-punk"? It appears easy for them to put on all kinds of new looks but they always come out looking hard and tough. In Hollywood the cosmetic mogul Max Factor used to say, "Give us your mother-in-law and we'll make her into a star tomorrow." The brains behind the Beatles, starmaker George Martin, dressed up his boys in Edwardian wigs. We can draw up an endless list of examples but I think I've proven my point on the subject.

'Permit me to round off another answer to your question by quoting artist-museum director John Wilde: "Art is not a circus, continually demanding new acts. Art states that things don't change, that genuine creativity is as much a matter of reverence and refinement as of invention and innovation." Now I feel it's about time to close this class meeting with a brief outline of what you can expect in future classes.

'It appears to me that we're off to a good start: a stimulating dialogue. An inquisitive attitude and an open mind is exactly what we are here for. In our search for truth we'll keep in mind what philosopher Whitehead proclaimed, that we all consist of ninety per cent emotions and ten per cent intellect. Although we can recognize an aesthetic truth by the way it feels, our response is not complete until mind tells us why. Integrated thoughts and feelings reveal why we like what we know as well as knowing what we like. This will require an open attitude and for some of us a new way of thinking. Unfortunately the ancient sophist notion of relativism is back in style. Relativism holds that true knowledge is impossible, sense perception (aesthetics) is very limited and all our thinking is only subjective anyway so there are no standards aesthetically or ethically. All values are levelled off and with a few exceptions all are equal in all things and so all views are of equal worth. At the other extreme, only scientists deceive themselves into believing in pure objectivity.

'Concerning the word truth, it is something like love. You have few words for analyzing it but you know it from your own experience of being alive. Words only describe truth to others who have had the same experience. Books are only words to help in making distinctions about truth. Knowledge cannot be restricted to words nor can one replace an interest in facts by an interest in words. Now that you are enrolled in my class I hope you will adopt an attitude that reason is never limited to intellectual activities. There is a concept called ideation which is the capacity of the mind to form, entertain, improvize and relate ideas like a dialectic where there is an instinct to become reflective and enlightened. When we discuss topics together let us grip the bow of our thoughts like a violinist prepared to play. This means placing one's hand on the frog of the bow just as if it were a little bird in the palm of one's hand. We must not squeeze it too hard nor open our grip too loosely. This is one way of developing an aesthetic attitude by discussing our points with empathy and sensitivity. After all we share this sensitivity to the way things ought to be in our fragile world and we're attracted to the rightness of beauty in life. Some might call it conscience, others a natural heart-felt self-feeling

167

that is almost spiritually profound. We desperately want to feel right about ourselves and conscience is not only our guide but our fate. Be aware too that relativistic minded people have always had contempt for the term "universal truths". They might as well be stating that wisdom is obsolete and there are a few who are that dogmatic too. Somehow they are unaware of the immense journey of mankind or perhaps prefer to belong to the "born yesterday" branch of the human race. They fail to consider that our planet is some five billion years old, that early man evolved approximately two million years ago, peacefully survived for 50,000 years, settled down for 12,000 years and philosophized and invented useful tools for another 6,000 years. Then during the last four hundred years scientists have indoctrinated us to believe that the real history of mankind has just begun. They have invited us to hop aboard the merry-go-round of technological progress to enjoy a brave new world of illusions. I tell you this because I'm convinced that we must grow up and out of this anthropocentric arrogance before we lose our minds and feelings in the information age of advanced computers which are bulldozing us into a robotlike future. Perhaps the ultimate truths of aesthetics can take us back home to the roots of humanity and the ultimate reality of life.

'Meanwhile, we are faced with a decline in cultural pleasures which used to uplift our spirits. Just ask yourself what powers demand that you adapt to a technological environment which zaps electronic sounds and trashes culture as though it were simply carnival entertainment? Only the uninformed express the platitude, "Time speaks another language." Those who know better realize that national languages are slow to change and the universal language of music needs an even longer time to mature and become refined. The finest quality music lives on for hundreds of years.

'The thin blue line between culture and commerce has faded away into oblivion, all categories are blurred and almost anything goes. Irony used to be a sad excuse for indifference but it's now the dominant aesthetic. Qualified critics must teach those with cultural interests to ignore the obvious as it is unworthy of the clear eye and the discriminating ear. Upon finishing this course some of you might well become self-appointed "gatekeepers" by simply speaking out and exposing the banal and mediocre art works rolling off the assembly lines. Under the guise of a new sensibility evoking a new lifestyle the Mafioso mob and Madison Avenue purveyors are promoting relativism in aesthetics which opens the door for any amateur dilettante to achieve super-star status by joining the industry. And if the "gatekeepers" fall asleep it's the duty of whistle-blowers to awaken them.

'One prominent "gatekeeper", a legendary New York music critic named Walter Kerr, probably defined aesthetic enjoyment better than anyone I know in his book entitled *The Decline of Pleasure*. He states that "relaxed reason is needed to contemplate music and art. One must let go completely to the joyous whipcracking of the intellect. Then one brings the senses and emotions into the ring for the specific purpose of letting one's mind draw a ring around them".'

Chapter X

LASSOING A TROIKA

(A MUSICAL ROUND-UP TIME)

Other nations of different habits are Godsends. Men require of their neighbors something sufficiently akin to be understood, and something different to provoke attention, and great enough to command admiration. We must not expect however all the virtues. We should be satisfied if there is something odd enough to be interesting.

Alfred North Whitehead

1

In winter light snow flurries pass through Santa Fé only fleetingly. A two-inch blanket covering at night melts away by noon the next day. The breath of winter blows softly down the Sangre de Cristo mountainside only to evaporate quickly in the high dry desert sun. On mid-winter weekends Monk and Anita drove on up into southern Colorado to enjoy some of the finest cross-country skiing in the west at the foothills of the Rockies. Better than he expected, Monk learned to adjust himself to his teaching schedule. There were times when he actually felt inspired by his students' progress and several of them respected him as their mentor. Back at the beginning of his college studies he had hoped some day to prove the relationship between aesthetics and ethnomusicology. From his teaching, field observations and PhD research he started to contribute his findings to leading academic journals. His holistic view of how these two areas converge stimulated response from several prominent professors who corresponded with him regularly. Their support encouraged him to explore further. By this time Monk was aware that he needed to apply his knowledge practically to verify his theory. Visiting the various Indian tribes with his ethnomusicology class offered him some of this experience. Occasionally they called on one of the legendary tribes living fifty-five miles north of Santa Fé. At the headwaters of the Rio Grande river high in the Sangre de Cristo mountains the famous Taos tribe resides in a completely restored Indian village. Picturesque and unique, it is popular for its Indian fiestas and ceremonial dances held throughout the year. On one of Monk's earlier visits he had met a Taos Indian who had been out in the white man's world doing his graduate work in North American Indian history. He was also a highly skilled dancer and a talented drummer. After ten years of living in that 'world of infernal annihilation' as he put it, Roving-Horse returned to the tribe to become a teacher. Impressed by this unique background and experience, Monk befriended him. Roving-Horse was often invited to lecture to Monk's students and together they spent long hours afterwards discussing American Indian history and philosophy. The tribe had such great respect for him that they appointed him Chief Trainer for the festival dances, some of which Monk's class had attended. Roving-Horse was especially sensitive and patient in teaching very young children the traditional dances and songs.

About the middle of February Monk and Anita attended her church which was known for its excellent children's choir. The director, Rita Fernandez, also taught general music in the local grade schools and supervised the elementary music program for the county.

The organist, one Francisco Alvarez, was a former monk and acted as assistant priest. On weekends he played for dancing in a downtown hotel. Monk was utterly amazed to hear such a beautifully disciplined choir. After the service Anita introduced him to Senorita Fernandez and Monk congratulated her for the excellent blend, balance and precision. She told him that none of the children were over eleven years old which further astounded him. How did she do it, he asked.

'Well, fortunately I studied the Carl Orff methods for three years and

171

decided to start these children right from the ground up, beginning at age three. In this way they learn to make music quite naturally and show it in their singing. And of course they internalize rhythm physically so that there are less of those typical problems to overcome later on.'

'That certainly does explain almost everything. As a music teacher myself I've used Orff methods on pre-school children with great success and I appreciate its value. Keep up this wonderful work and I'll be around to hear more again soon.'

One Saturday morning as Monk drove around the plaza on shopping errands he heard the live sounds of a big jazz band blowing its energetic vibrations all over town. He stopped immediately, pulling into a free parking space, and finally spotted the band playing at the far end of the square in front of the Indian bazaar. For about twenty minutes he listened to modern arrangements of Johnny Richards, Sammy Nestico and Manny Albam. How really groovy, he thought, that Santa Fé had a band capable of playing professional level repertoire. Monk stepped out of his car and walked through the crowd for a closer look to discover that this was actually a teen-age high school band. During the intermission he met the director to tell him how surprised he was to hear a young band of musicians playing difficult arrangements so well. Monk mentioned that he was a musician now teaching at the College of Santa Fé and asked if he could attend one of their rehearsals sometime. Xavier Cavellero, a former Hollywood studio musician, gave him his telephone number and suggested he call first so he could plan some extra time to get acquainted. At that very moment his mind clicked into gear when he felt Cecilia's nudge and her words, 'This is it, Monk. It's time for you to fulfill that pledge that you made to yourself and Anita.' Then Monk thought to himself how right she was but realized too the time, sweat, organization and money needed to invest in such a project that was still only a vision.

Between classes and field trips Monk found time to start organizing his project step by step. His ideas were beginning to take shape and now he had a clear picture of what he wanted to accomplish. He and Xavier hit it off so well that Monk was invited to improve the band's soloists ability to improvize on Saturday mornings. Roving Horse and his Taos

Indian group were enthused about contributing their talent. Rita Fernandez and Francisco Alvarez agreed to join too but for them it was a question of researching appropriate repertoire. They planned to contact an ethnomusicology professor at the University of New Mexico who specialized in old Spanish folk-lore. In the meantime they were prepared to present a program of popular standard folk songs and simple dances, some of which were performed earlier. Eventually Monk hoped it would be possible to organize a preview sample production in June. This meant that the other two groups had little time to rehearse new repertoire and they too decided to 'recycle' their old material. The main idea was to get all three ensembles together on one program.

2

Monk called these music leaders to set a date to meet and discuss all the details and logistics. All were enthusiastic but unsure that it could be organized in four months. Monk tried to reassure them that the programs he had heard them perform were quite sufficient for an introductory concert. Considering that all three groups were participating in one concert one could assume that any potential audience would not have heard all their repertoire earlier. And even if they had, some of the best pieces were worth seeing and hearing again. Gradually all four directors came around to agreeing that it was June or never. Finally Monk asked the inevitable question. 'Can any of you suggest who we might contact to sponsor us by covering the basic expenses like transportation, advertizing and necessary meals?'

Francisco knew several members of his parish who were bankers or store owners and also happened to be members of the local Rotary Club. He thought he could ask them for contributions. Rita thought she might persuade her principal to find money in the budget to hire extra school buses. The school cafeteria could possibly serve meals but the funding must come from other sources. Roving-Horse was sure that his young students might work on creating original Indian style posters. Rita added that some of her students would help to make more posters if needed. Perhaps both groups of students could co-operate in hanging them up all over town. They all agreed to a thirty minute performance by each ensemble. Monk acted as chairman-coordinator and later persuaded Anita to take telephone messages. About a month later the town council granted them permission to play in the city plaza on 10 June.

3

The project was launched, rehearsal times doubled and endless details and questions had to be settled but the co-operation from sponsors was more than they expected. Newspapers, TV and radio were notified, hundreds of posters placed, invitations to prominent people mailed and the whole event looked promising. Monk's old friend Barry informed his booking manager in Albuquerque who in turn contacted a friend who was chairman of the Albuquerque Music Festival. All too soon the big day arrived. Anita and Dr Eisenbach followed Monk to the box seats arranged for the organizers and sponsors. His professor colleague was quite proud of Monk's initiative to apply his knowledge for the benefit of the community and told him so.

'Entirely too many Sante Féans think we college instructors are a bunch of eggheads. What you are doing will certainly enhance our image in the community. And what's more, by applying your research practically you'll be learning some valuable lessons too.'

The media, including TV coverage, were on the spot and newspaper reporters interviewed Monk persistently. A professional recording technician was hired to make a tape of the entire production. An authentic Spanish fiesta pageant opened the program as fifty boys and girls dressed in gaily colored folk costumes marched around the plaza singing old Spanish songs. After making the round five of them broke ranks, picking up instruments, three violins and two guitars, to accompany themselves singing an old Santa Fé folk song. When they finished singing the first chorus a choir joined in with three-part harmony. At the very end, this five-piece combo increased the tempo, breaking into another song for a folk dance. Ten couples took the stage to demonstrate how one dances to ranchero music. This was followed by another ten couples who presented their dance interpretation of mariachi tunes. A trumpet player joined in on this last piece. Immediately after this the whole company marched off singing the Spanish text to the trio of an old Spanish march. The huge crowd applauded thunderously and added shrieking whistles to punctuate their approval.

By this time it appeared that the whole population of Santa Fé had filled the plaza. But now it was time for the high school jazz band to perform. The applause died down to a dull roar when suddenly the brassy sound of a seventeen-piece band broke through the pause. Trombones, trumpets, saxophones and a bass drum blasted off a version of 'Seventy-six Trombones'. Meanwhile on stage a pianist and an acoustic string bass player lightly fingered their part of the accompaniment. A complete set of drums awaited the drummer along with music stands and chairs for the rest of the band. Marching in time the band approached the stage as the last chorus faded away. In less than five minutes the musicians were seated and the director Xavier announced, 'We kick off the program with a special new arrangement named after our own land of enchantment entitled "New Mexico", written by Stan Kenton's favorite arranger, Johnny Richards.' It was such a powerful swinger that even the audience seemed to be lifted off their feet. Next came Sammy Nestico's 'Quincy and the Count', a new chart by Bill Holman, a calypso style arrangement by David Baker, Marty Paiches' 'The Big Chase', 'My How the Times Do Change' by Manny Albam and more charts by Don Sebesky and Russ Garcia. The grand finale was an 'everybody happy' piece by that funky jazz pianist Horace Silver entitled 'The Preacher'.

Never before had Monk heard such a high level performance by young musicians and he beamed over the soloists he had trained. In fact, so thrilled and excited was he that he grabbed his bullhorn and jumped up, shouting at them as they passed by, 'Beautiful, just beautiful!' Xavier smiled, bowing with a wave toward him.

Assembled in the street the band stepped off smartly wailing Glenn

Miller's Air Force band arrangement of 'The St Louis Blues March' while the crowd cheered them on. Gradually the big band sound died off in the distance and a far off booming of tom-toms accompanied by jingling rattles introduced the Taos Indian tribe stomping toward the plaza as if prepared to go to war. Resembling drum majors gone wild, two ceremonial clowns led the way into the plaza. Tall boys of about sixteen, they looked to the sky in all directions spying for rain clouds and gesticulating with all sorts of motions to lure rain. A long soft droning chant built up gradually to a crescendo as the 'singers of power' approached the plaza. Following the clowns these young people formed an arc in the middle of the square as the tom-toms and singing faded into a morendo. Even the metal rattles strapped from their waist to their ankles stopped ringing while all heads were directed skyward. Hands over their foreheads, feet rooted in the earth, they beckoned to the rain gods, then bowed their heads in prayer. The clowns begin to improvize dance steps, first with a flat-footed trot then a foot lift and a solid tramp. One clown clapped from his hands ashes representing a cloud then glanced toward the heavens, shading his eyes as he tried to see far into the distance. Finally both these clowns repeated the same gestures, directing them toward the four points of the compass. Accompanied by the drummers a droning pentatonic chant began while the clowns persisted in the dance hopefully expecting rain clouds to appear. Roving-Horse told Monk that there had actually been occasions when this procedure produced rain within minutes but on this day the rain gods were apparently sleeping. No raindrops. No miracles. However the drummers made one last effort to awaken them by beating their drumheads mercilessly to create thunderous sound effects. The group of twenty-five 'power-singers' began to chant again, gathering themselves into a circle moving counter-clockwise for about five minutes before finally trotting softly back to the street. Heads looked skyward again, drums pounded them forward into a stomping movement and the energetic vibrations of their singing shook the sleep of anyone caught taking a siesta. This triple threat production ended with broad smiles on the faces of nearly everyone in the plaza crowd.

Anita embraced Monk with a long kiss and Dr Eisenbach gave him a hug of congratulation, exclaiming, 'Monk my man, this is a record production and you can be sure that neither the city nor the college will ever forget it!'

On the way to the hotel for a drink a short dark middle-aged gentleman approached Monk, introducing himself as José Mondragon, chairman of the Albuquerque Music Festival. He congratulated Monk for his work and left a card saying that he'd promise to call him soon. Then Barry Stein met them all on the way to the cocktail lounge, greeting Monk with tears of joy.

'That was the most spectacular musical event I've seen in many years. How in the world did you ever organize such fine young talent?'

Monk looked up and over his right shoulder, replying, 'I guess I've got pretty good connections somewhere up there in the great beyond. You've never met my angelic friend Cecilia, have you?'

Upon hearing this comment Francisco made the sign of the cross as his head tilted upward.

As they all sat in the lounge drinking, suddenly Monk stood up, raised his glass, nodding to each of his leaders and shouting 'Skål! You four were the ones who made this achievement possible. All of your students and I are most grateful. And one more special Skål for my beloved secretary, Anita. It looks to me like we have a great future ahead of us. What do you think?'

'I think we're ready to hit the road, Monk,' cried Xavier.

'That's quite possible and I'm planning to go to work on that very soon. In the meantime I'll keep in touch with you all. *Muchas gracias* everyone!'

The next day José Mondragon called to tell Monk how impressed he was by the performance and that he was now prepared to book them to participate in the Albuquerque Music Festival at the end of August. He apologized for inviting them so late but an unexpected cancellation by another group made this opening possible. Would they be interested?

'Thanks for your proposition but all I can tell you now is that I am definitely interested. First I must check with the others involved. What can I tell them about your terms?'

'Altogether I can promise you 3,500 dollars plus transportation and a free lunch and dinner for everyone. How does that sound?'

'Fair enough. I'll call my colleagues immediately so we can meet to discuss it. What are the times and dates and when is the deadline for confirmation?'

'The program calls for your performance 30 August from 8:00 to 9:30 p.m. Please contact me within a week. If you are all positive then I'll mail copies of the contracts for all three groups to sign.'

Monk telephoned all four leaders who agreed but had to check the availability of their students. Within a few days they called back to confirm their OK. In the meantime the local radio and TV station mailed the concert tapes and the newspaper sent clippings which Anita filed away for future PR needs. Shortly after this the contracts arrived and were signed and mailed in time. Anita was almost as excited by the project as Monk and offered to stand by for all secretarial work.

4

In April Monk and Anita had planned to take a four-week tour of some National Parks in the south-west and they decided that now was the time to get started. They rented a Safari-type caravan with a fold-up bed and a small kitchen lay-out and set out for Arizona. For the entire month they cruised around into what they thought was some of the world's most panoramic landscape. The July weather was heavenly with a sunny blue sky following them wherever they went. Riding mules down the Grand Canyon, viewing the sculptured desert monuments of Utah, the Rocky Mountains of Colorado, Yellowstone Park and the yawning wide open spaces of Wyoming were the highlights that captivated them most. On the way back home they found that Colorado offered the most idyllic camping places. Driving through a State Forest area they discovered an ideal spot tucked into a small valley by a mountain stream where they camped for the night. As they sat around a campfire sharing a bottle of wine Monk was overtaken by a romantic instinct when he blurted out quite impulsively, 'This is almost like being on a honeymoon, isn't it?'

'Say that again, Monk, or was it just a Freudian slip?'

His face flared up as red as the coals in the fire until he finally confessed.

'All right, Anita, my love. Now I know what I have to do to get you to move in with me permanently. You win. Let's do it and get it over with, OK?'

'Now what kind of a proposal is that, Monk Freeman?'

'All I'm saying is that I'm sure that I love you enough to want to marry you, OK?'

'OK, Monk. We both win and we've certainly been waiting long enough.'

A long kiss and a passionate hug, then Anita asked softly, 'When, Monk? When do we do it?'

'As soon as possible. How about sometime in August? The big question is – which church will marry us? My Unitarian Church will have no problems for us but I must say that I would have a difficult time converting to Catholicism just to get married.'

'Monk, I have the greatest respect for you Unitarians and I do like your minister. My priest may not recognize the marriage and my parents will not be happy about it but they know I'm mature enough to decide for myself. Frankly I'm exasperated by certain Catholic dogma. Actually I prefer the open-mindedness, following your own conscience and letting God steer the individual attitude that prevails among Unitarians. And you know our friend Francisco, deep inside, is an unusually liberal Catholic and he will be the first to understand.'

When they arrived home in Santa Fé Monk called Web Connelly, the Unitarian minister, and related his marriage plans. Web suggested Sunday afternoon 20 August. Anita consented but pointed out that time was short for mailing invitations and making party plans. It would only be possible if she took several days off from her library work and he helped out. Monk asked Barry Stein to be his best man and invited all his colleagues to attend. The news of the wedding spread all over town and both Unitarians and Catholics were among the first to know. Monk's parents flew out several days in advance and had a very enjoyable time meeting Anita's family. Roving-Horse, Rita, Xavier and even Francisco planned to show up.

Finally, the big day of the wedding. Monk's friend Carlos Romero played several Spanish classic guitar pieces as a prelude to the ceremony which was followed up by a fanfare of three trumpeters from the school jazz band. This introduced the traditional wedding march performed by the church organist. Immediately after the nuptials Web finished the service by quoting several lines from Kahlil Gibran's 'Prophet' (On Marriage)

Sing and dance together and be joyous,
But let each one of you be alone,
Even as the strings of a lute are alone
Though they quiver with the same music
Give your hearts but not into each other's keeping
For only the hand of life can contain your hearts.

Proceeding down the aisle and out the main door they stepped into a rented Cadillac convertible to be driven to a local hotel dining room where Anita's parents played host. The music was furnished by one of Santa Fé's popular mariachi bands. They played on for the dancers until midnight when Monk and Anita made a dramatic exit to take off in his VW convertible for a brief honeymoon in Colorado. Both were enraptured and exhilarated by the festivities, so much so that little was said until they approached a quiet little hotel in a mountain valley close to their old trysting place. Anita spoke first.

'Well, Mr Freeman, whether you like it or not, this is the real honeymoon. The last time was only a rehearsal!'

Laughing heartily, Monk exclaimed, 'Oh God, not only do I like it but I really love it and Mrs Freeman too!'

Anita then added, 'I think we should congratulate each other. When it comes to choosing mates we both have rather good taste, don't we?'

'You just confirmed my opinion and let's add to that a special wish for lots of good luck, too.'

A glorious five days awaited them in the San Luis Valley near the foothills of the Rockies. They loafed, hiked, fished and swam in some of the deeper pools of the mountain stream not far from the lodge. These happy days seemed to rush by like hours and all too soon they had to face the reality of returning home. Anita had taken out all her paid vacation time and needed help moving into Monk's more spacious apartment. Besides the Trio project required Monk's attention before the Albuquerque concert. Four days before the festival they returned home to start their new life together. Most of Anita's belongings were moved within a few days by Monk while Anita worked in the library. Monk contacted his musical teams and ironed out the final logistical details.

5

The following Saturday morning Monk and Anita drove behind three busloads of musicians and dancers on the highway to Albuquerque. Throughout the month of August rehearsals were intensive to brush up any rough spots. Like all performing artists, amateur or professional, they demanded nothing less than perfection.

En route they tried to think of a name for this motley group of ensembles. Anita thought out loud, 'Now they consist of Spanish, Indians and Anglos and they are all sort of a tribe. One could make up an anagram out of this, like SP-IN-GLO. That's it! What about calling them the "Spinglo Tribe"?'

'That sounds great, Anita. I can't dream up a better name. I'll ask our directors how they like it. I hope they'll approve.'

Upon arrival they mapped out the area and rehearsed going on and off the stage at this football stadium. The central high school contributed dressing rooms for everyone and served them lunch and dinner in the cafeteria. As evening closed in many members were nervous even though it was a repeat performance of the Santa Fé concert.

At 8 o'clock sharp the Spanish troupe marched in as majestically as Coronado's conquering army, demonstrating discipline and artistry in perfect balance. Thunderous applause continued for five minutes but they were unprepared for an encore. We'll have to work on one for the next time, thought Monk. Next came the big jazz band sounding more professional than ever and the audience was so enthusiastic that they demanded two encores for which Xavier had prepared the band. The Taos Indian tribe invaded the stadium casting a spell upon the audience until they were hypnotized into a trance while observing this mystical ceremony. As the tribe proceeded to leave the entire audience stood up, whistling, stamping and clapping until the grounds trembled like an earthquake. Meanwhile backstage under the stadium there were tears of joy as everyone felt proud, jubilant and triumphant. The conductor of the Albuquerque Symphony Orchestra congratulated Monk and his colleagues, saying, 'I expected your performance to be good but not that professional. In fifteen minutes we're next on the program and it won't be easy to follow your act. Good luck to you all in the future!'

José Mondragon stepped in as the conductor left, bubbling over with delight. He hoped they would return next summer and then introduced his companion, the regional co-ordinator for many south-west cultural events. Donald Baker shook hands, gave Monk his card and asked him to call his office the next day to discuss booking possibilities.

After assisting the leaders and checking that all students were accounted for, he thanked them all for their efforts, saying, 'This was a unique achievement for which you can all be proud and I hope you will think seriously about future performances because it looks like we're going to be in demand. But before you get your hopes too high, please remember that this is not nor can be a commercial business venture. Just to begin with there are limits for such a large aggregation as this. Your directors and I will discuss these plans later on and let you all know what comes out of it. In the meantime keep up with your fine work. And good luck!'

The next day Monk called Donald Baker who greeted him in a warm friendly manner and then came right to the point. Presently he was booking artists for south-west music festivals for next summer and wanted to know if they were interested in playing more engagements under the same conditions as Albuquerque.

'That sounds promising but we'll have to have a meeting of the Spinglo

Tribe to discuss it. Can I call you back in about a week?'

'Yes, certainly. I'll look forward to hearing from you then.'

Three days later his music directors confirmed the proposal, knowing that parents and students would approve later. Another item on the agenda was discussing the possibilities of organizing a co-operative non-profit foundation for the Spinglo Tribe activities. Unanimously they agreed that theoretically it was an ideal alternative to avoid commercialism but what were his suggestions for getting established? Monk proposed electing officers first, then drawing up a simple and practical constitution. Next he thought that since all the students were minors perhaps one fourth of all the proceeds could be deposited in long term bank accounts until the age of eighteen. In that way the compound interest amount might help contribute to their future education. The five leaders of the organization ought to be entitled to twenty-five per cent for their services. Retiring at eighteen, younger talent already in training would take the new positions. Approximately one fourth of the yearly income ought to be divided equally among all three tribes for new music, instruments, costumes, supplies. etc. The remaining amount might be distributed to worthy local, national and global charities. All five of them agreed to this and elected Monk Chairman, Roving-Horse Vice-chairman, Xavier treasurer, Rita secretary and Francisco business manager. Obviously they volunteered to take on these responsibilities as there were too few for voting procedures. Each year they agreed to rotate officers' positions. All three ensembles worked on renewing their repertoire for next year's program.

6

During her work at the main library Anita met all kinds of interesting people. One day she had a long conversation with a PhD graduate from Stanford, a young woman, one Sylvia Henderson, who happened to be a qualified consultant in applying for cultural funding. Anita invited her home for dinner to get acquainted and to meet Monk. After enjoying a spicy meal of chili con carne washed down with several shots of tequila,

Sylvia told Monk she had heard the Spinglo Tribe's last concert on the plaza and was highly impressed. She wanted to help in some way but first had to see some PR media material. Did he have any clippings or TV tapes to show her? Monk passed it on to her and as she looked it over she asked more about how they were organized and if they needed a 'culture subsidy' in the future. If they were interested she offered to keep a low fee, realizing it was a co-operative effort with limited finances. Also Sylvia reminded Monk that both state and national (NEA) grants were only meagre and symbolic. The best they might hope for would be the prestige, better connections nationally and internationally and perhaps a matching of funds from big business. As an afterthought she added, 'By the way, have you met Oliver Buckminster, the oil millionaire who lives by himself in a large mansion in the northern hill district overlooking Santa Fé?'

'No, I've never even heard his name. Is he some kind of eccentric?'

'No. Not really. He serves on the board of directors of the Santa Fé Summer Opera and has a special interest in all music activities. He's very shy and likes to operate incognito. I got acquainted with him three years ago shortly after arriving in Santa Fé and he seems to respect my opinions. Although he has a secret telephone number I'll give it to you if you simply greet him with my regards. One never knows but he just might be interested in helping your project. In the meantime I'll do all I can to contact the right culture authorities with the information you've given me. We'll keep in touch for answering any questions or signing any necessary papers.'

Upon these final words she left and Monk exclaimed to Anita, 'Wow, Anita! I'm really glad you discovered her. It looks like I'm now ready to marshal more new forces.'

Calling Mr Buckminster the next day, he passed on Sylvia Henderson's greetings.

'Ah yes, that lovely intelligent young lady! I can almost say that any friend of hers is also a friend of mine. Besides I do think I've heard your name in connection with our college and a music festival. Well now, I'm looking forward to meeting you. You just bring your wife along to my place and we'll all have dinner together tomorrow night. Is that a good time for you?' Then he gave details on how to find his house.

It was a Friday evening when they drove up to park in front of his Spanish style mansion. He welcomed them exuberantly at the door and showed them around the various rooms completely furnished with museum pieces, paintings and antique furniture he had collected during his four-year assignment as America's ambassador to Spain. President Eisenhower had appointed him to this position which he considered to be the high-point in his life. He mastered Spanish, learned much about its place in European history and finally became a Spanish 'culture vulture' as he put it.

'Actually I turned into a Spanish-American when I retired and my wife and I could only feel at home again in Santa Fé. My wife died ten years ago and I chose to stay on here. *Comprende español, señor Freeman?*'

'*Muy poco. Solo dos años en la escuela,*' answered Monk.

'Well, that's not bad to begin with but I'm sure your wife can do better than that.'

What appeared to be a long enjoyable dialog in Spanish continued for at least five minutes until Mr Buckminster said, 'Pardon us, Mr Freeman, but I assure you there were no secrets shared between us.' He added jubilantly. 'Now let's go to my den and have an aperitif. What's your pleasure? Would you like to try some port or do you prefer something else?'

'Thank you. We'd be glad to taste your port, wouldn't we, Anita?'

'Of course, I always like port.'

'That's the spirit, the real fine red spirits! Wait until you taste this.' Generously he filled the glasses three quarters full and toasted them – '*Saludos, amigos!*'

Anita sipped it slowly, then exclaimed, '*Delicioso.* Just *exquisito.* It's like pure liquid red velvet!'

'Don't tell anyone but it's twenty-five years old, "Graham's Vintage", and I have a barrel of it down in my cellar *bodega.* Now, before we indulge in our evening meal, maybe you can fill me in briefly on that special project you mentioned.'

Monk then related the whole story of how they started and where they'd come so far and his plan for the future.

'Well now, you're a musician with vision and creative imagination. This is a unique production that needs all the support it can get. And because it's an idealistic venture with so many gifted young people involved, I'll tell you right now I'm interested in backing you. As you said, Miss Henderson has your essential papers and I'll meet her soon to check things out. Let me tell you generally how I operate for a start. I usually give a substantial grant, eventually match any others which come in and guarantee to compensate for any losses along the way. But for now I won't make any promises until I talk with Miss Henderson. And of course I'll keep in touch with you. Now that business is over let's go in and enjoy our dinner.'

Mr Buckminster was curious about Monk's life experience, especially his work in Sweden, the West Indies and his stint as a Navy musician.

He too was an old Navy man who had served aboard an aircraft carrier during World War II and recalled the time when Artie Shaw's Navy Jazz Band surprised the crew by landing on the flight deck to present a concert one night. Later a Japanese kamakazi plane nearly blew up the ship and 250 members of the crew were killed. Then he asked Monk about his Navy memories during the Korean War. Finally he was curious about how Monk and Anita met. Nodding toward Anita she related several amusing times they had shared at the beginning of their romance which made Buckminster roar hilariously.

When she finished he nudged Monk saying, 'You are indeed one lucky man, Monk Freeman!'

'Thank you,' replied Monk, 'I am well aware of that and you've just confirmed my feelings.'

To these remarks a slight blush covered Anita's face.

The medium rare Texas T-Bone steak was juicy and tender but also more than either of them could manage. To top it all off, for dessert they were served a three-flavored ice cream sundae followed by a half a glass of 'Lepanto' brandy.

'You know, Mr Buckminster, the exotic Spanish atmosphere I feel in your house must bear much likeness to old Spain. Some day I hope Anita and I can visit her motherland but first I'll have to brush up on my Spanish.'

'If I'm as impressed by Miss Henderson's material as I am by you personally a trip like that is quite possible. I have lots of friends there and good contacts in the State Department. Let's wait and see what develops. If you have anything more to add to Miss Henderson's papers please mail them on to me. We'll look it all over together and decide where to go from there.'

The hour was late and they were all beginning to feel a little drowsy so Monk and Anita arose to thank him most graciously for his hospitality. 'It was my pleasure to have you. Let's keep in close contact and feel free to call me at any time. *Hasta luego. Buenas noches mis amigos.*'

Three weeks later Monk received papers from Sylvia which she asked him to sign so that she could mail them on to state cultural authorities and the National Endowment for the Arts in Washington. He noticed that Mr Buckminster had recommended him highly. In her letter she added that Monk could expect a surprise decision from Buckminster in the near future. Another month passed by and a letter arrived with a check enclosed for 30,000 dollars which he explained would be his grant for the project. Also Buckminster reassured him about matching funds and guaranteeing any losses. Monk called him immediately, thanked him profusely and hoped they would all live up to his expectations.

'This gives me more pleasure than you'll ever know, Monk. And by the way, as you are now my friend, please call me Oliver from now on. If you need me for further contacts concerning a European tour just let me know when you're ready. Recently I heard that you are booking a south-western tour next summer. How would you like to use the Santa Fé Opera House for a kickoff concert? You'd have to do it before the middle of April as the opera rehearsals begin about that time. If you can give me a tentative date I'll check with my fellow board members.'

'Many many thanks for that invitation. I'll discuss it with my colleagues and let you know soon.'

'*Buena suerte, amigo.* This is just the beginning, believe me!'

7

About this time Monk was overjoyed at the prospects lying ahead and he needed this inspiration. Along with his teaching load he was busy studying for his PhD, and working out endless details for the Spinglo Tribe engagements. Anita assisted him in typing letters, copying papers, collecting important PR material, etc. In preparing for the summer season the tribe played several weekends and holiday concerts. Eight musical festivals were booked and more were promised if all were so inclined and able. The grant from Oliver B. made it possible to buy necessary office equipment and printed letter head stationery. The balance was deposited in the bank for reserve needs. In January the NEA approved their project and offered a grant of 15,000 dollars, a generous amount which surprised Sylvia H. The Spinglo Tribe leaders agreed that 10 April was the best date for the Opera House concert and Monk called to confirm it with Oliver. With all the support and engagements coming in Monk felt the time was ripe to ask his colleagues what they thought about the possibilities of planning a European tour the summer after next. Of course this sounded exciting to them but they realized that intensive organization and resources were necessary. Maintaining the consistent standard of performance quality when old members graduated and newly trained students moved in was a challenge in itself. Monk reminded them of Buckminster's grant and added his offer to contact highly placed friends in the State Department to consider the tribe for a government sponsored European tour.

'Let's all give it a good try and see what Buckminster can do for us,' said Xavier.

Monk contacted Oliver B. and confirmed their interest for the tour and he was delighted to help them. However he warned that the old 'Foggy Bottom' was a rabbit warren maze and the process could take many months even for an answer in spite of his close friends working there. He promised to call and with luck he might get one of them on the phone.

'Be patient, my friend, and I'll just promise to do my best for you. I have copies of your papers so I'll send them special delivery air mail and we'll wait for their response. Let's give them about three months although I may get a personal letter earlier on. I'll keep you informed.'

The Opera House concert was an outstanding success. Intensive advertising made it a near sell-out and the local newspaper reviews had nothing but positive comments. Some of the reporters pointed out that this kind of project along with the Summer Opera and Chamber Orchestra could well make Santa Fé a cultural mecca in the south-west.

By early June the Spinglo Tribe had signed ten contracts for appearances in New Mexico, Arizona, Colorado, Wyoming and Texas. Booker-manager Donald Baker held to the minimum fee of $3,500, transportation and lodging included, while several paid close to $5,000. However Baker insisted that they must reduce the number in the troupe to seventy members because it was oversized logistically. Fortunately about sixteen members graduated which levelled it off to the preferred size.

During the tour these young people had the time of their lives seeing new places, meeting new faces, feeling important for the media and being asked for autographs by other teenagers as though they were 'pop super-stars'. Not only did they take pride in showing off their artistic abilities but they actually improved with each performance. Monk and Anita beamed as they watched them growing in confidence. Everyone along the way treated them as professionals while showing generous hospitality toward them at all times. The tour ended up as a spectacular success and everyone was ecstatic as the buses approached Santa Fé. Just before they stepped off the bus to meet their parents, Monk gave a short farewell speech: 'We're all getting off to a flying start so just stay with us through the next school year. I love you all and I'd like to kiss and hug each one of you but I'm sure your parents will take care of that. Enjoy your summer, good luck and see you all soon again!'

The next evening Monk, Anita, Donald Baker and all four music directors held a dinner party at the Hotel Estancia. Each of them was exuberant with the glow of success. Finally Monk got up to remind them of the plans being made for a European tour next summer. He felt confident that Buckminster's friend in Washington ought to be interested.

Roving-Horse held up his hand. 'It's a fantastic idea, Monk. Even though our "Big House" is getting smaller all the time do you really think there's room at the top for the Spinglo Tribe?'

Half-jokingly Baker interjected, 'Now that your project is such a big sensation you're going to leave me high and dry next summer.'

'First, my answer to Roving-Horse is that we have some of the finest support and contacts any artistic group would ever need to arrange this tour. At our next meeting I hope I can spell out more preliminary details so that we're prepared if and when we get the confirmation. And Donald, we are all most grateful to you for all you've done to make our western tour possible but I think we can all agree to give you exclusive managing rights for all future American tours. Managers as competent and reliable as you are rare indeed. And don't worry that we'll have to leave you for only a few weeks.'

A week later the Spinglo Tribe leaders met to discuss the details involved in a European tour. They expressed their gratefulness that Buckminster had taken a hand in launching it and agreed to retrain their ensembles for a new program. While rehearsing new repertoire for school year engagements they could prepare a program for the European tour. In October Oliver called Monk to say that his old friend in the State Department wrote telling him that he had recently been promoted to Culture Advisor for the US Information Service and all embassy cultural attachés. In this new position he was given full authority to seek the best American talent available for assignment to overseas tours. After looking over all of the Spinglo Tribe material, listening to tapes and considering the NEA grant, he was now prepared to approve a State Department sponsored European tour starting early in July the following year. All flights, buses, trains and lodging would be provided for the seventy-member troupe. Embassy personnel in each country would take care of all organizational details immediately upon arrival. Each member of the group would receive 350 dollars for pocket money. The official agreement was being drawn up and mailed within a few weeks with copies for all concerned. The chief advisor, one Grover Hotchkiss, promised to keep Monk informed with more detailed information.

'Oliver, you know that I have a guardian angel but for all of us you are really a saint. We can never thank you enough for all your persistent efforts. What in the world can we ever do in return?'

'Just keep right on making those kids happy and proud of their musical achievements and I will be grateful to you!'

The music directors were overjoyed at hearing the news and could hardly restrain themselves from announcing it to the parents and students. The local newspapers picked it up and photographed the leaders and ensembles on the front page of the Sunday edition. For the rest of the school year they worked for perfection playing seven engagements within the state which Donald Baker booked for them. Inspired and eager to show the world their talent, they performed with more youthful enthusiasm than ever. Grover Hotchkiss notified Monk that the following countries were on the tour list: Spain, Italy, Germany, Denmark and England. Seventy-five official government ticket vouchers to cover the whole trip had just been mailed.

8

All too soon the day arrived and with wild anticipation they all hopped aboard chartered buses waiting to take them to the Albuquerque Airport, on to Chicago, New York and the destination of the first stop, Madrid. All the cultural attachés from the respective embassies were notified to stand by and contact the local media in time for the arrivals of the Spinglo Tribe. Each embassy planned a formal reception for the leaders and a lawn party for all participants. Monk and his colleagues felt relieved and secure that the embassies had everything under control for them when they reached their destinations.

While on the plane and underway to Madrid one of the cheerleading type Spanish boys belted out a hammy version of that old chestnut, 'Viva España'. Those who knew the words joined in for more rousing choruses until Francisco calmed them down to a dull roar and the serving of dinner distracted them. Finally after eleven hours flying time plus three hours as transients the plane cruised down for a soft landing in Madrid.

The American cultural attaché welcomed them all to Spain and reassured them that they were all in good hands. He was accompanied by his staff of two American men and two Spanish women fluent in both languages. Meeting in the conference room of the airport he introduced himself as Richard Ellsworth and presented his colleagues one by one. His assistants passed out detailed information and schedules for their two-day visit to Madrid. Mr Ellsworth reminded them that his staff was at their service to guide them and to answer any questions they might have.

'In the meantime,' he went on, 'let me say that it is an honour and a privilege for us that you young American artist-performers are here to represent your country by sharing your gifts. We know that your performances here in Spain will be as successful as they were in the USA. And you may be sure that before and after your concerts we as your hosts will help you enjoy your visit. May you all have a wonderful time in Spain! *Bienvenido!* And now my staff will take over to show you to your buses and on to your hotel.'

Three performances were booked for them in Spain: Madrid, Granada and Seville. Spanish TV covered the whole production in Madrid and newspapers raved enthusiastically about them. At the embassy party Monk met several Spanish colleagues in ethnomusicology who invited him for an informal lecture at the University of Madrid the morning before they left for Granada. After viewing them on TV Granada was especially well prepared to receive them at the airport where an authentic flamenco troupe welcomed them with a special performance at the airport auditorium. Needless to say that the Granada City concert hall was filled to overflowing that evening. At Seville the city mayor greeted them accompanied by a one-hundred piece band which escorted them all the way to the city plaza. With such super-star ceremonies the tribe was bubbling over from the sheer joy of it all. The buses stopped at the plaza where they were invited to watch a National Folk Dance Festival which happened to take place at that time. From all over Spain various provincial costumed dancers participated in this yearly event. The Spanish guide told them that Spain held over three thousand fiestas annually and that ideally there were more participants than spectators.

The city arena was so jam packed for the concert that evening that there was hardly room for standing. The morning paper printed in headlines their praise: 'The Spinglo Tribe Conquered Seville!'

Next stop Rome. Crossing over the Mediterranean one of the girls broke out singing 'Arrivederci Roma' until Rita gently reminded her that one sings that song upon leaving Rome, not when one is on the way there. But this alert young lady quickly answered, 'I know, but the trouble with hello is goodbye!'

As the plane flew in for a landing several of the members peeked out the windows to spot some of the ancient ruins they had read about in school. One of them picked out the Roman Forum and the Baths of Caracalla but the plane landed before they had time to identify anything else. As the plane pulled into the terminal one of the boys inquired quite seriously, 'I wonder if any of the Romans still speak Latin.' To which a bright young girl replied, 'Only the power elite ever spoke Latin but that was two thousand years ago, silly boy!'

Both the embassy cultural attaché and the mayor of Rome were on hand at the airport to greet them. The mayor welcomed them with the help of an embassy translator and the logistical procedure resembled that in Madrid. The next day they were invited for an all day tour of the high points of Rome and during the trip more of the students recognized the classical ruins which they had studied in world history classes. That evening the concert took place in Rome's Radio City auditorium because the city as yet had no public concert hall. Rome's national radio and TV networks relayed the performance to all of Italy.

The day after the performance one of Rome's most notorious critics smothered them all with verbal bouquets. Early the same morning they took a half day tour of the Roman Forum using plastic diabild maps to help reconstruct the ancient ruins. During the afternoon they were guests at the American Embassy reception. Going to bed early that evening, they slept well before waking up for a quick breakfast and a bus ride to the airport where they flew off to Munich.

They were met by the consul general and bussed to the consulate where they had a lavish lunch followed by an official reception. Later in the afternoon they rested before arriving early at the city concert hall to get the sound and feel of it all with brief warm-ups. The auditorium filled early and a grateful audience showed their appreciation with resounding applause, stomping and cheering for two encores after the finale. The media coverage could not have been more generous or positive and at this midway point Monk had planned a well deserved two day break. On the first free day Monk was invited by German ethnomusicologists to a discussion seminar at the local university while the others joined in on a full day tour of the city. On the second day they arose at six a.m. in order to take a day trip to nearby Salzburg, Austria. It was a special treat to visit Mozart's original home and the Mozarteum Academy of Music as part of the city tour.

The morning after, all were aboard the 10:20 SAS plane bound for Copenhagen. Many of them had seen the Hans Christian Anderson film starring Danny Kaye so that all the way to Denmark everyone took turns singing 'Wonderful, Wonderful Copenhagen, salty old queen of the sea, with her harbor lights', etc., while a half-drunken Dane refilled his glass of aquavit and shouted 'SKÅL!' at the end of each verse. When they were about to land Monk suggested they'd heard enough and he was concerned lest this lusty Dane might have to be poured off the plane.

Departing from the plane into the 'suction tunnels' and mile long corridors through the baggage belt and customs they were met by the cultural attaché and his assistants who welcomed them all to Copenhagen. They were guided to the buses which took them directly to Tivoli amusement park, Europe's finest. Stepping through the main gate they were confronted with what appeared to be a marionette brass band in toy soldier like uniforms. It was the famous Tivoli Boys Band who greeted them with a welcoming blast of 'Stars and Stripes Forever'. Waiting for them at the palace-like main restaurant was the American Ambassador who delivered a brief but warm welcoming speech. A royal Danish smörgåsbord was laid out, filling the entire dining room and incredibly, within an hour it was nearly demolished by these hungry teenagers.

About two o'clock, the cultural assistants guided them around this 150-year-old world famous amusement park with its beautiful gardens, lovely lakes, exotic atmosphere, numerous fine restaurants, rides, live music and circus acts nightly. Some stayed on to enjoy the roller coaster and other rides but were reminded to take a taxi to the Hotel Copenhagen before five o'clock in order to rest up before dinner – if they didn't feel like fattened Danish pigs already.

The performance took place in Tivoli Concert Hall, a very ornate building with a 150-year-old tradition and home of the Zeeland Symphony Orchestra. The acoustics were found to be excellent and the sound technicians had everything well under control during the short dress rehearsal. One half hour before concert time the hall was nearly full to capacity. For the first time during the tour the audience demanded encores after each ensemble appeared, causing a break in the smoothly rehearsed transition between introducing each group. When in Denmark, do as the Danes do, so give them what they want, thought Monk. After the Indian ritual show there were three final encores and the jazz band had to blow everyone out the doors but not before the mayor of Copenhagen expressed his thanks for appearing in his city. 'Please feel very welcome to visit us again very soon,' said he.

Fortunately Monk had taken his clarinet along with him and was itching to do some playing. He was told by some Danish musicians that the Club Montmartre had a late night jam session going on that evening and they were sure he would be welcome. Monk mentioned it to Xavier, who was unprepared without his trumpet but decided to accompany him to the club with some of his young jazz soloists. Monk blew up a storm that evening and the Danes were positively ecstatic over his playing. The leader of the session told him, 'There are so few really fine jazz clarinetists in our country. All they know is Dixieland and Benny Goodman so it's very refreshing to hear someone like you with an original style. Keep swinging and come on back any time. You're so welcome!'

The music critic for Denmark's leading newspaper *Politiken* complimented the Spinglo Tribe by saying it was the finest music production he had seen for the last ten years.

Another day's tour awaited them and twenty members decided to take a quick hydro-plane boat over to Sweden with Monk as their guide. In the meantime the embassy assured Monk that all newspaper reviews from the various countries would be translated and mailed to his office in Santa Fé.

Everyone slept soundly that night anticipating the last leap of the tour ending up in London. Leaving Kastrup Air Terminal at eight a.m. was not an easy task but all were punctual and accounted for. The flight from Copenhagen was merely a hop in the air allowing them just enough time for breakfast to be served. Once again some of the high strung characters among them decided to sing the only English song they knew – 'Rule Britannia, Britannia rules the waves, Britons never, never never shall be slaves!' Although Monk thought that verse to be somewhat arrogant and controversial he hoped the Englishmen on board would excuse such youthful exuberance. Then others recalled 'London Bridge is falling down' and 'God Save The Queen'. Finally the bright young lady who had quipped about Rome and Latin had to point out that the melody to America's national anthem is actually an old English drinking song and the US had had to borrow the tune of 'God Save the Queen' to put words to 'America – My Country 'Tis of Thee'.

'All right, smartie pants,' said one of the jazz band members. 'I still like Britannia rules the waves and never will be slaves. Let's all wail it one more time!' Several English-looking passengers started to raise their eyebrows and make grimaces during their encore until Monk cried out: 'OK, gang. Enough of that. Take it easy. We're about to land.'

The embassy routine at Heathrow airport was the same procedure as usual, warm and extremely polite. Everyone received printed schedules and information covering the final three-day visit ending up with a performance at the Albert Hall. The buses drove them to their hotel while the embassy staff answered questions along the way. At the hotel they found their rooms and unpacked in time to indulge in an English roast beef luncheon in the dining room. At 1 p.m. the buses prepared to take them all on a three-hour tour of London with proud English guides. Later in the afternoon they were driven to the embassy for a reception where the ambassador greeted and shook hands with each member of the troupe. This included a generous buffet serving soft drinks and bar service for the adults. Appetites were well quenched and at 6:30 the buses and guides took them all on a tour of London By Night which fascinated everyone. They became enchanted by the dramatic colored lighting illuminating many of the downtown buildings.

Compared to New York City, London appeared to have more stability and an appealing style that made one comfortably at home in spite of its size. And London citizens seemed to be so very polite and helpful. Several of the anglos traced their ancestors to England and one was certain that his forefathers came from London and landed with the pilgrims in Massachusetts. Suddenly one of the restless Indians spoke up, exclaiming, 'You and I don't know which boat your ancestors took to America but I know one thing for sure, that my forefathers were already settled down in New Mexico when they arrived. Besides, tribes back east met your folks on the beach.'

Everyone roared with laughter and one Spanish member slapped him on the back saying, 'He asked for it and you said it!' Then he added, 'And my old forefathers came up north from old Mexico to settle Santa Fé long before you anglos landed at Plymouth Rock.'

Finally one anglo confirmed their opinion with a sigh. 'OK, the historical facts are on your side. Both you guys won that round long ago. Unfortunately American history has been silently censored. Our ancestors were not the first Americans and it's not so easy to admit.' Then he turned to the other anglo, saying, 'If your old folks could see London today they probably never would have left.'

At 10 p.m. the trip was over and Monk hoped they would sleep well because tomorrow they planned a whole day's tour with lunch and dinner at some typically English pub restaurants.

In the morning they all had an early breakfast as the buses were waiting to take them on to a Thames River boat right through the center of London. Afterwards the bus picked them up for a drive to 'Ye Old Cheshire Cheese Pub' where they had lunch. Then they spent the afternoon at Westminster Abbey and with a visit to parliament. For dinner that evening they were guided to 'The Anchor Bankside Pub' noted for its beef and kidney pies and fig puddings.

On the last day they visited the British Museum and later went to Buckingham Palace just in time to watch the changing of the guard. Upon witnessing this royal ritual they were released to go shopping downtown for several hours before the buses met them and they returned to the hotel for an early dinner. They had plenty of time to warm up at the Albert Hall but forty minutes before concert time the auditorium was filled. Rumors circulated that the Prince of Wales was spotted sitting in the royal box.

In spite of all the routine and experience behind them, many of the members suffered from stomach butterflies and several vomited ten minutes before curtain time. Anita's motherly care calmed them down in time. When the performance got underway it came off so professionally that it had no sooner started than it ended. The applause lasted fifteen minutes with five curtain calls and three encores.

The troupe slept deeply and awoke at nine the next morning to eat breakfast and read the sensational reviews in the papers. The embassy personnel reassured them all that all clippings would be mailed on as usual. Hundreds of pictures were taken by various members of the troupe throughout the tour and a few had luck getting their films processed at instant photo shops. On the way to the plane they looked them over.

Arriving in good time at the airport they had one hour before departure. The cultural attaché thanked them again and hoped they would have a good trip home. Many were in a wistful mood, some in tears and others snapped pictures of the final farewell scene. When the plane took off they were both keyed up and sad that the tour had come to an end. A number of them reminisced about favorite memories while others shared their photos with each other.

After lunch was served nearly all of them took a long siesta and sooner than they realized woke up landing at Kennedy airport. With only one hour to change planes Monk and the leaders had to hustle them through the transit corridors to the Chicago plane which continued on to Albuquerque. Now they were all wide awake and eager to come home again. A few of them began to sing some of the songs they had sung in the show until lumps in their throats choked off the words and tears came to their eyes. Anita and Monk had worked so hard to organize and concentrate on the needs of all these young people that it finally dawned on them that the tour was actually over.

9

Monk dozed off for a much needed rest until Anita awakened him saying, 'Just look at all those beautiful kids, Monk. Did you ever see happier faces anywhere? They literally poured out their hearts and souls into this project and real reward for them is a wonderful lifetime memory. When we study the pictures of them before and after I'm sure we'll see maturity in their countenance. What do you think?'

'Well frankly, I can only envy them. This kind of tour would have been impossible when I was their age. And we can all be grateful for the smooth organization, relaxed efficiency and appreciation from all concerned, not least of all the embassy personnel. However when I think of all the sweat everyone has put into this production and the unusual amount of pure luck we've had, and consider the bloody sacrifices that other creative amateurs and highly gifted artists invest just to get started, I'm convinced it's a tragic irony that the wealthy western world still remains relatively underdeveloped in cultivating and promoting artistic talent. A much greater number of Americans revere our millionaire baseball and football stars than our world class band leaders such as Duke Ellington and Count Basie for example. There is such a waste of potential talent begging for the privilege simply to be recognized. The entrenched one way track of technology and business share much in common. On the one hand the entertainment conglomerate makes it possible for a handful of amateur 'pop-players' to become multi-millionaires while on the more destructive side 'Pentagon parasites' reach billionaire status all to the tune of a trillion dollar military-industrial complex. Many of these creatures are nothing but the scum of the earth.

'All these factors distract too many Americans away from cultivating an empathy and a sensitivity for human values. Until a change of attitude in our thinking and feeling evolves, the majority of highly trained and gifted musicians in America will never receive the appreciation, respect nor minimal support necessary to make a decent living. Both Barry and the New York City Science supervisor I mentioned earlier believe that the pendulum of science has swung too far right and the time is already late for music to swing civilization back into balance. However I am very thankful that the state department recognized our talent and found a few crumbs in their budget to launch our tour. Anyway, as a rough educated guess try estimating America's annual military budget of approximately 200 billion dollars and figure out .001 per cent of that and you can be sure that it's enough to pay for twenty groups our size for a similar tour. So far the USA is most powerful on the military and science side but that's the least important half for our future. We must learn very soon how to evolve aesthetically and ethically. For me that is plain realistic-idealism. Have I made my point?'

'One thing I love about you, Monk, and that is that you are one of the few who practice what they preach.'

'No, you're wrong, Anita. In this dark world I'm still looking for a contemporary Albert Schweitzer to inspire me.'

As the plane flew out of Chicago toward the south-west one boy stood up to lead the group in singing 'Albuquerque, here we come, right back where we started from', to the tune of 'California, here I come'. Three hours later the plane skated over the dry sandy hilltops and landed on the tarmac with a gentle bump. Going through the terminal they stepped down into the main entrance to catch sight of Oliver Buckminster shouting joyfully to them, 'Welcome home, super-stars! *Muchas gracias.* Thank you one and all. *Bienvenito!* I love every one of you!' From left to right he began shaking hands with all the boys and hugging the girls. Then, waving a large black book in the air, he asked everyone to sign their autograph for him. 'And I can hardly wait to see the photos, clippings and hear the tapes,' he exclaimed to Monk. 'When you collect everything please call me and we'll have a dinner party to celebrate. Now I want to escort your buses to Santa Fé because I think the citizens have a little surprise for you.'

While everyone climbed aboard the buses Oliver hopped into his Mercedes Benz convertible, ringing a fire truck siren wildly, and they all charged off to Santa Fé. About one hour later they arrived at the town plaza where the local high school band greeted them with a royal fanfare. All the parents stood patiently waiting for their sons and daughters to step off the bus into the arms of home. Just as the sun began to set and the family reunions were completed fireworks shot off into the sky to the accompaniment of the town band and the mayor approached the microphone to welcome them home with a heartfelt thanks for showing Europe a sample of Santa Fé's cultural life. He invited Monk and his music directors up to the stage to receive specially engraved plaques honoring the occasion. They were presented with thundering applause and whistles from hundreds of the town's citizens.

On the way home Monk told Anita, 'Nice to get all this recognition but none of us are the kind of heroes who deserve that much celebration. Now it's time to sleep it all off for a few days.'

The next morning at lunchtime Donald Baker called to pass on his congratulations.

10

For the rest of the summer they relaxed, taking short weekend drives to the mountains and neighboring Indian tribes. Occasionally Monk wrote to his European ethnomusicology colleagues to suggest the possibilities of organizing an international foundation for the preservation of native folk music.

Several of them thought it was a good idea and offered to advertize for members in their journals if he would do the same in the US. Monk checked with the college burser and he agreed to contribute funds for such ads as it directly benefited the college in the future. Toward the middle of August the NBC-TV channel in Albuquerque informed Monk that the filming of the Spinglo Tribe from the local music festival had been sent to the New York studios. The TV star host Dave Garroway and his staff were enthusiastic about inviting all the ensembles to participate in a dynamic new TV production entitled 'Wide, Wide World'. The program consisted of two hours of live direct cultural events occurring in various parts of the US on a Sunday afternoon. General Motors and Standard Oil agreed to sponsor it, using discrete one liner commercials. They hoped to film them live on the second Sunday in December and were willing to pay 70,000 dollars to the Spinglo Tribe fund for all TV rights.

Monk called all his leaders to spread the news and make plans to meet the following week to discuss it. They were all thrilled and excited by the offer when they met. All of them realized that only the Europeans had seen their last production so it was only necessary to repeat most of it for the American TV audience. Monk called NBC in New York to confirm the date and conditions. The producer promised to mail the contract, adding that Albuquerque would handle all technical details and keep them informed. In the meantime he requested a copy of the European tour film so they could make suggestions for timing.

During the first week of September Monk returned to college to start his fall term classes. Dr Rudolf Eisenbach was all aglow, congratulating him for the successful tour and hoping he would write a report on it for the *National Ethnomusicology Journal.*

'You can be sure I'll do that, Rudolf. And what's more, it looks like I'll finish writing my PhD dissertation by next June.'

'Splendid! That's more good news. That will give you an incremental raise and promotion to assistant professorship while securing your tenure too.'

'And here's one more item for the headlines. In December the Spinglo Tribe will appear on a national prime time TV show out of New York. Albuquerque plans to beam it direct from Santa Fé.'

'Wow! Cecilia has certainly been bestowing heavenly gifts upon you lately! Is there anything we here at the college can do to help? For example, I can think of filming it from our campus football arena and showing a few glimpses of our college buildings in the background?'

'Rudolf, you are a first class PR promotion man. You missed your calling. You could have made a million on Madison Avenue. Of course we must take you up on that offer.'

Much to the envy of his colleagues, Monk was becoming a celebrity at the college of Santa Fé. His classes were more popular than ever and some students were rejected because of limited enrolment. He introduced both subjects in much the same way as the preceding year. However for his music ethnography class he required a final essay making original suggestions for stimulating and promoting serious interest in all kinds of folklore activities.

Later in October he began to receive letters from ethnomusicologists in the US, Canada, Mexico and Europe who expressed keen interest in joining the new foundation. Monk decided it was time to discuss this movement with Rudolf to find out how they could collaborate in making the College of Santa Fé the international headquarters. Dr Eisenbach approved and offered to co-operate personally by inviting all prospective members to a conference in Santa Fé sometime the next summer to establish the foundation. His secretary would offer to help with mailing and other paperwork. Using his mailing list of potential members Monk wrote a form letter of invitation asking them to confirm their interest by a certain date and Rudolf's secretary mailed copies to all concerned.

In November the Spinglo Tribe showed up at the college to rehearse for the big TV production. Technicians from Albuquerque stood by to supervise all the movements, perspectives and various angles. Several TV cameras and a mobile 'studio bus' checked out the transmission of pictures to Albuquerque which would later be relayed on to New York.

On Sunday 14 December all seventy-five members of the Spinglo Tribe gathered at the college football field for a final dress rehearsal. The mobile transmitter bus, an army of technicians and eight TV cameras were all in position standing by for the show to go into action. Precision was the greatest challenge in adapting themselves to the shortened version and the sudden switches from one ensemble to the next. Tightly timed synchronization of all three groups was needed, not a chance to be out of step nor to drop a beat.

The countdown time arrived and the troupe went into action like real professionals. It came off so smoothly that few were aware of the time until it was all over. They took care of themselves as if nothing at all had happened. Hundreds of local spectators watched the whole procedure and later at a picnic of the Spinglo Tribe they reviewed the replay tapes. Dave Garroway who also hosted the morning 'Today' show invited Monk and the leaders for a TV interview in New York which delighted them all. Among other things they discussed was Monk's initiative to organize an International Folk Lore Society. While there the producers of the 'Wide Wide World' show told him they were experimenting on future satellite telecasts of the show and promised to keep him informed on how their work developed.

One week after the interview, Monk received dozens of letters from TV viewers and a number of ethnomusicologists interested in joining the new organization. Encouraged by all this response Monk asked Rudolf's secretary to notify all members of the conference dates which the college authorities agreed on – 15-19 June. In the meantime he checked logistical details for hotel space, B and B rooms and the maximum number of delegates which could be accommodated in Santa Fé at that time.

Then Monk's dissertation work demanded more of his time so Anita and Dr Eisenbach's secretary took over all correspondence involving bookings and applications for the conference. At one of the Spinglo Tribe meetings Monk asked the leaders if they could persuade all members to perform at the summer conference. The performance would be paid for from candidates' registration fees and inviting the public for admission fees. They thought there would be no problem as the spirit of the members was exceptionally high and summer vacation plans usually came later.

About the end of May Monk received a letter from the head producer at NBC in New York thanking them for their co-operation and announcing a special experimental program which 'Wide Wide World' expected to produce during the fall season. By satellite they hoped to connect folklore events in Liberia, India and the US to begin the series of world cultural activities. As usual these programs would be televised live – direct on the spot. Besides the countries involved they planned to build a co-operative web of other nations who would in turn relay it on to their own TV audiences. They sensed that there was a growing demand for grass roots culture in countries all over the world and they were prepared to invest in the risks involved. On the American side NBC had invited authentic folk musicians from Tennessee to divide time with the Spinglo Tribe. Would Monk's group like to participate in this kind of a project?

Monk thanked him for the offer, adding that they would be honored to perform for a world audience via television. And of course they must allow time to rehearse a brand new repertoire. He requested more detailed information concerning fees and contract deadlines so that his staff could discuss it as soon as possible. Once again the Spinglo Tribe and its directors were overjoyed at the news but knew it meant summertime rehearsals to hold up a high quality standard for a potential world audience of a billion viewers. However, for the present they had to repeat their old routine show for the last time at the folklore organization conference.

11

Sixty delegates from seven countries arrived on campus for the conference in the middle of June. During the four days of the meeting a charter, constitution and election of officers took place. The great majority voted Monk for president, an Italian for vice president, a Canadian secretary and a German treasurer. The Spinglo Tribe concert was an overwhelming and inspiring success and many members hoped to organize more folk groups in their own countries which could eventually participate in future conferences. On the last day Monk suggested that they consider seriously the prospects of presenting an 'Olympic' size folklore production based upon a step by step five year plan. Essentially these were his proposals:

1. At next year's conference members from each country present some kind of folklore ensemble, any size at all depending on financial support. Ask each teacher leader to hold a brief seminar-demonstration on training methods.
2. The second year recruit all available and outstanding folklore groups

from each country to demonstrate their talents at a conference festival open to the public. Hopefully find sponsors to pay transportation and expenses for the best ensembles. Get all media involved.

3. Campaign and/or lobby for folklore support from both government and private funds to start a national academy for all indigenous music and dances for which a two to four year diploma could be awarded. Send the best groups and teachers to a conference each year.

4. Find an ideal city with well developed cultural demands and persuade its mayor to take an initiative in placing his city on the cultural map of the country by welcoming in a national folklore festival some summer in the near future. The organization would contribute their share to promote it.

5. Out of the various cities holding these national festivals we will select one with the best potential to attract a global audience, the first truly international folklore Olympic size festival. To make that possible the organizations must beg or borrow the finances to support such an endeavor.

'As I mentioned to some of you earlier America's huge TV media is already on my side and there is no reason why they could not help us all promote this kind of project in the coming years. Hopefully we could avoid as much commercialization as possible and promote a co-operative, not a competitive, spirit. Judges might select three so called 'winners' who would receive a plaque naming each participant an honorary life member of our organization and all three would be invited to attend the following year's conference all expenses paid.'

All members appeared to be impressed and inspired by the conference and twelve of them stayed over for a week to tour Santa Fé and the surrounding Indian reservations.

Toward the end of November the Spinglo Tribe had the honor of performing for a global audience on the first satellite production of 'Wide, Wide World'. In spite of each new challenge the groups faced in their short career it astonished Monk every time that they could perform so magnificently under pressure. The congenial host Dave Garroway was

206

amazed the second time around and could not refrain from announcing a two liner plug for the International Folk Lore Society. During the weeks to come several hundred letters expressing compliments and interest in the organization arrived.

The 'Wide, Wide World' satellite TV series continued through the years and the programs were so successful that NBC presented six national folklore shows annually from various parts of the globe. The persistence of his organization in pursuing the five-year plan was well rewarded and the name of the society was changed to the 'Global Folk Lore Network'. In less than five years the membership of the association increased to over two thousand. Oliver Buckminster together with the Ford and Rockefeller Foundations contributed generously to the yearly budget. Dozens of other independent folk lore organizations from around the world joined and sent participants to the 'Olympic' size international folk lore festival held at Soldiers Field Stadium in Chicago where a maximum of sixty and a minimum of twelve performers was permitted for each group. The Global Folk Lore Network decided against any kind of plaque or prize awards because finding neutral judges to evaluate each national cultural standard was absurd. Eventually these 'Olympic' festivals became an established yearly tradition with various cities around the world playing host.

The years rolled on and Monk remained at the College of Santa Fé where he took over Rudolf Eisenbach's position as full professor when he retired. He and Anita eventually had a family of two children, a boy and a girl, both of whom showed musical inclinations. Anita often half joked about most librarians being boring and musicians having more fun, feeling that their kids were already blessed with the right spirit. Monk kept active on the board of the Global Folk Lore Network serving along with Barry Goldstein, Oliver Buckminster and Sylvia Henderson. The Spinglo Tribe was by now a world famous tradition and younger leaders took over as the older ones retired.

12

*One thing that is new is the prevalence of newness, the changing scale and
scope of change itself, so that the world alters as we walk in it, so that the
years of man's life measure not small growth or rearrangement or moderation
or what he learned in childhood, but a great upheaval.*
    J. Robert Oppenheimer (The man who gave birth to the first
                atomic bomb at Los Alamos, New Mexico)

Monk the visionary, a realistic-idealist, had committed himself to his life
project until it was fulfilled. In this hard core world he broke through the
concrete only to feel distressed witnessing the 'realistic' asphalt men of
our times marching compulsively into a ravaging neo-dinosaurian age.
Observing this rapacious, unholistic world view Monk recalled the Indian
tradition of sending adolescent boys out into the woods to search for a
vision and not to return until they had one to report. The Indian elders
placed great significance on interpreting and sharing dreams. Collectively
they believed that dreams revealed the God of the nation which naturally
helped them plan for the future visions to realize ideals. Monk learned
many lessons about earth wisdom from his Indian friends who lived with
nature and had developed their 'inner space' for thousands of years. Such
things as stability - sustained development - concentrating on and
accepting earth conditions without over-exploiting its resources: simply
facts of life. Nor did they have a compulsive obsession about change for
the mere sake of change. For them 'progress' was always a myth because
they were deeply convinced that one can only master the future by realizing
that all time is eternal and the only eternity we'll ever know is each
present moment. Sounds in motion, the hidden powers of music, recharged
them spiritually in their songs, chants, and dances while they experienced
the deeper meaning of being and becoming in this present time of their
lives.

Growing older, Monk reminisced about the by-gone era of steamboat
jazz on the river, the big-time circus in town, his sessions in New York
and San Francisco jazz clubs, college days, his Navy band tour of the

Pacific, Sweden, the West Indies, and finally the Santa Fé era. All this good fortune had enriched his life with a series of momentous events never to be forgotten. If he were to write the story of his life everything would be perfectly logical with few changes.

But as he looked at the world around him it appeared that physical changes were occurring as rapidly as a television film at high speed while living styles were being transformed like patterns in a kaleidoscope. For example, he contemplated the number of dynamic turning points in history which he had lived through: a ten year world depression, World War II, the Atomic Age with fifty years of nuclear missile threats, 250 American interventions, Korean and Vietnam Wars, the Post-industrial Age, thousands of farms selling out to agro-industry, the Space Age landing man on the moon (only sixty-six years after the first airplane took flight) the accelerating web of communications and transportation world wide, the global technological revolution and the birth of the Digital Age and its computers. Piles of strata had been laid down in just a few generations but in spite of being a fossil in a new Dinosaurian epoch Monk felt very much alive and still swinging strong. Although he adapted reasonably well to these jet speed changes he could not help but consider the fate of younger generations caught up in the vortex of this whirlpool of 'progress'. How much more speed can the human mind and body tolerate and still live a healthy life? Long ago Monk had learned to slow down his pace in a fast moving environment and in the act of creating music he made himself independent of everything that exists in the outer world. His playful spirit in the dance of life was an expression of his freedom and vitality of joy in following the swinging inner pulse of his own body rhythm.

In retirement years Monk found it more difficult to feel at home in this rollercoaster maelstrom of our 'Brave New World'. He and Barry often met to talk over old times and one day Monk revealed to his friend that before the Great Spirit called to take him away to the Happy Hunting Grounds he planned to write a book, more for therapy than to impress anyone at this late stage.

'I'll be writing for people who belong to an entirely different culture from our own. And I'll keep in mind what science philosopher Bacon suggested - to send out your little book upon the waters and hope that your will may be worked beyond you in another and more favorable age.'

They both agreed that only the thrust of a new Renaissance greater than that which grew out of the Medieval period, a humane enlightenment, a holistic way of thinking and an awakening of our sensitivity, will be adequate to point the direction toward nothing less than a Utopia.

Hanging on Monk's wall was a frame with four lines from Edna St Vincent Millay's poem 'Renascence':

> *The world stands out on either side*
> *No wider than the heart is wide.*
> *Above the world is stretched the sky*
> *No higher than the soul is high.*

EPILOG

Increasingly there is but one way into the future: the technological way. The frightening aspect of this situation lies in the constriction of choice. So great is the power of western technology over men that any other solution, any other philosophy is silenced. Men, unknowingly, and whether for good or ill, appear to be making their last decisions about human destiny. To pursue the biological, it is as though, instead of many adaptive organisms, a single gigantic animal embodied the only organic future of the world.
(Loren Eiseley: distinguished anthropologist, science historian and author)

Monk's eighty-five year old mother, a Bible-belting fundamentalist, faced the jet speed changes and twentieth century inventions uttering an old familiar bromide, 'Oh my Lord, miracles never cease!' Now, for some of us it appears that God is abandoning us and letting us spin around to lose our way among ten billion other stars and galaxies. Whatever church one belongs to, the dominant creed of our times is still scientism. The brainwashed majority are true believers in the miracles progressive technicians produce for us. Moreover futurologists have been predicting for years that our future may well be stranger than any present day science fiction writer can imagine.

Technology has conquered man's individuality and his traditional life values to the extent that he is losing all contact with nature and lives completely in a technological environment. Cyberspace, the successful cloning of sheep and apes (who's next?) and the guinea pig experiment with consumers unknowingly being forced to buy unmarked genetic grain and vegetable products are samples of nefarious contributions to our modern lifestyle.

We are all aware that the most powerful institution in the world is the electronic communications system and America controls it strictly for its own profit. Only six recording companies produce eighty-five per cent of all the world's recordings and in 1989 Japan's Sony purchased two of them to become the world's largest entertainment industry, a conglomerate which includes billions of dollars invested in films and television corporations. Another member of this 'six-pack' of entertainment groups is Polygram, ranking number 3 in Europe and number 9 globally, followed by EMI which rates number 4 on the continent and 10th in the world.

But neither Monk nor Barry ever dreamed that in the 1990s an ingenious Frenchman would invent a one-man composing-recording apparatus using the latest electronic devices. If it weren't such a serious effort one might guess that this contraption was conceived by Rube Goldberg for one of his famous cartoons. Marc H'Adour is a gifted electronic sound technician who cannot read or write a note of music. Never mind that, because he has filled his apartment with literally a one man musical(?) sound factory. He features as his main equipment: a Macintosh Quadra 700 computer, 14 synthesizers, 4 drum machines, 2 sequencers, 5 keyboards, 1 electric 'grand' piano and 2 samplers. All gear is linked up to a MIDI (Musical Instrument Digital Interface). As he tinkles out stray tones on a keyboard they are automatically harmonized and orchestrated including a complete score print out while the final results are fed in to master recording process. No spools, no recording tapes, no razor blades nor snippets, no music, no fuss needed to manufacture another kind of electronic sound production. Fully equipped, he is independent and needs no assistance. In his hubris, he comments, 'The synthesizer is still in the Stone Age, something like a piano in Mozart's time.' This kind of Rube Goldberg* project brings back memories of an old song from the Gay 1920s – 'You push the first valve down and the music goes round and round, Oh ho ho ho ho ho and it comes out here.'

---

* *Rube Goldberg, a famous old American cartoonist who specialized in making fun of many new inventions.*

A comical contraption if it weren't so deadly serious. Typical how all reductionists are infernally clever at eliminating the human element to make electronics the great leveller, predictable as always. In the future this kind of techno-progress will make it possible for everyone to amuse and amaze themselves by becoming both a composer and a record producer. Isn't it a shame to think how many great composers missed this opportunity to 'create' 'scientifically improved' music almost instantly?

About the time the Global Folk Lore Network presented their first 'Olympic' concert, informed citizens were becoming concerned about the technical-economic web encompassing the planet in the form of mega-technology. The key components of this phenomenon are interlocked and converge with one another. This global web consists of television, computers, satellites, corporations and banks (including the forty-two year old 'Bilderberg Group', a nefarious secret power elite of world leaders conspiring for a New World Order, laying the track for a technocratic regime), space technology (NASA, America's government-sponsored space agency, has already invested 200 million dollars to make space safe for American business), genetics and the final scientific solution for humanity – the post-biological machinery of robotics and nanotechnology. We are all highly indoctrinated to believe that megatechnology will continue to invent more magic marvels to lead us into the Third Millennium. The real truth of the matter is that these developments are forming something new, almost like living cells. And the loaded question is: are they benevolent for our mental and physical evolution or malignant as the cancer-like slime mold of the world's cities?

Concerning communications, TV opened the door and paved the way for the new world of computers which are the latest 'automatic gurus' and high pressure slave-drivers for those forced to use them. 'Info-Tech' and the computer has become everyone's instant wonder tool for leaping into the future. Digital streams of text images and sounds feed the user with second hand facts, trivia and junk information. Even industry must hire experts to 'filter out' the vital facts. But when one is well stuffed with computer 'knowledge' then the user is hypnotised by the illusion of brilliant thinking and a sense of creativity going on in the mind. Memories are no longer to be relied on and person to person contact is obsolete. Both TV and computers are competing to make book reading unnecessary for many people. Sound bites and shrinking attention spans are the new trend. Info-tech at best is inferior to the human brain which has a quadrillion connections between its nerve cells. That adds up to the total number of telephone calls made in the USA in a ten year period. Ah well, anything goes for the sake of push button 'virtual reality'! Incidentally the toxic pollution from manufacturing computers is nearly as dangerous as radioactivity emanating from nuclear reactors: actually the most deadly chemicals ever synthesized.

And finally, the real top heavy power behind computers lies in the hands of multi-billion dollar companies who manufacture and sell them to the Pentagon in preparation for future computerized wars. The government and police are now planning to interlock locally into any and all PCs in the very near future. Indeed the leading espionage author John Le Carré revealed recently: 'As the systems for propagating information and speeding it around the globe are becoming ever more sophisticated, so do the opportunities to manipulate information, political correctness or sound bites or family values. Finally the manipulation of truth seems to go hand in hand with the availability of information.' Another exciting contribution from the best of all scientific worlds is the earlier mentioned expanding area of molecular engineering, a hot ticket called nanotechnology. One of America's foremost ecologists, Jerry Mander, in his recent book (*In the Absence of the Sacred* (1992)) interviews Mark Dowie, a prominent environmental researcher who describes this phenomenal scientific breakthrough:

'It's beyond genetics, it's the new physics all right here and now. The idea is to zero down into the atomic structure of all materials and re-arrange the molecules to get completely new forms, materials and creatures. It's a technological fix to end them all. We won't need resources anymore since the resources are the molecules themselves from which they can make anything; trees, houses, animals, weapons and people. Eventually they promise to eliminate death. Jerry, nanotechnology will make the industrial revolution look like a hiccup. These kids (nanotech. researchers) are the ultimate technological nerds. They really believe more in machines than people or nature. To them human beings are kind of out of date.'

These contemporary nerds have given us another utopian innovation in a new area called bionics (biological electronics, a division of cybernetics). Bionic convergence makes it possible to implant computers that can send messages to and from our brain and have the capacity to stimulate electronically our creativity and response to pleasure. Fifth generation computers are now working overtime to 'create' artificial intelligence. It makes one curious about what kinds of joy our molecules will respond to then, poor things. And of course if our gung-ho happy nerds fail to create their 'paradise' they can always jump off into the escape hatch of a rocket ship and find another planet to pulverize. One can only hope that these scientific determinists with their colossal insensitivity and lack of moral responsibility will eventually fail to suck us all into the accelerating whirlpool of materialism which they call 'progress'. This mythical Garden of Eden, the 'American Dream', the cornucopia of technological 'progress' is deceptive as it leads to an endless movement of pursuit of happiness at any price. In this age of disruption and its fragmentation of values it appears that all that remains is the 2,500 old sophist concept of relativism to guide our 'new' sense of ethics. And like the whirlpool, shifting human values begin to circle without direction. 'Survival of the fittest' notions applied to humanity ought to be obsolete as we approach the Third Millennium. Survival itself is inadequate if we do not have a life quality society worthy of surviving. And western governments which continually thrive on lying to their citizens are abominable and unworthy to be called 'democracies'. In the evolution of man there remain natural and positive attributes which need an outlet but are going into atrophy. Perhaps it is time to rediscover our roots by inquiring just how natural is 'natural'? With intuitive sensitivity Pascal prophesied this problem in modern science by stating, 'There is nothing we cannot make natural and there is nothing natural which we do not destroy'. To carry the point one step further it is not too late to question the unnatural nature of science.

Barry Stein once told Monk that in the entire history of technology the so called 'best scenario' result has never once been achieved. The ingenuous true believers among us attempt to defend that criticism with their favorite cliché: 'That may be true but would you prefer to sacrifice technology and go back to live in a teepee with the Indians?' The logical answer to that is simply to accent the negative by challenging and questioning scientific authority, analyzing and criticizing all side effects of new technology, simplifying one's own needs in life and working actively toward sustained development for an economy where people come first.

Too often environmentalists are accused of being romantics. What is truly a romantic notion is to believe that the promoters of technology will fulfill all their promises and can fix - or free us from - its dangerous side effects. Ironic as it may be, the only ethnic groups who know this to be absolutely false are the more realistic North American Indians who have successfully experienced tens of thousands of years of nature-based living.

In his later years Monk began to feel less at home in our new world of 'Isms'. It disturbed him deeply to witness the latest trend toward solipsism - the 'Me-Me' Yuppies, the ego-tripping technocrats and the narcissistic adolescents of science. He became aware that both technological 'idealism' - worshipping the scientism cult - and the cyberbetic term 'virtual reality' are misnomers. To begin with, science only holds contempt for the dreams of idealists while plugging oneself into a computer is another kind of escape from the real world.

The famous futurist writer Arthur C. Clarke in *Profiles of the Future* summarizes our technological era by imagining human beings hundreds of years from today reading our history with a feeling of wistfulness as he describes it in the following statement: 'But for all that, they may envy us, basking in the bright afterglow of Creation; for we knew the universe when it was young.' Quite probably these future generations will never know the pleasure we once knew in natural acoustic music-making. Possibly too this present generation is growing old too fast, moving toward entropy and a spider web society.

Monk contemplated further on why so many people are in such a hurry to ride the merry-go-round of 'progress' at a prestissimo tempo, faster, bigger, better and louder. Then he reflected on Lester Young, the

216

president of all tenor saxophonists. 'Pres' would have taken one quick glance at these 'progressive' hotheads and brushed off his left shoulder, saying, 'Uncool man, very uncool!' Then, adjusting his pork pie hat and bending his saxophone at a 45 degree angle, he took off and swung into the space, freedom and joy of playing in his own galaxy.

References

Eiseley, Loren, *The Unexpected Universe* (Harcourt-Brace, NYC 1964)

Eiseley, Loren, *The Man who Saw through Time* (Francis Bacon) (Macmillan, NYC 1973)

Heaton and Groves, *Wittengenstein for Beginners* (Icon Books 1994)

Mander, Jerry, *In the Absence of the Sacred* (the Failure of Technology and the Survival of the American Indians) (Sierra Club Books, San Francisco 1991)

Monk, Ray, *The Duty of Genius* (Wittgenstein) Jonathan Cape Ltd 1990)

Price, Lucien, *Dialogues with Alfred North Whitehead* (Atlantic Monthly Press, Boston, USA, 1954)

Stravinsky, Igor, *Poetics of Music* (Harvard University Press, Cambridge, Mass., and London England: First Edition 1942)

Tame, David, *The Secret Power of Music* (Destiny Books, Rochester, Vermont 1984)

The Smithsonian Collection of Jazz: five CD volumes (Smithsonian Institute Press, Blue Ridge Summit, Pa., USA)

218

Postlude

'Only the artists are on the right path. It may be that they can give this world some beauty but to give it reason is impossible'.

(Georges Clemenceau, legendary premier of France 1906-9, 1917-20). 'A soldier of democracy', Doctor of Medicine, humanist and friend and supporter of French artists.

219